Garfield says a mouthful

BY: JIM DAVIS

BALLANTINE BOOKS · NEW YORK

Copyright © 1991 United Feature Syndicate, Inc.
GARFIELD Comic Strips: © 1990 United Feature Syndicate, Inc.

All rights reserved under International and Pan-American Copyright Conventions. Published in the United States by Ballantine Books, a division of Random House, Inc., New York, and simultaneously in Canada by Random House of Canada Limited, Toronto.

Library of Congress Catalog Card Number: 91-91856

ISBN: 0-345-37368-5

Manufactured in the United States of America

First Edition: October 1991

10 9 8 7 6 5 4

Top Ten Signs That Your Cat is a "Garfield"

10. Your food bill surpasses the national debt
9. He gets a court order requiring you to pamper him
8. He takes over everything in the house except the mortgage payment
7. Dogs in the neighborhood get anonymous hate mail
6. He has never strayed farther than three feet from the house
5. He treats you with no more respect than the drapes
4. Your plants die mysterious deaths
3. He's sometimes mistaken for Rhode Island
2. He tries to have *you* declawed
1. Can't tell if he's sleeping or dead

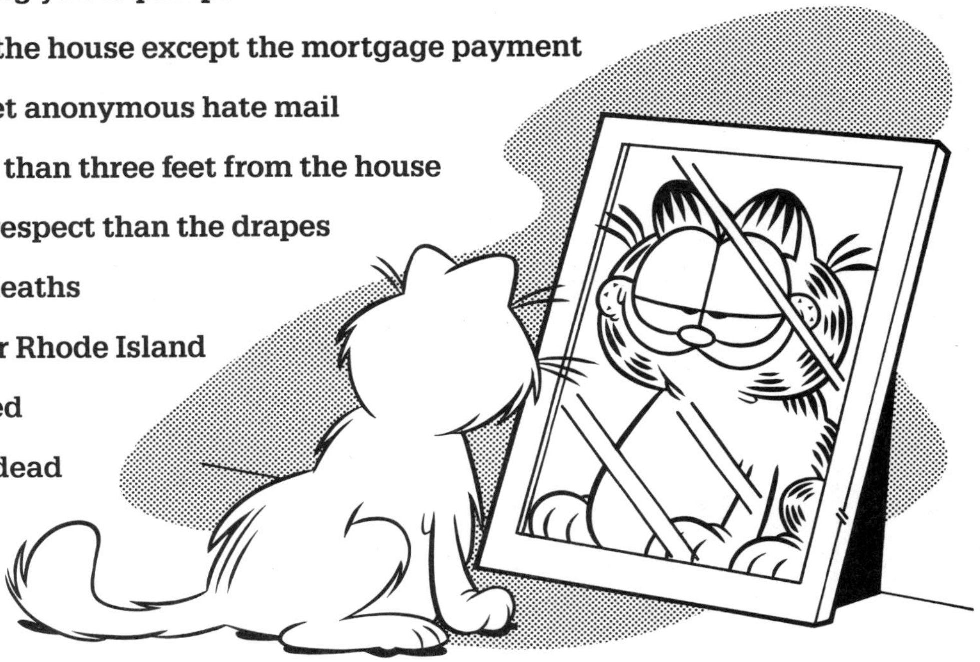

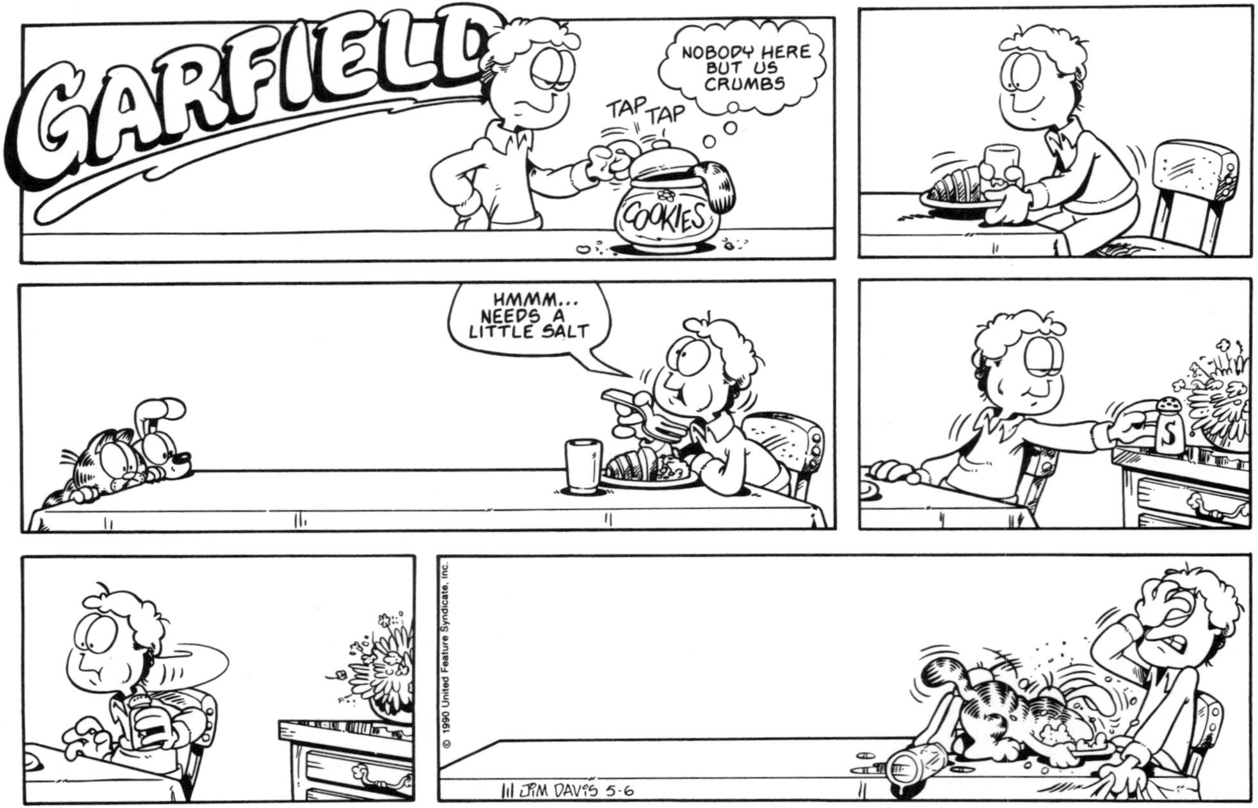
GARFIELD
TAP TAP
NOBODY HERE BUT US CRUMBS
COOKIES
HMMM... NEEDS A LITTLE SALT
S
© 1990 United Feature Syndicate, Inc.
JIM DAVIS 5-6

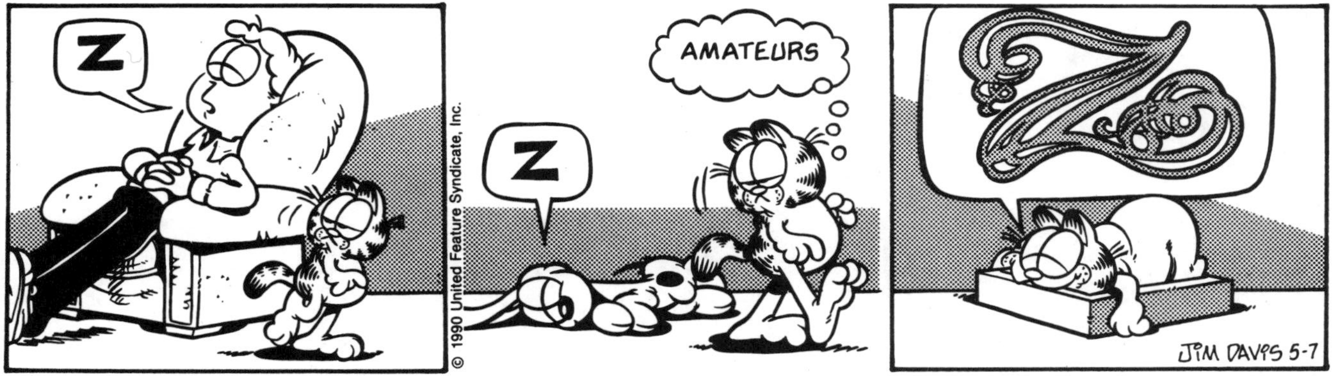
Z
Z
AMATEURS
JIM DAVIS 5-7
© 1990 United Feature Syndicate, Inc.

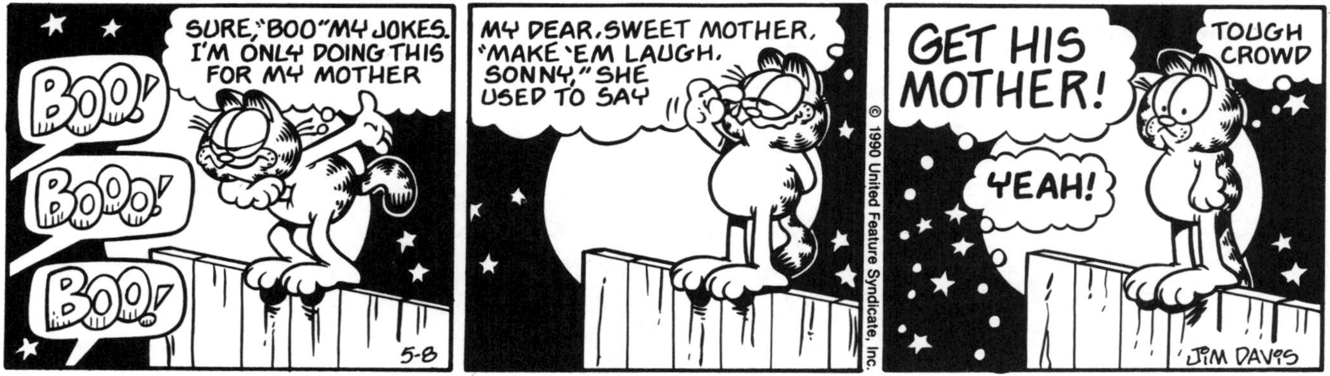
BOO!
BOOO!
BOO!
SURE, "BOO" MY JOKES. I'M ONLY DOING THIS FOR MY MOTHER
5-8
MY DEAR, SWEET MOTHER. "MAKE 'EM LAUGH, SONNY," SHE USED TO SAY
© 1990 United Feature Syndicate, Inc.
GET HIS MOTHER!
YEAH!
TOUGH CROWD
JIM DAVIS

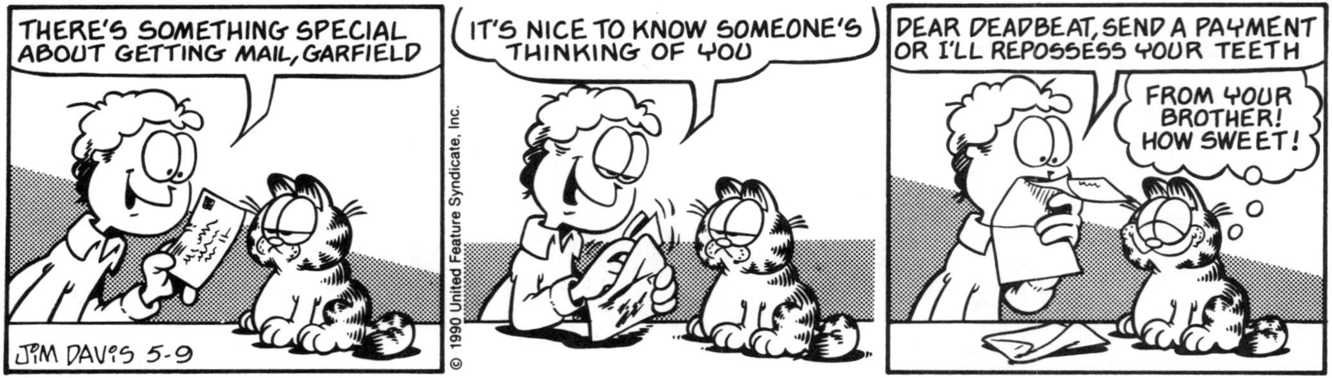
THERE'S SOMETHING SPECIAL ABOUT GETTING MAIL, GARFIELD
JIM DAVIS 5-9
IT'S NICE TO KNOW SOMEONE'S THINKING OF YOU
DEAR DEADBEAT, SEND A PAYMENT OR I'LL REPOSSESS YOUR TEETH
FROM YOUR BROTHER! HOW SWEET!

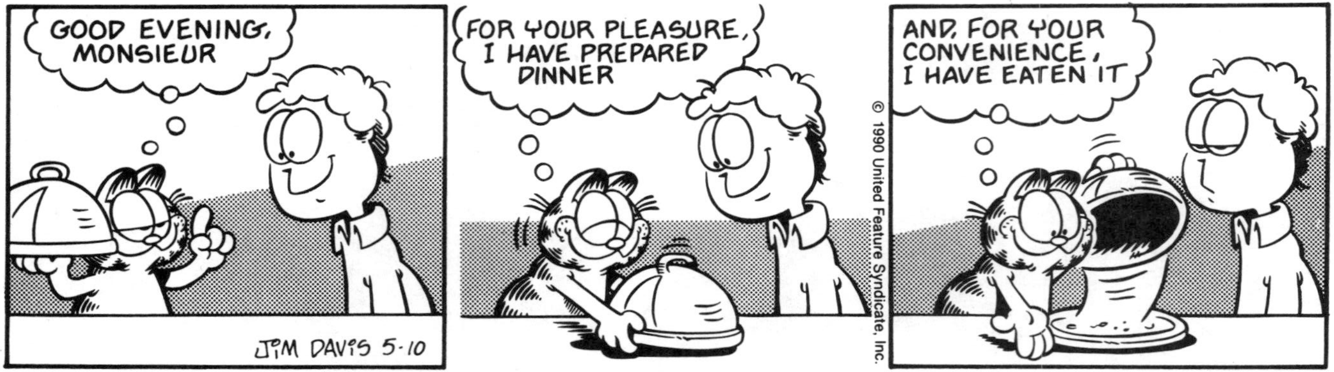
GOOD EVENING, MONSIEUR
JIM DAVIS 5-10
FOR YOUR PLEASURE, I HAVE PREPARED DINNER
AND, FOR YOUR CONVENIENCE, I HAVE EATEN IT

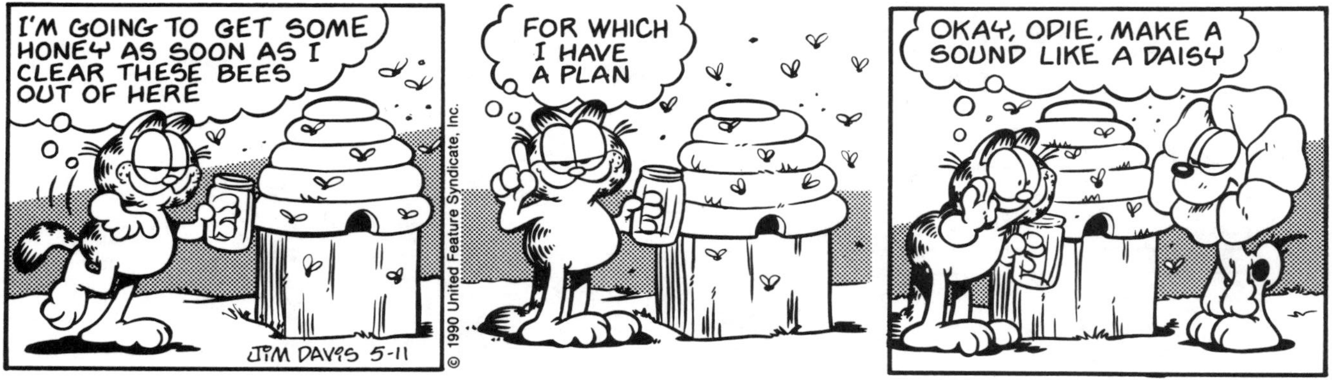
I'M GOING TO GET SOME HONEY AS SOON AS I CLEAR THESE BEES OUT OF HERE
JIM DAVIS 5-11
© 1990 United Feature Syndicate, Inc.
FOR WHICH I HAVE A PLAN
OKAY, ODIE, MAKE A SOUND LIKE A DAISY

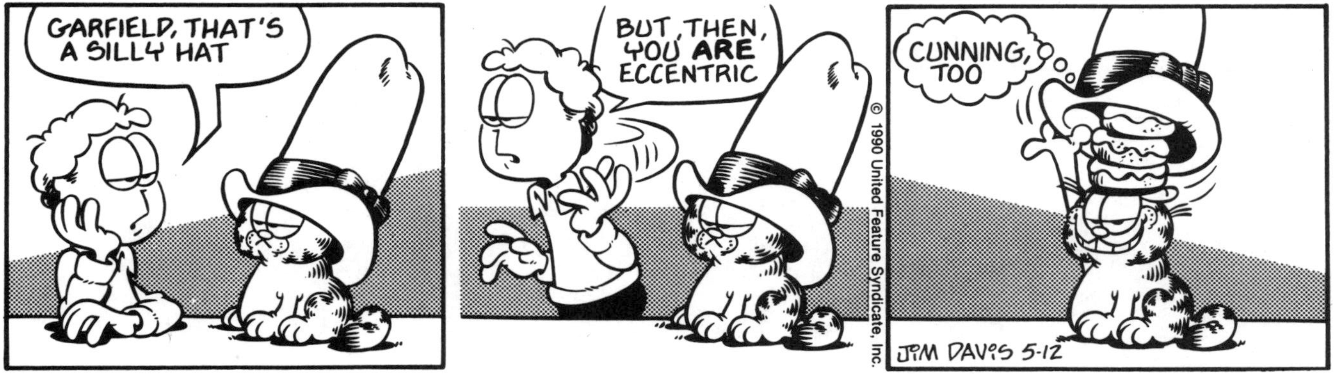
GARFIELD, THAT'S A SILLY HAT
BUT, THEN, YOU **ARE** ECCENTRIC
© 1990 United Feature Syndicate, Inc.
CUNNING, TOO
JIM DAVIS 5-12

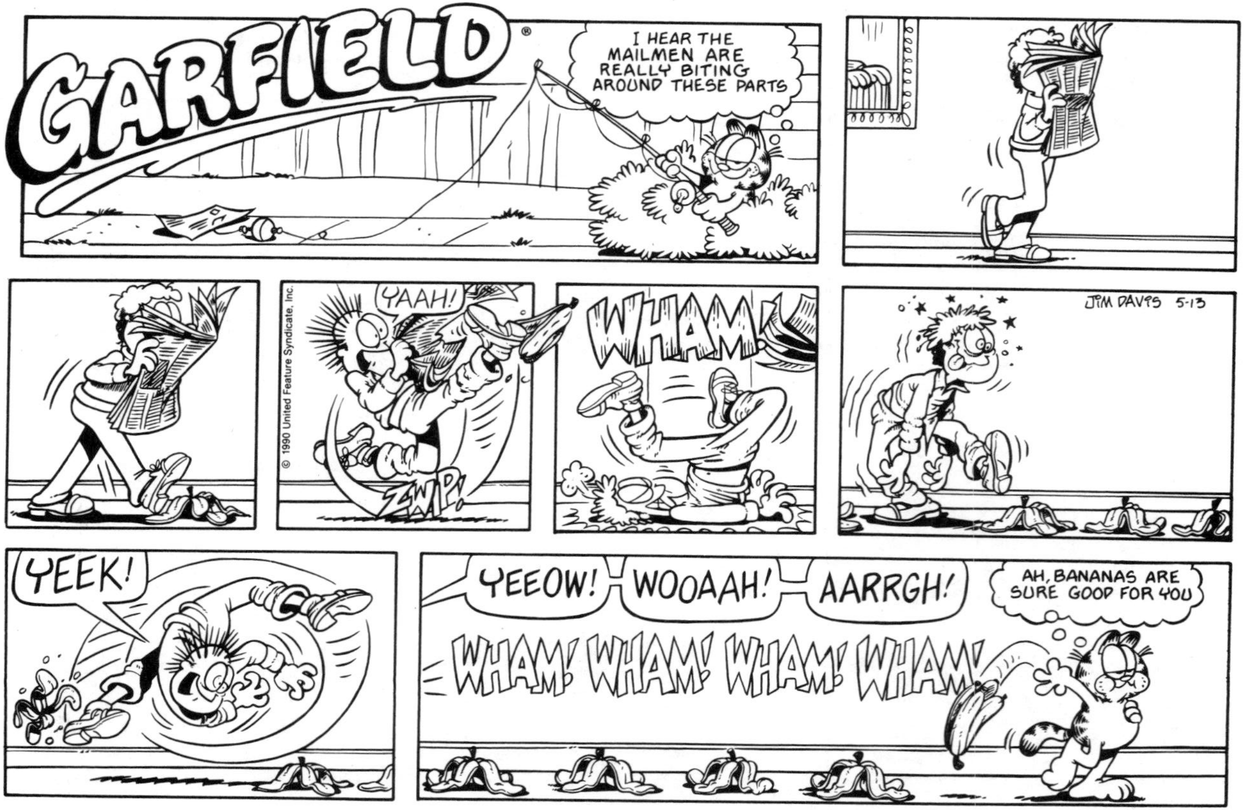
GARFIELD®
I HEAR THE MAILMEN ARE REALLY BITING AROUND THESE PARTS
© 1990 United Feature Syndicate, Inc.
YAAH!
ZWIP!
WHAM!
JIM DAVIS 5-13
YEEK!
YEEOW!
WOOAAH!
AARRGH!
WHAM! WHAM! WHAM! WHAM!
AH, BANANAS ARE SURE GOOD FOR YOU

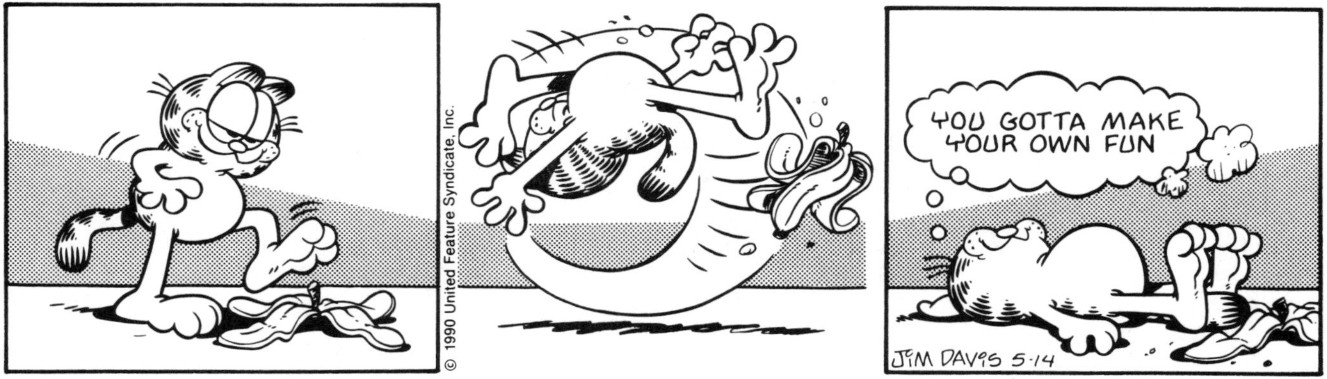
© 1990 United Feature Syndicate, Inc.
YOU GOTTA MAKE YOUR OWN FUN
JIM DAVIS 5-14

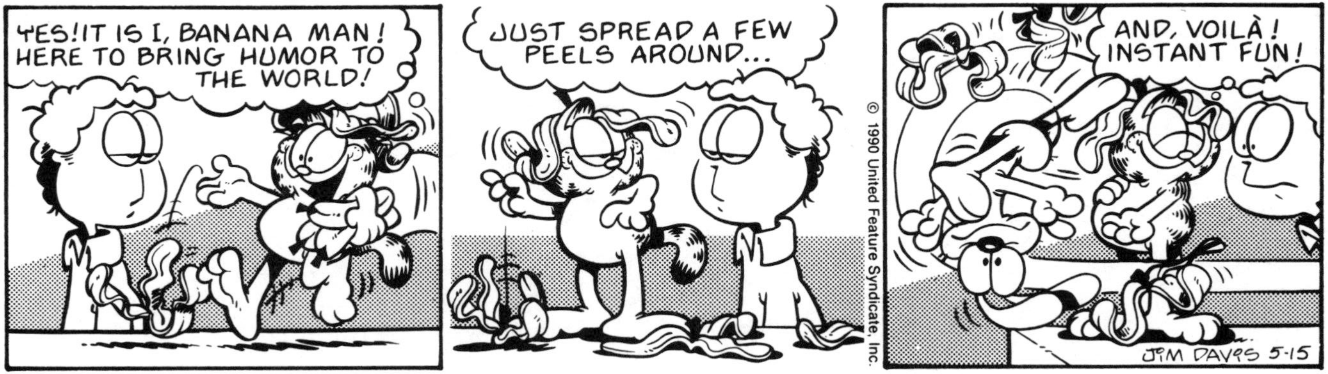
YES! IT IS I, BANANA MAN! HERE TO BRING HUMOR TO THE WORLD!
JUST SPREAD A FEW PEELS AROUND...
© 1990 United Feature Syndicate, Inc.
AND, VOILÀ! INSTANT FUN!
JIM DAVIS 5-15

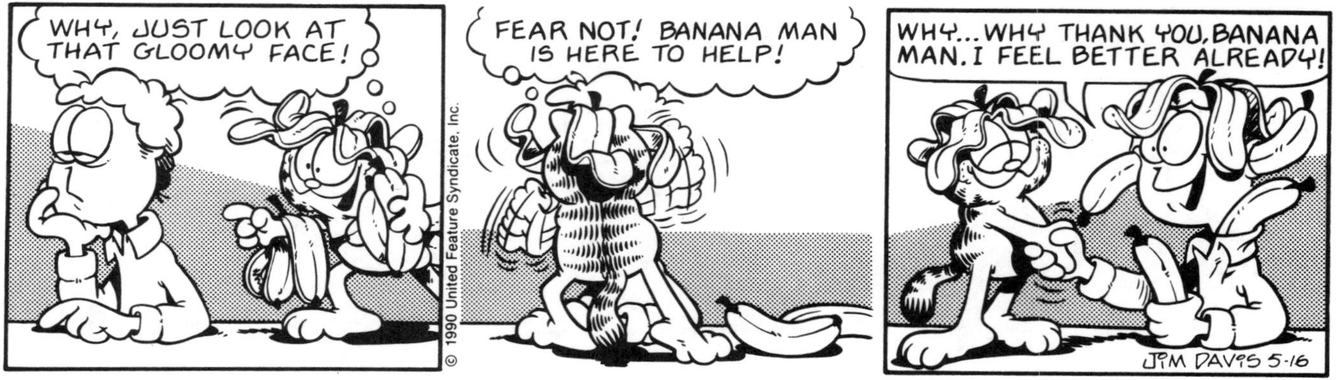
WHY, JUST LOOK AT THAT GLOOMY FACE!
FEAR NOT! BANANA MAN IS HERE TO HELP!
WHY...WHY THANK YOU, BANANA MAN. I FEEL BETTER ALREADY!
JIM DAVIS 5-16
© 1990 United Feature Syndicate, Inc.

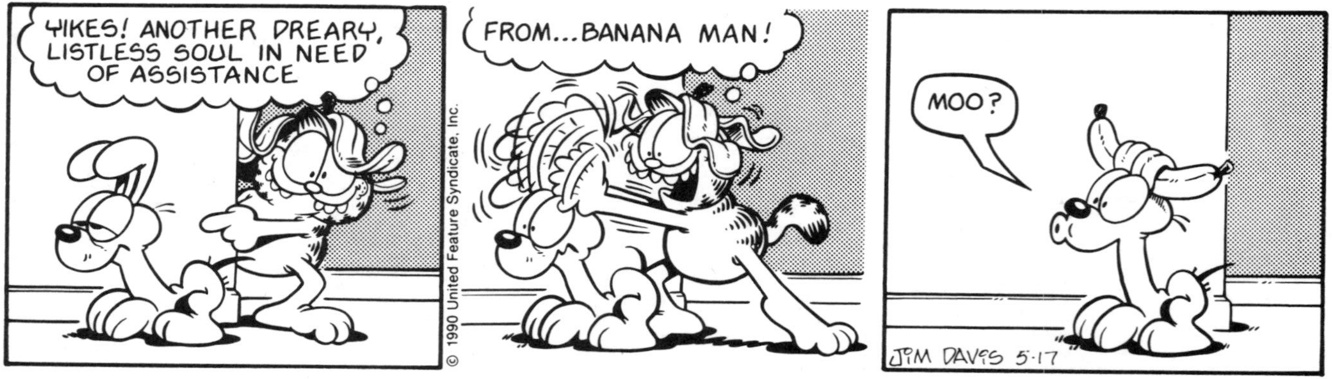
YIKES! ANOTHER DREARY, LISTLESS SOUL IN NEED OF ASSISTANCE
FROM...BANANA MAN!
MOO?
JIM DAVIS 5-17
© 1990 United Feature Syndicate, Inc.

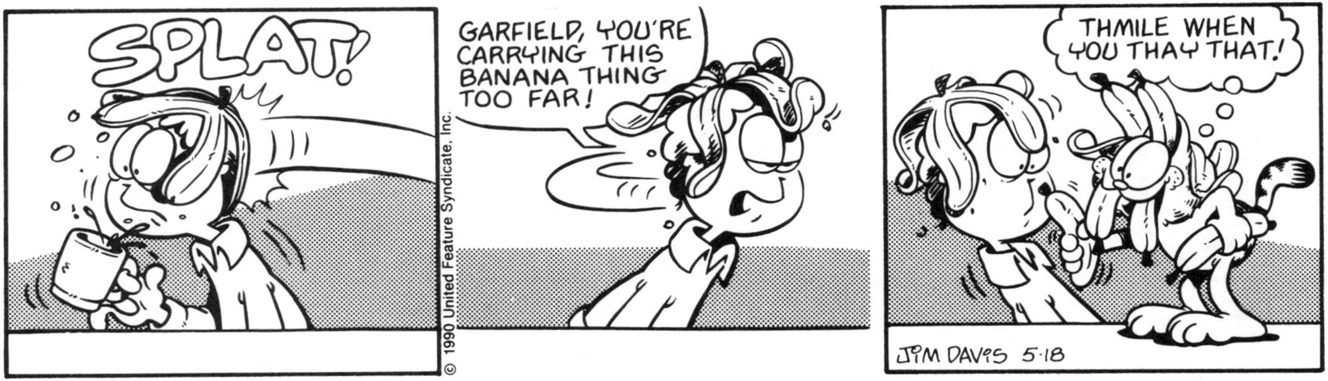
SPLAT!
GARFIELD, YOU'RE CARRYING THIS BANANA THING TOO FAR!
THMILE WHEN YOU THAY THAT!
JIM DAVIS 5·18

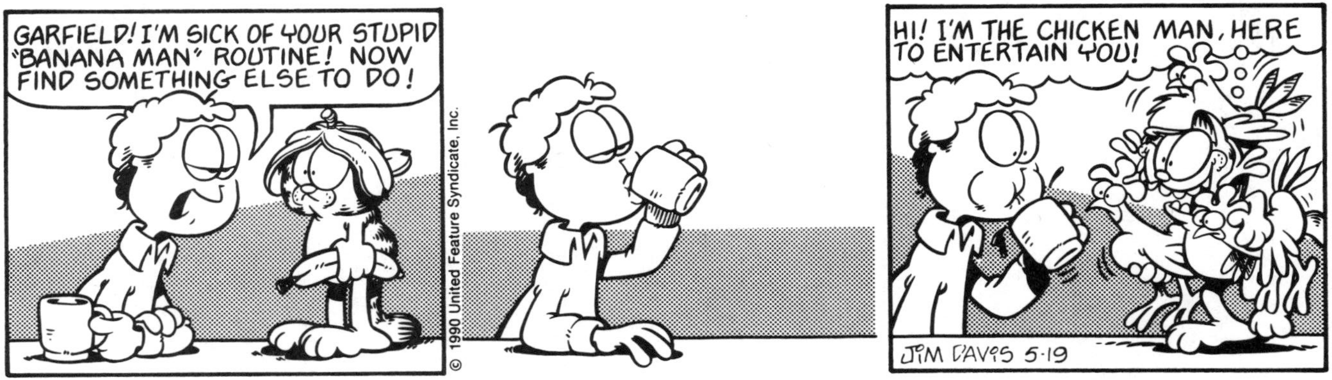
GARFIELD! I'M SICK OF YOUR STUPID "BANANA MAN" ROUTINE! NOW FIND SOMETHING ELSE TO DO!
HI! I'M THE CHICKEN MAN, HERE TO ENTERTAIN YOU!
JIM DAVIS 5·19

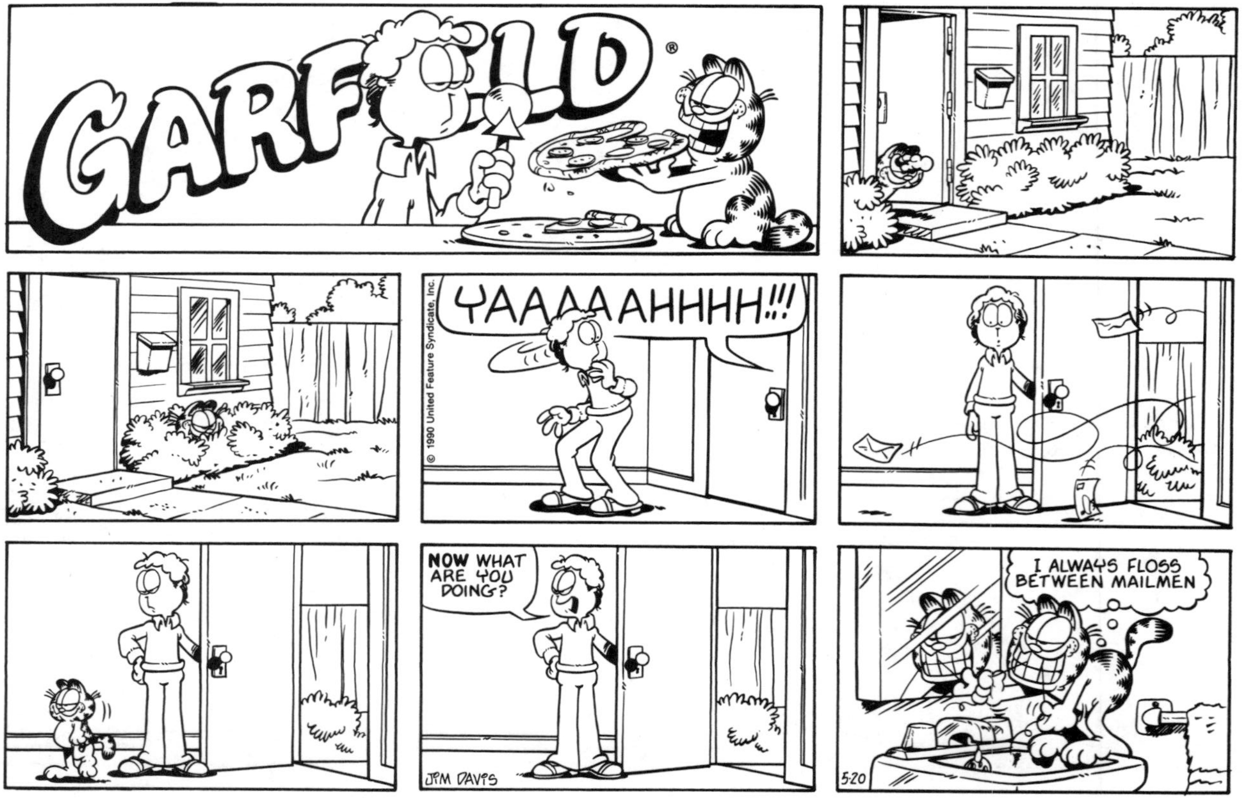
GARFIELD®
© 1990 United Feature Syndicate, Inc.
YAAAAAHHHH!!!
NOW WHAT ARE YOU DOING?
JIM DAVIS
I ALWAYS FLOSS BETWEEN MAILMEN
5-20

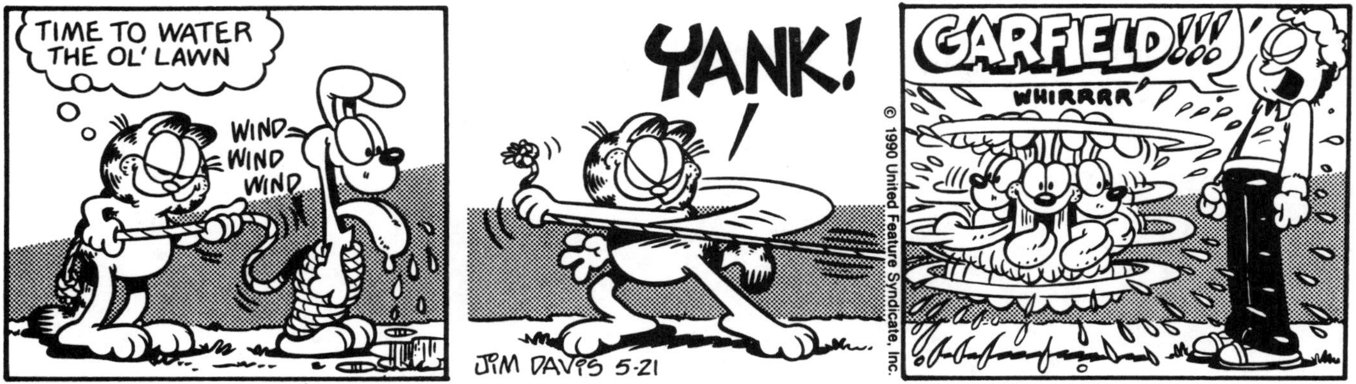
TIME TO WATER THE OL' LAWN
WIND WIND WIND
YANK!
JIM DAVIS 5-21
WHIRRRR
GARFIELD!!!
© 1990 United Feature Syndicate, Inc.

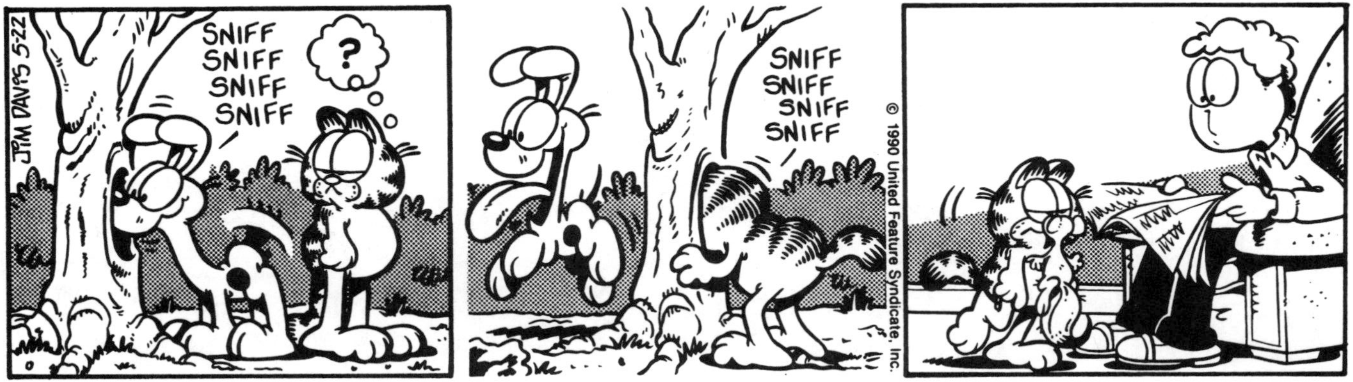
JIM DAVIS 5-22
SNIFF SNIFF SNIFF SNIFF
?
SNIFF SNIFF SNIFF SNIFF
© 1990 United Feature Syndicate, Inc.

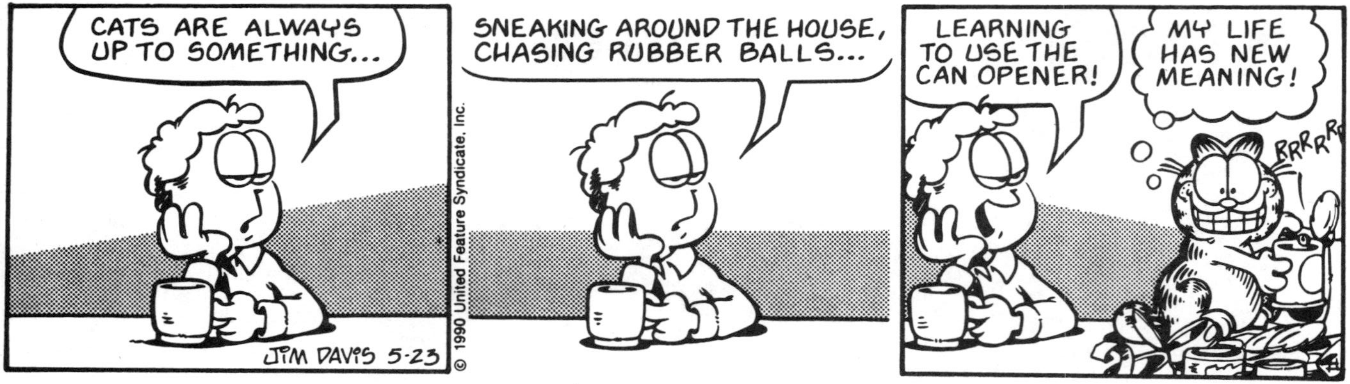
CATS ARE ALWAYS UP TO SOMETHING...
SNEAKING AROUND THE HOUSE, CHASING RUBBER BALLS...
LEARNING TO USE THE CAN OPENER!
MY LIFE HAS NEW MEANING!
RRRRR
JIM DAVIS 5-23
© 1990 United Feature Syndicate, Inc.

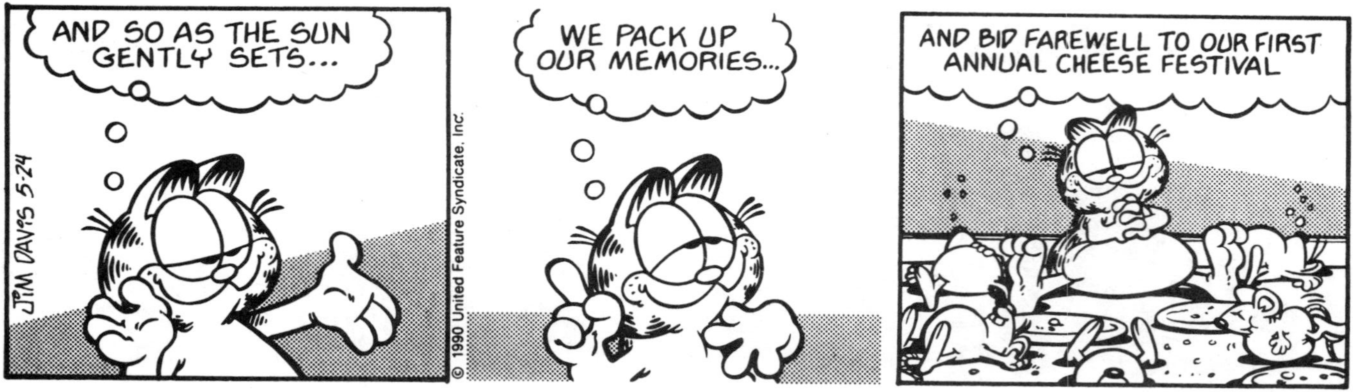
AND SO AS THE SUN GENTLY SETS...
WE PACK UP OUR MEMORIES...
AND BID FAREWELL TO OUR FIRST ANNUAL CHEESE FESTIVAL
JIM DAVIS 5-24
© 1990 United Feature Syndicate, Inc.

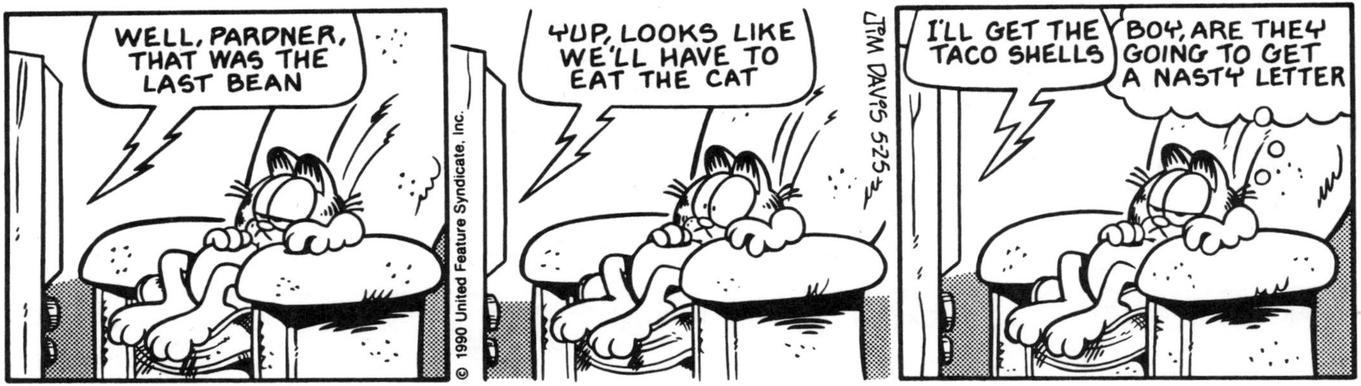
WELL, PARDNER, THAT WAS THE LAST BEAN
© 1990 United Feature Syndicate, Inc.
YUP, LOOKS LIKE WE'LL HAVE TO EAT THE CAT
JIM DAVIS 5-25
I'LL GET THE TACO SHELLS
BOY, ARE THEY GOING TO GET A NASTY LETTER

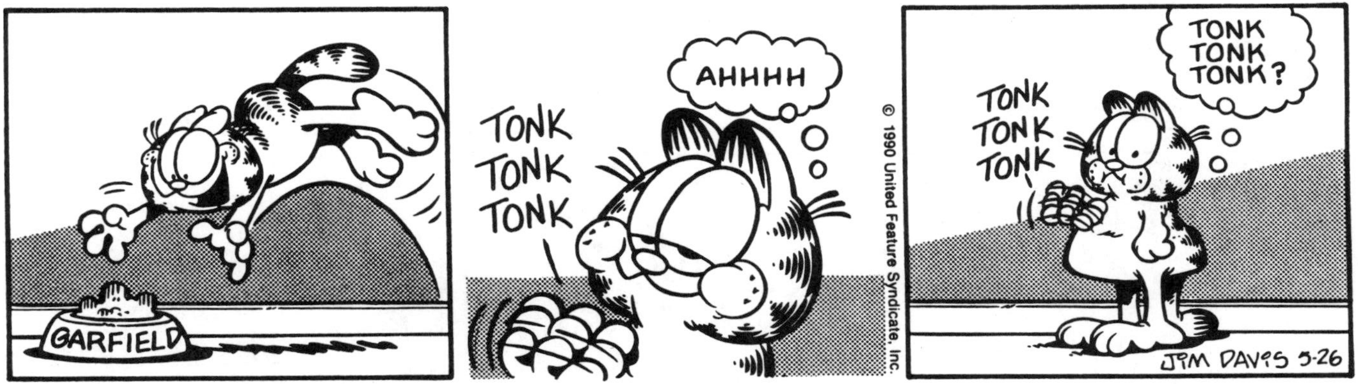
GARFIELD
TONK TONK TONK
AHHHH
© 1990 United Feature Syndicate, Inc.
TONK TONK TONK
TONK TONK TONK?
JIM DAVIS 5-26

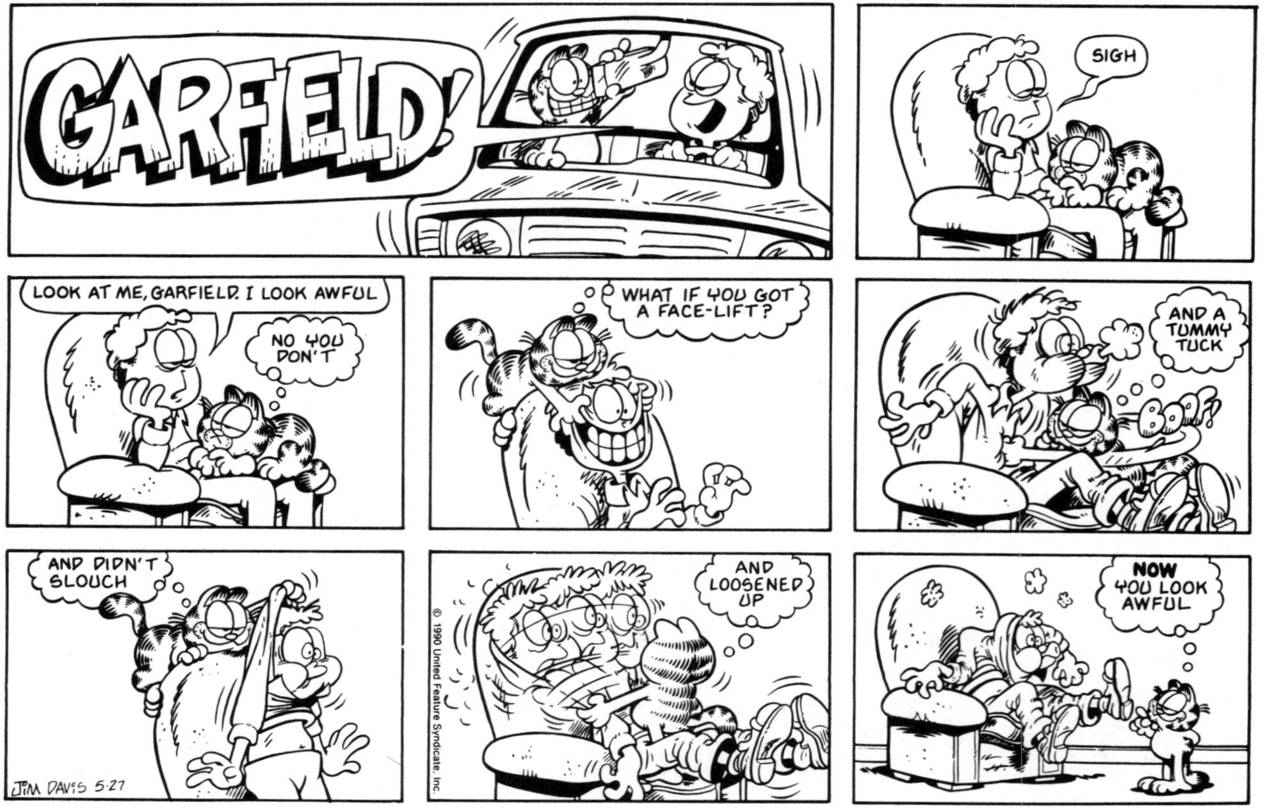
GARFIELD
SIGH
LOOK AT ME, GARFIELD. I LOOK AWFUL
NO YOU DON'T
WHAT IF YOU GOT A FACE-LIFT?
AND A TUMMY TUCK
BOOF!
AND DIDN'T SLOUCH
AND LOOSENED UP
NOW YOU LOOK AWFUL
JIM DAVIS 5-27
© 1990 United Feature Syndicate, Inc.

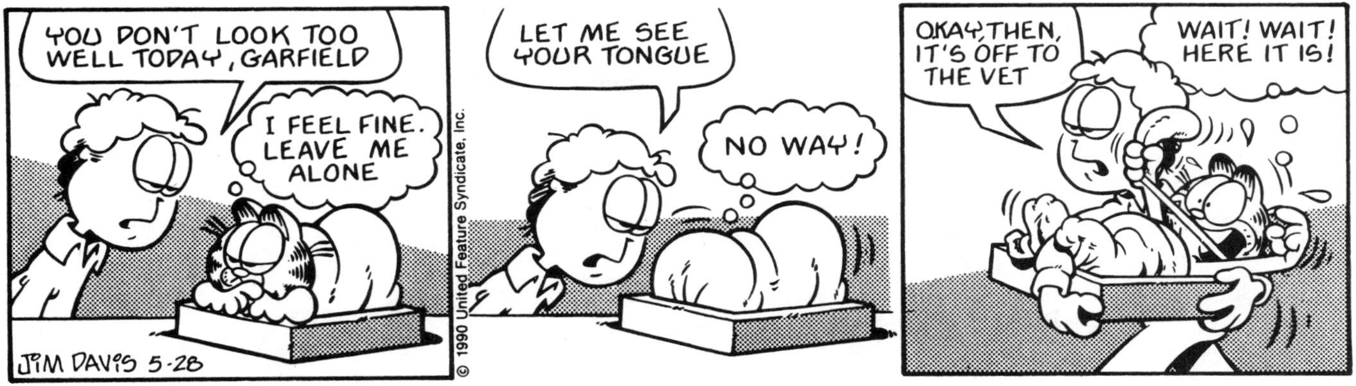
YOU DON'T LOOK TOO WELL TODAY, GARFIELD
I FEEL FINE. LEAVE ME ALONE
JIM DAVIS 5-28
© 1990 United Feature Syndicate, Inc.
LET ME SEE YOUR TONGUE
NO WAY!
OKAY, THEN, IT'S OFF TO THE VET
WAIT! WAIT! HERE IT IS!

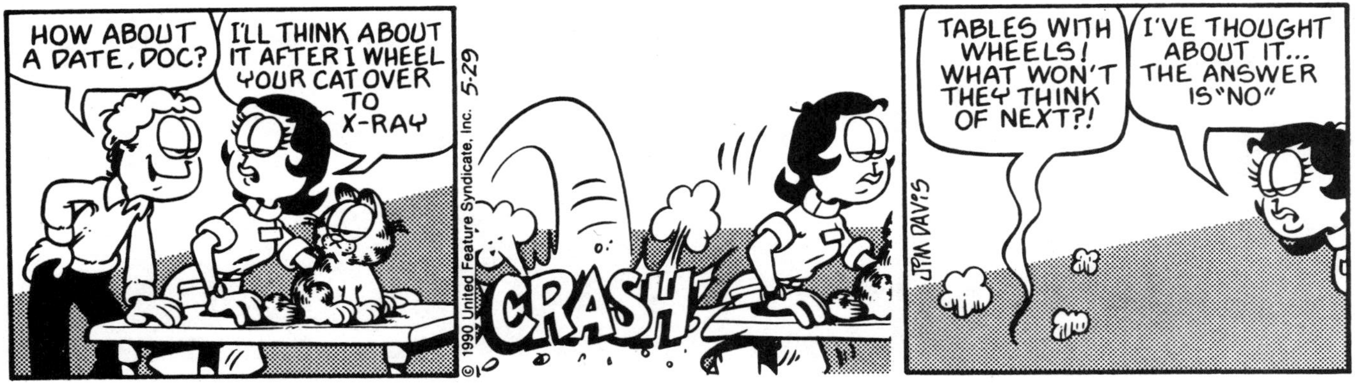
HOW ABOUT A DATE, DOC?
I'LL THINK ABOUT IT AFTER I WHEEL YOUR CAT OVER TO X-RAY
5-29
© 1990 United Feature Syndicate, Inc.
CRASH
JIM DAVIS
TABLES WITH WHEELS! WHAT WON'T THEY THINK OF NEXT?!
I'VE THOUGHT ABOUT IT... THE ANSWER IS "NO"

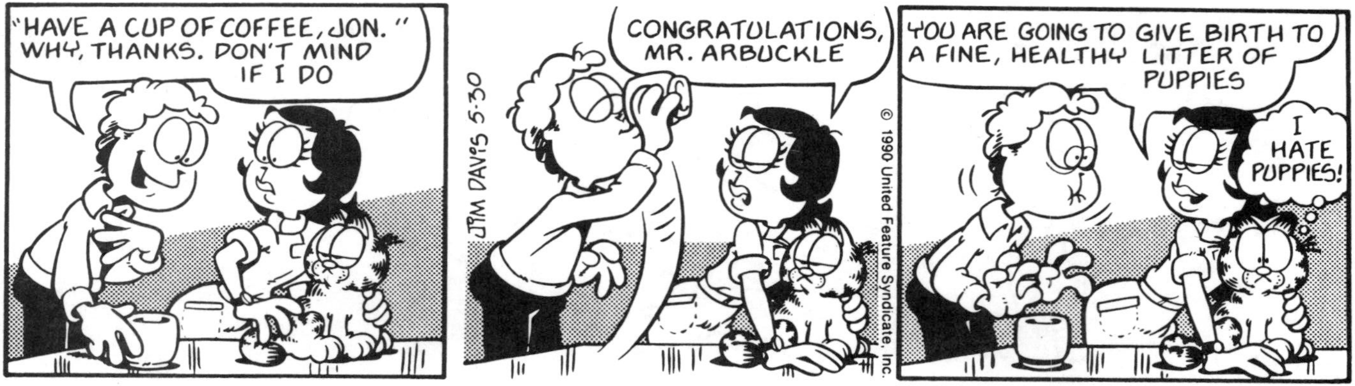
"HAVE A CUP OF COFFEE, JON." WHY, THANKS. DON'T MIND IF I DO
CONGRATULATIONS, MR. ARBUCKLE
YOU ARE GOING TO GIVE BIRTH TO A FINE, HEALTHY LITTER OF PUPPIES
I HATE PUPPIES!
JIM DAVIS 5-30
© 1990 United Feature Syndicate, Inc.

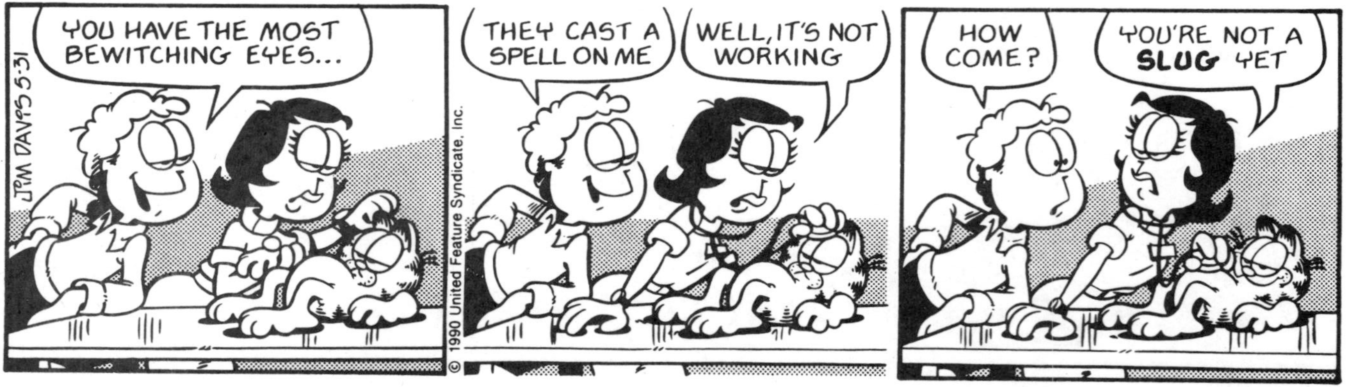
YOU HAVE THE MOST BEWITCHING EYES...
THEY CAST A SPELL ON ME
WELL, IT'S NOT WORKING
HOW COME?
YOU'RE NOT A **SLUG** YET
JIM DAVIS 5-31
© 1990 United Feature Syndicate, Inc.

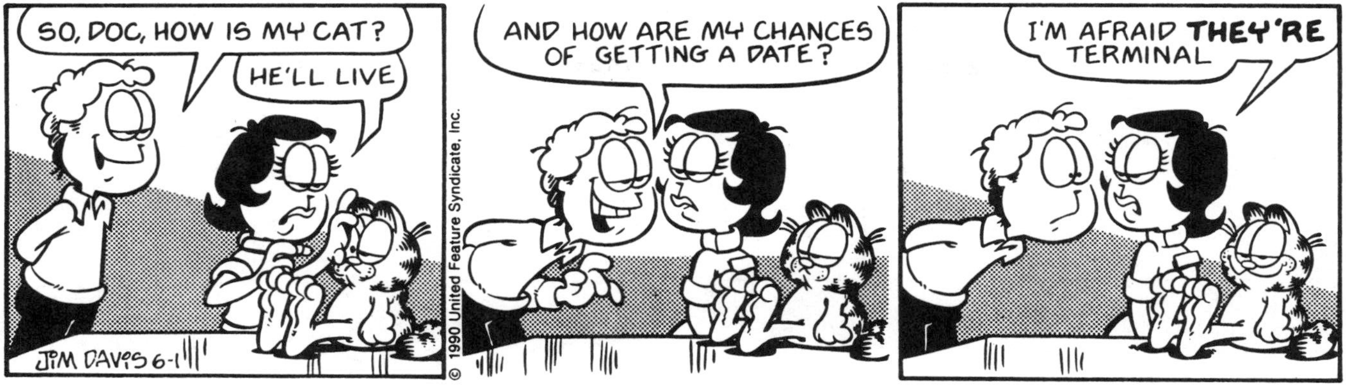
SO, DOC, HOW IS MY CAT?
HE'LL LIVE
JIM DAVIS 6-1
© 1990 United Feature Syndicate, Inc.
AND HOW ARE MY CHANCES OF GETTING A DATE?
I'M AFRAID **THEY'RE** TERMINAL

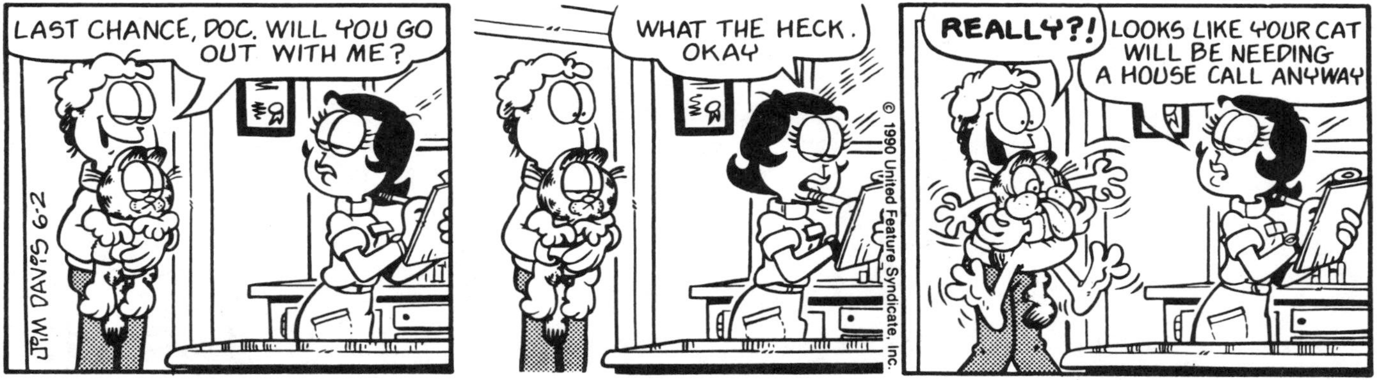
LAST CHANCE, DOC. WILL YOU GO OUT WITH ME?
JIM DAVIS 6-2
WHAT THE HECK. OKAY
© 1990 United Feature Syndicate, Inc.
REALLY?!
LOOKS LIKE YOUR CAT WILL BE NEEDING A HOUSE CALL ANYWAY

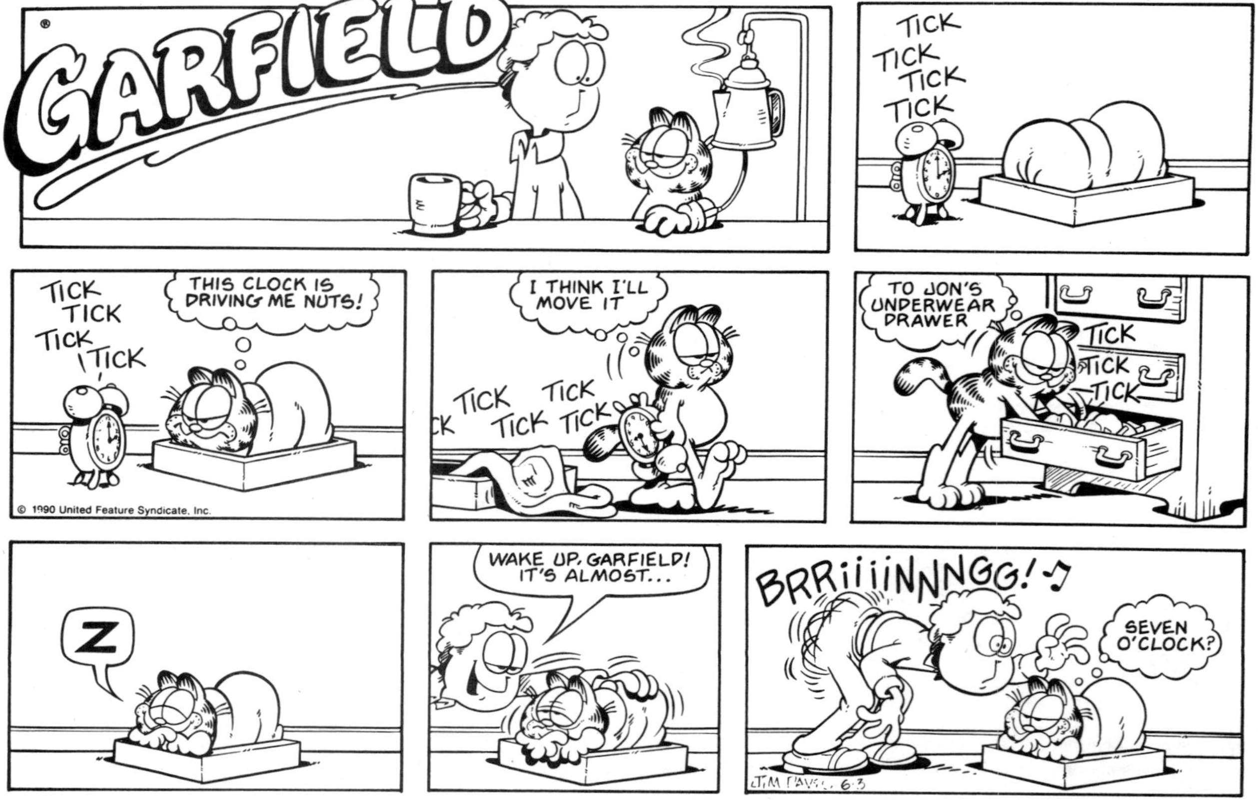
GARFIELD
TICK TICK TICK TICK
TICK TICK TICK TICK
THIS CLOCK IS DRIVING ME NUTS!
TICK TICK TICK TICK
I THINK I'LL MOVE IT
TO JON'S UNDERWEAR DRAWER
TICK TICK TICK
Z
WAKE UP, GARFIELD! IT'S ALMOST...
BRRiiiiNNNGG!
SEVEN O'CLOCK?

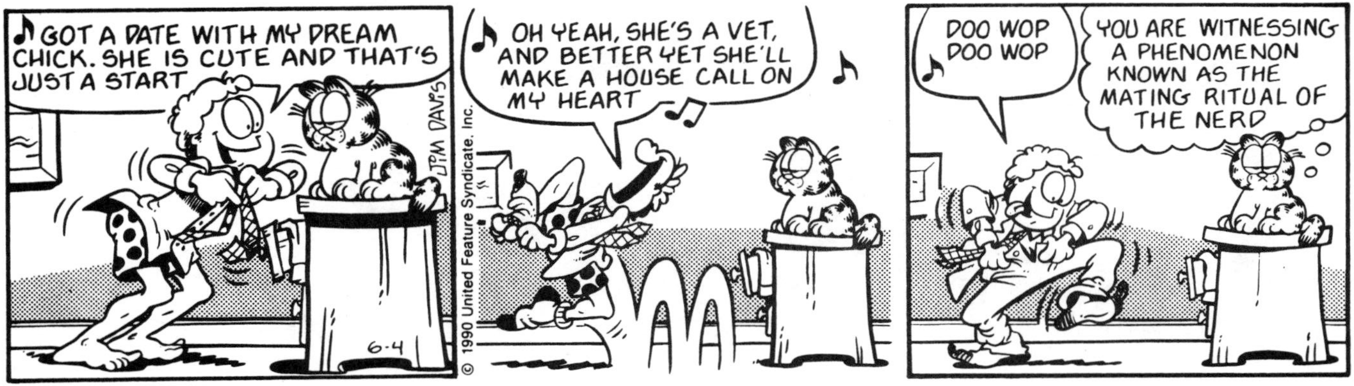
GOT A DATE WITH MY DREAM CHICK. SHE IS CUTE AND THAT'S JUST A START
JIM DAVIS
6-4
© 1990 United Feature Syndicate, Inc.
OH YEAH, SHE'S A VET, AND BETTER YET SHE'LL MAKE A HOUSE CALL ON MY HEART
DOO WOP DOO WOP
YOU ARE WITNESSING A PHENOMENON KNOWN AS THE MATING RITUAL OF THE NERD

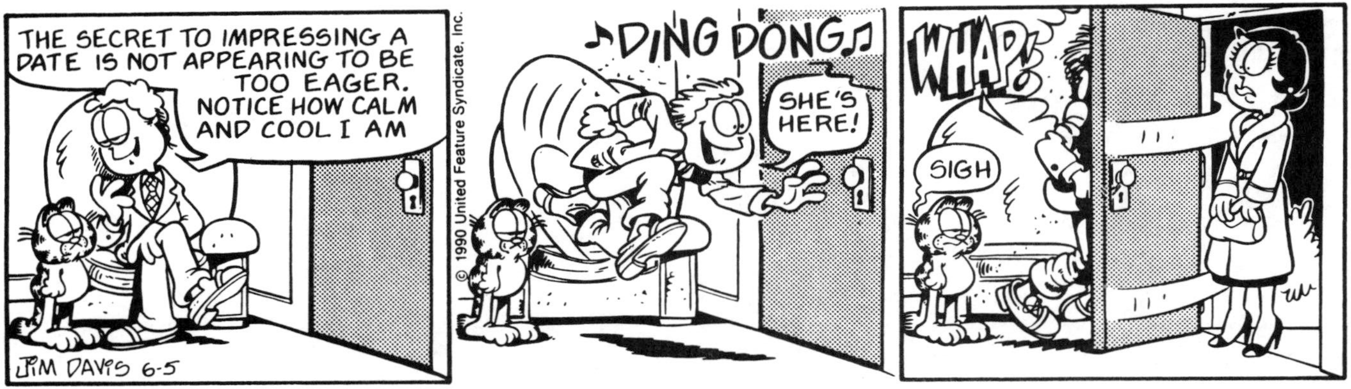
THE SECRET TO IMPRESSING A DATE IS NOT APPEARING TO BE TOO EAGER. NOTICE HOW CALM AND COOL I AM
JIM DAVIS 6-5
© 1990 United Feature Syndicate, Inc.
DING DONG
SHE'S HERE!
WHAP!
SIGH

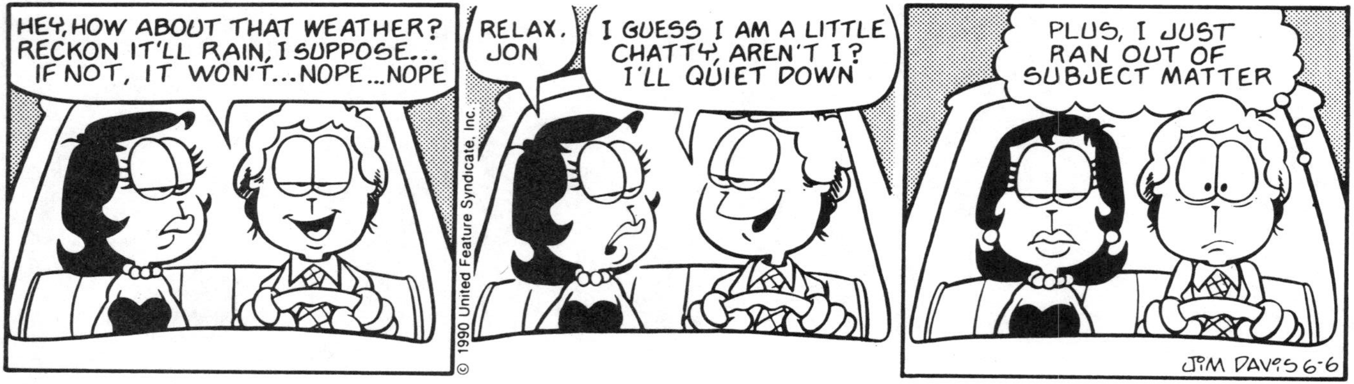
HEY, HOW ABOUT THAT WEATHER? RECKON IT'LL RAIN, I SUPPOSE... IF NOT, IT WON'T...NOPE...NOPE
RELAX, JON
I GUESS I AM A LITTLE CHATTY, AREN'T I? I'LL QUIET DOWN
PLUS, I JUST RAN OUT OF SUBJECT MATTER
JIM DAVIS 6-6
© 1990 United Feature Syndicate, Inc.

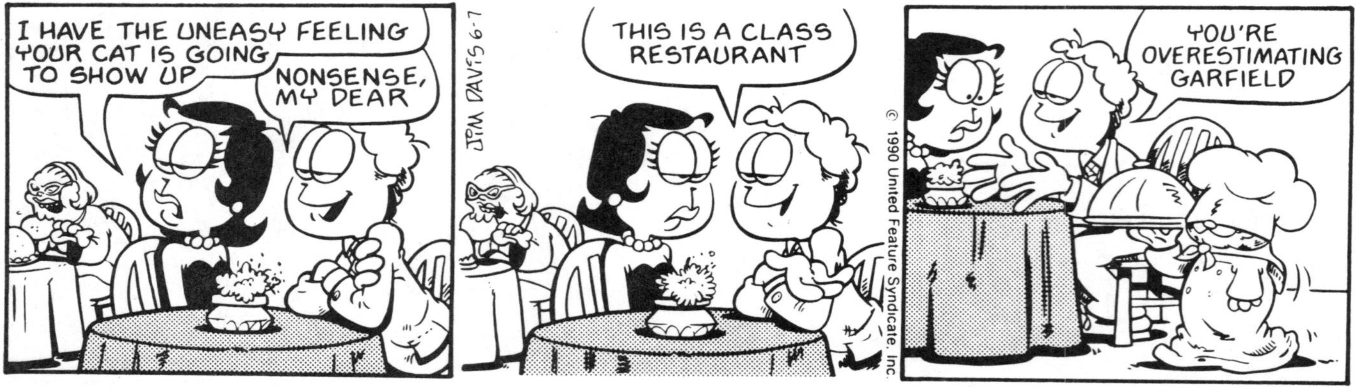
I HAVE THE UNEASY FEELING YOUR CAT IS GOING TO SHOW UP
NONSENSE, MY DEAR
JIM DAVIS 6-7
THIS IS A CLASS RESTAURANT
YOU'RE OVERESTIMATING GARFIELD
© 1990 United Feature Syndicate, Inc.

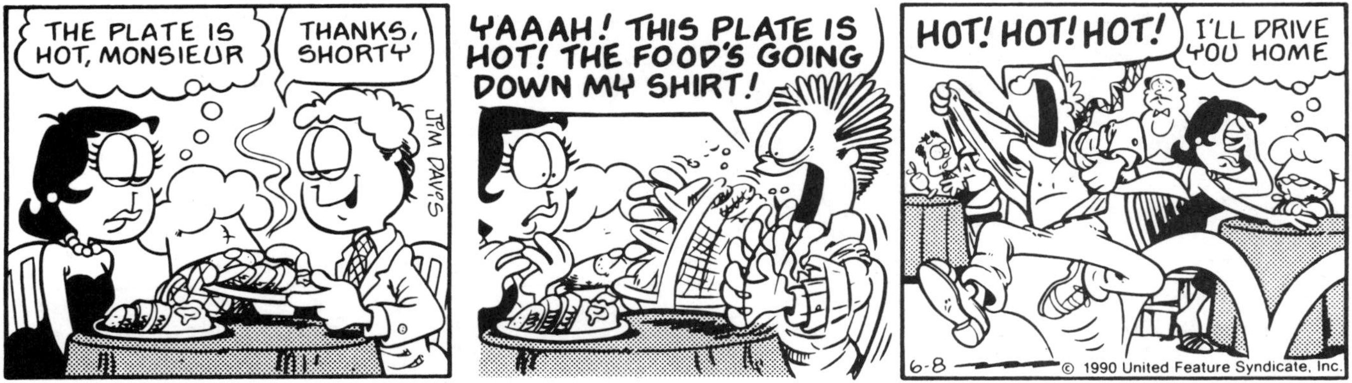
THE PLATE IS HOT, MONSIEUR
THANKS, SHORTY
JIM DAVIS
YAAAH! THIS PLATE IS HOT! THE FOOD'S GOING DOWN MY SHIRT!
HOT! HOT! HOT!
I'LL DRIVE YOU HOME
6-8
© 1990 United Feature Syndicate, Inc.

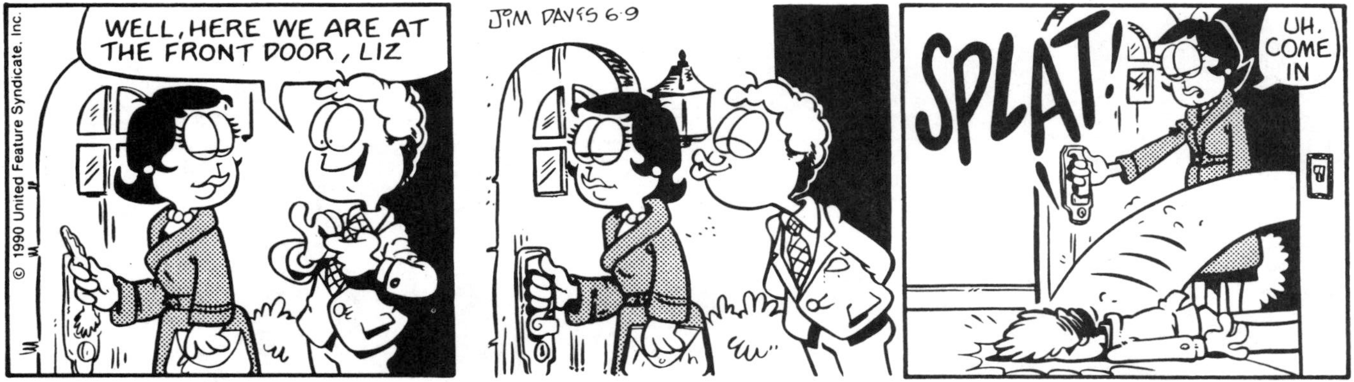
© 1990 United Feature Syndicate, Inc.
WELL, HERE WE ARE AT THE FRONT DOOR, LIZ
JIM DAVIS 6-9
SPLAT!
UH, COME IN

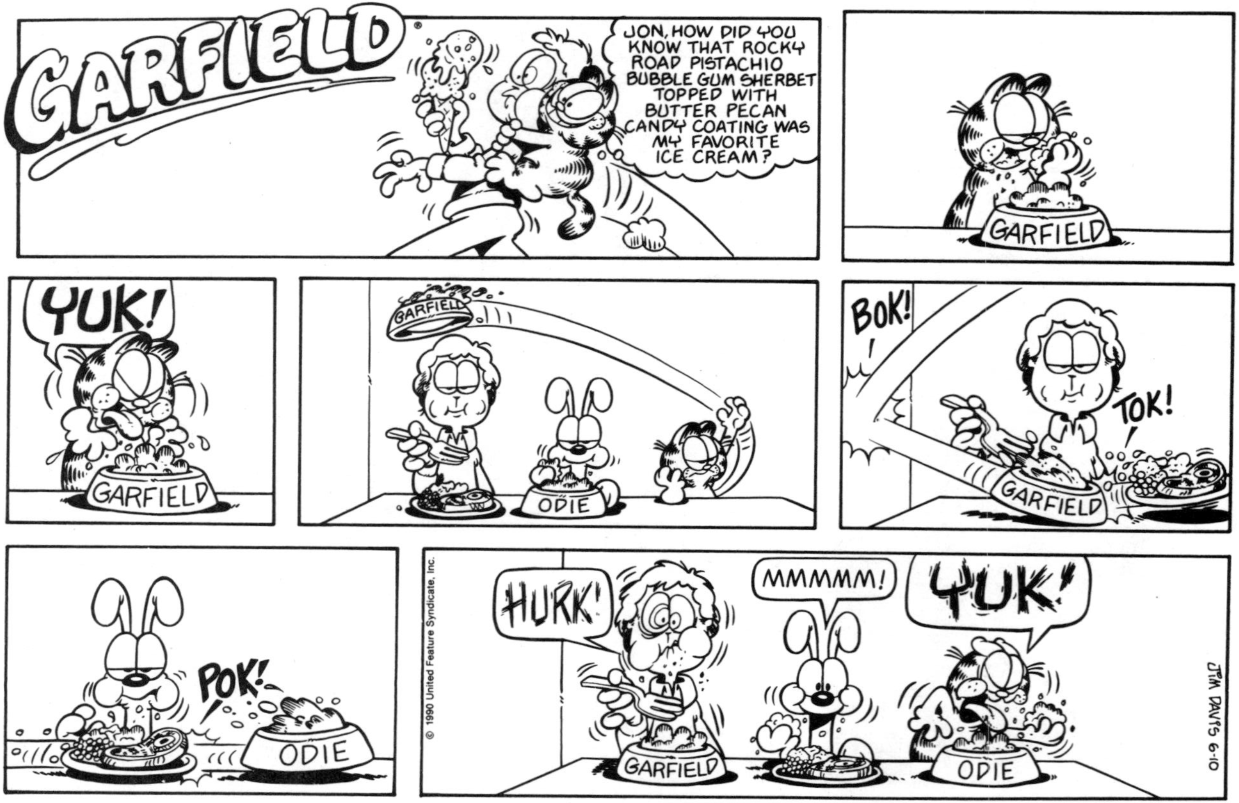
GARFIELD
JON, HOW DID YOU KNOW THAT ROCKY ROAD PISTACHIO BUBBLE GUM SHERBET TOPPED WITH BUTTER PECAN CANDY COATING WAS MY FAVORITE ICE CREAM?
GARFIELD
YUK!
GARFIELD
GARFIELD
ODIE
BOK!
TOK!
GARFIELD
POK!
ODIE
HURK!
MMMMM!
YUK!
GARFIELD
ODIE
JIM DAVIS 6-10
© 1990 United Feature Syndicate, Inc.

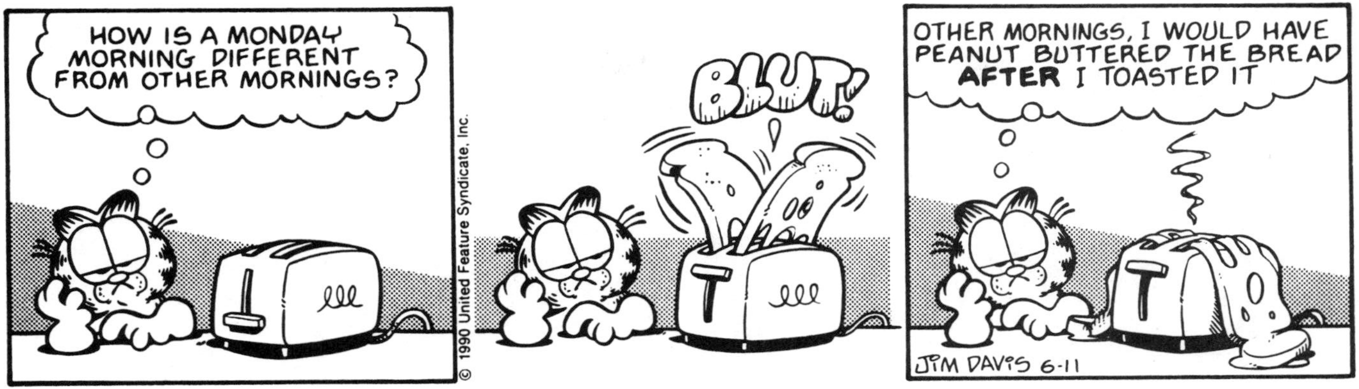
HOW IS A MONDAY MORNING DIFFERENT FROM OTHER MORNINGS?
BLUT!
OTHER MORNINGS, I WOULD HAVE PEANUT BUTTERED THE BREAD **AFTER** I TOASTED IT
JIM DAVIS 6-11

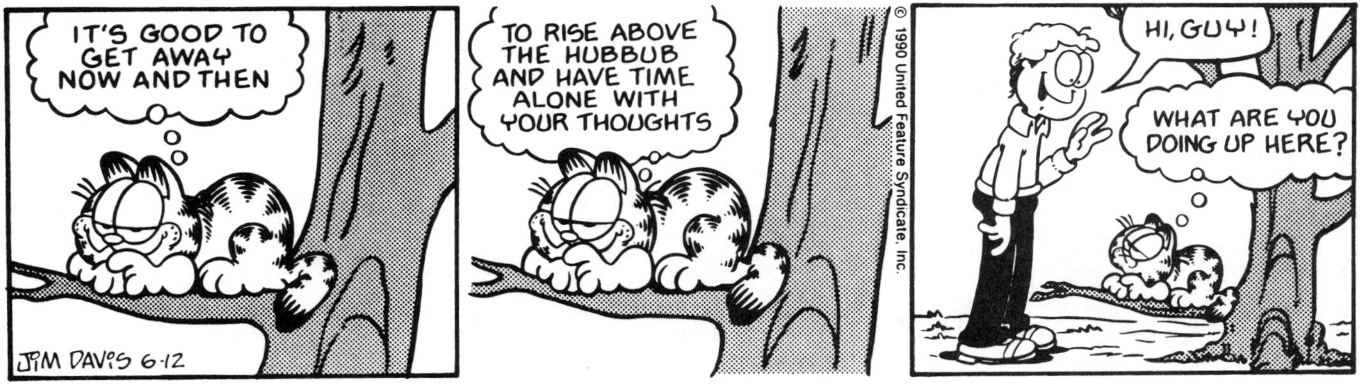
IT'S GOOD TO GET AWAY NOW AND THEN
TO RISE ABOVE THE HUBBUB AND HAVE TIME ALONE WITH YOUR THOUGHTS
HI, GUY!
WHAT ARE YOU DOING UP HERE?
JIM DAVIS 6-12

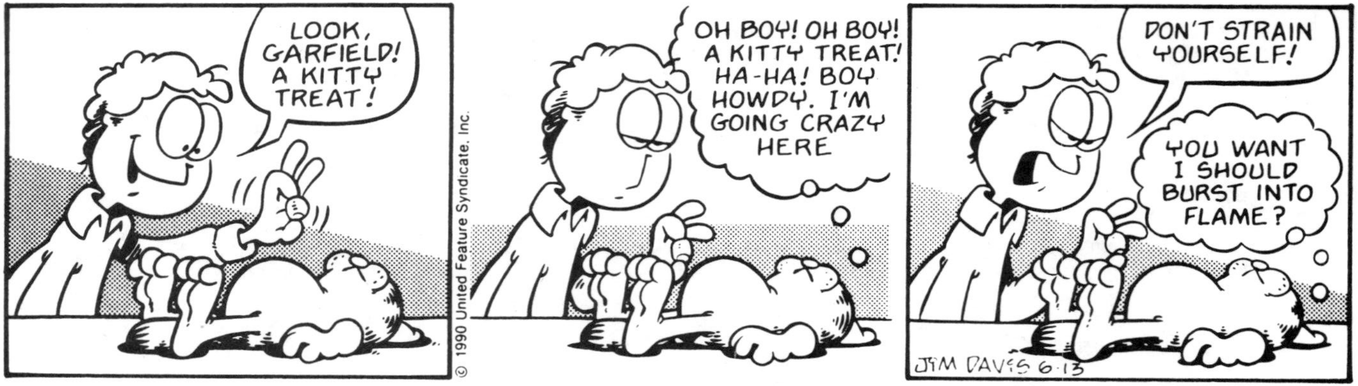
LOOK, GARFIELD! A KITTY TREAT!
OH BOY! OH BOY! A KITTY TREAT! HA-HA! BOY HOWDY. I'M GOING CRAZY HERE
DON'T STRAIN YOURSELF!
YOU WANT I SHOULD BURST INTO FLAME?
JIM DAVIS 6-13
© 1990 United Feature Syndicate, Inc.

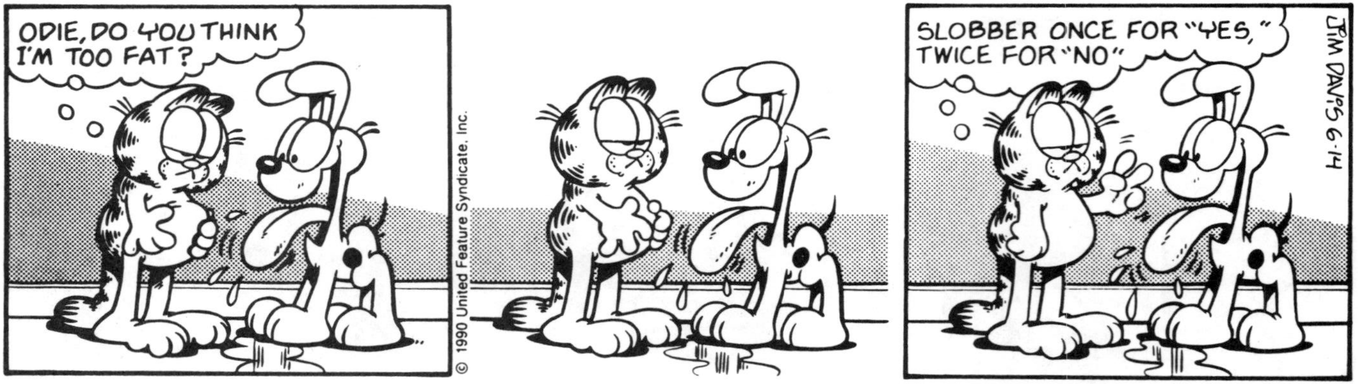
ODIE, DO YOU THINK I'M TOO FAT?
SLOBBER ONCE FOR "YES," TWICE FOR "NO"
JIM DAVIS 6-14
© 1990 United Feature Syndicate, Inc.

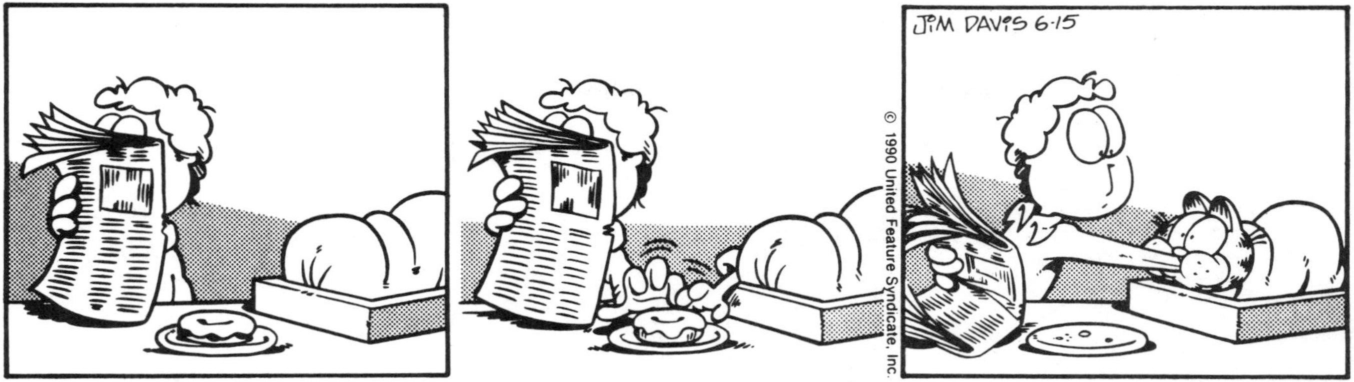
JIM DAVIS 6-15
© 1990 United Feature Syndicate, Inc.

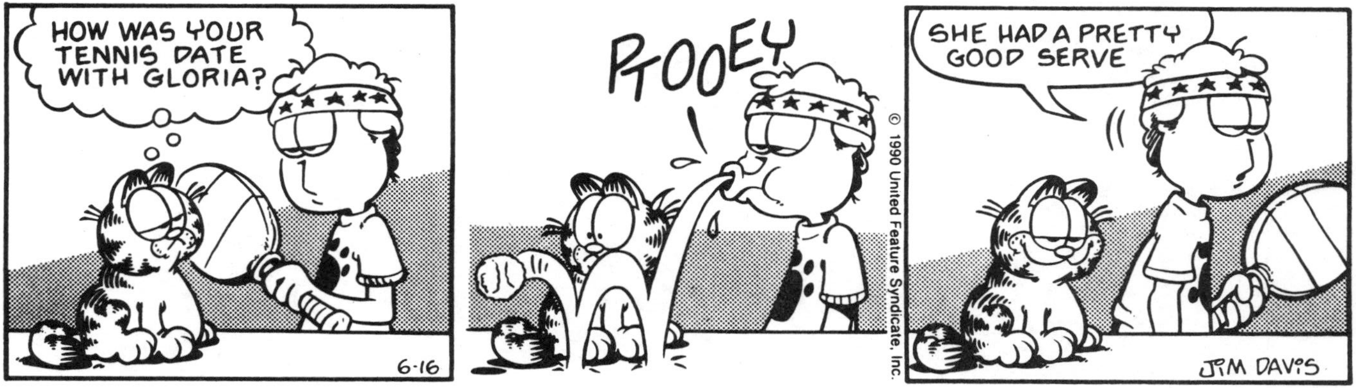
HOW WAS YOUR TENNIS DATE WITH GLORIA?
6-16
PTOOEY
SHE HAD A PRETTY GOOD SERVE
JIM DAVIS
© 1990 United Feature Syndicate, Inc.

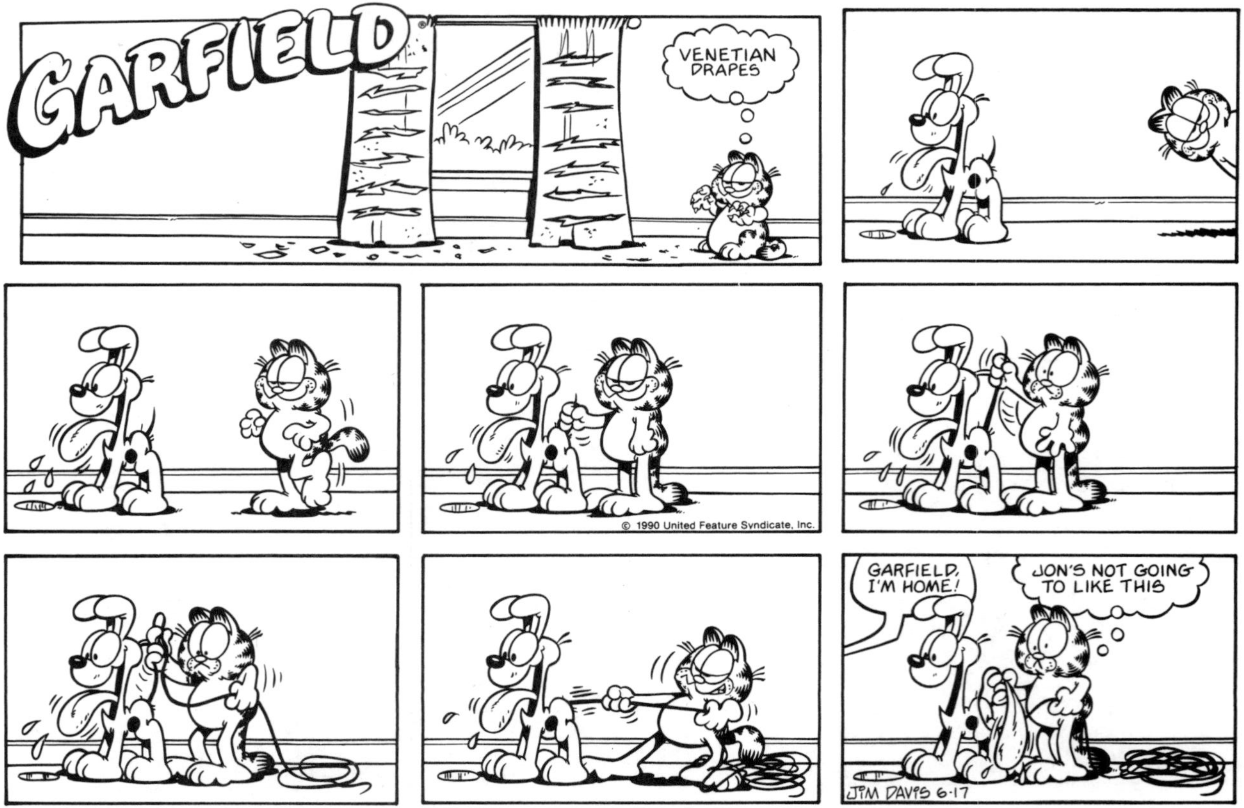
GARFIELD
VENETIAN DRAPES
© 1990 United Feature Syndicate, Inc.
GARFIELD, I'M HOME!
JON'S NOT GOING TO LIKE THIS
JIM DAVIS 6-17

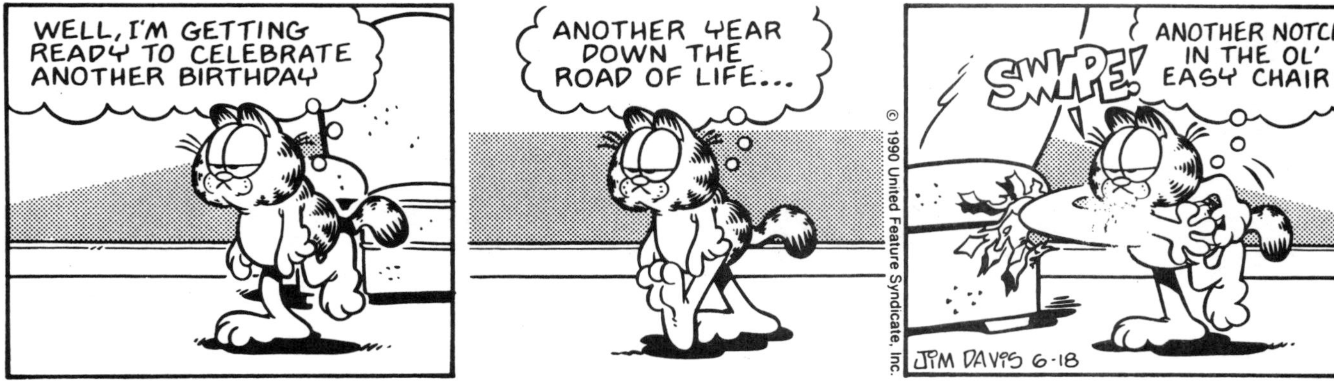
WELL, I'M GETTING READY TO CELEBRATE ANOTHER BIRTHDAY
ANOTHER YEAR DOWN THE ROAD OF LIFE...
SWIPE!
ANOTHER NOTCH IN THE OL' EASY CHAIR
JIM DAVIS 6-18

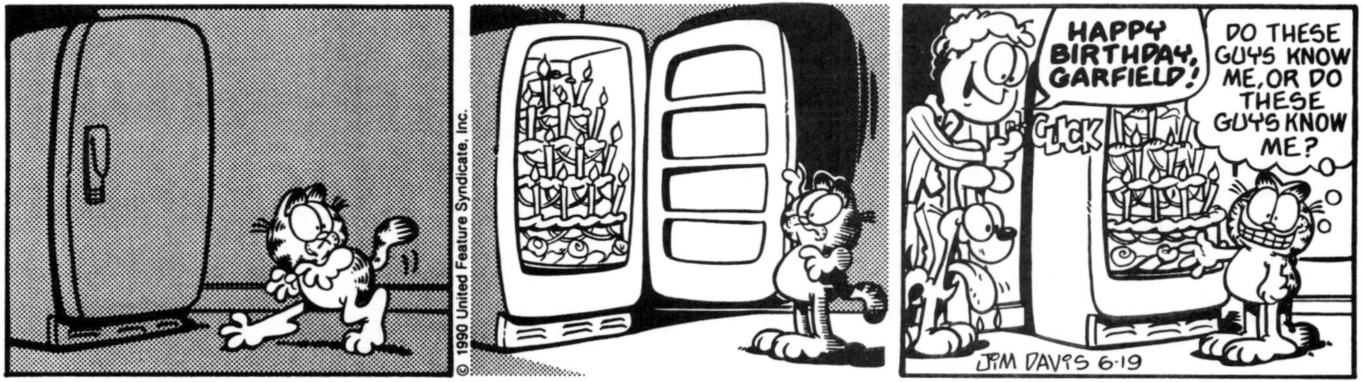
CLICK
HAPPY BIRTHDAY, GARFIELD!
DO THESE GUYS KNOW ME, OR DO THESE GUYS KNOW ME?
JIM DAVIS 6-19

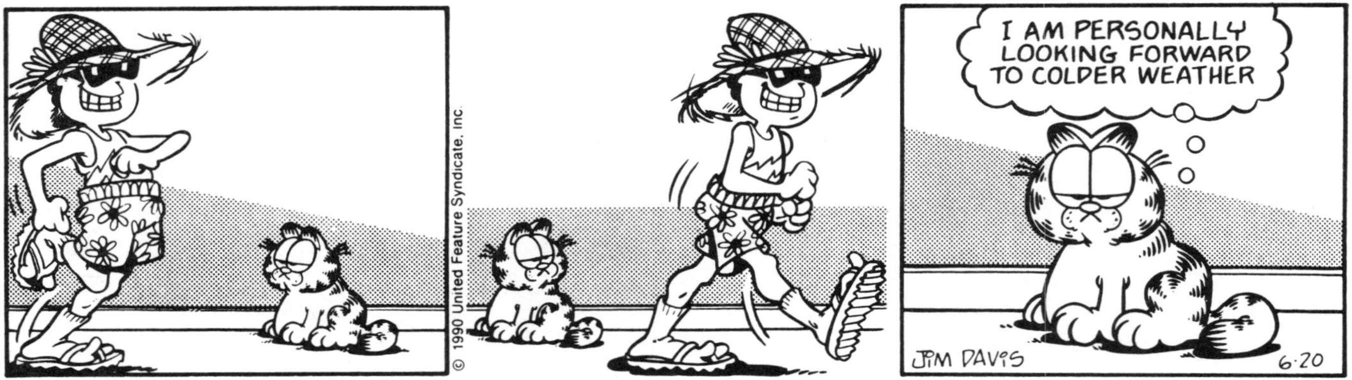
I AM PERSONALLY LOOKING FORWARD TO COLDER WEATHER
JIM DAVIS 6·20

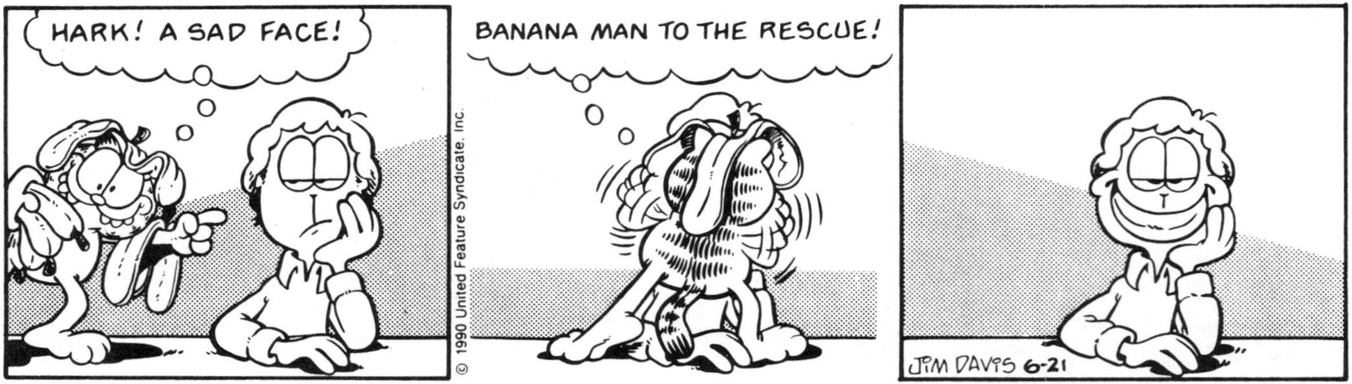
HARK! A SAD FACE!
BANANA MAN TO THE RESCUE!
JIM DAVIS 6-21

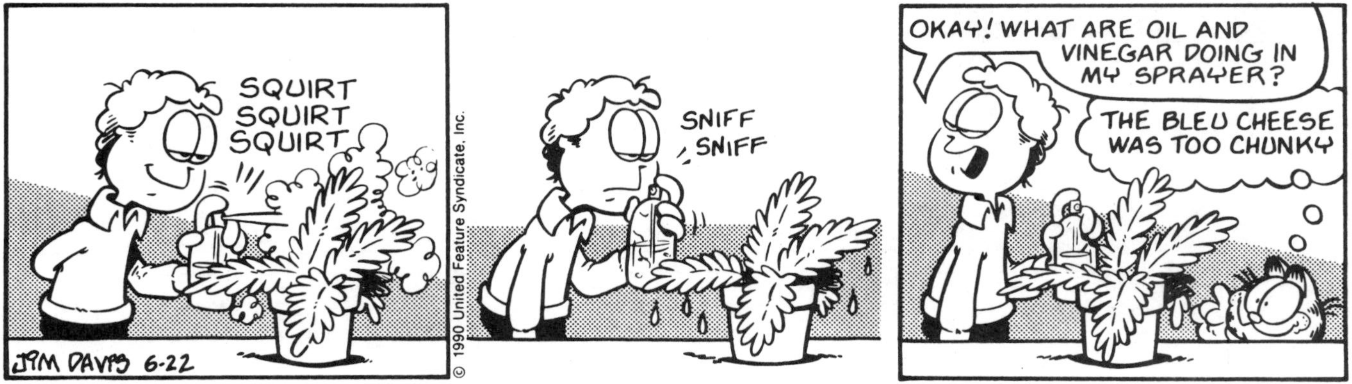
SQUIRT
SQUIRT
SQUIRT
JIM DAVIS 6-22
© 1990 United Feature Syndicate, Inc.
SNIFF
SNIFF
OKAY! WHAT ARE OIL AND VINEGAR DOING IN MY SPRAYER?
THE BLEU CHEESE WAS TOO CHUNKY

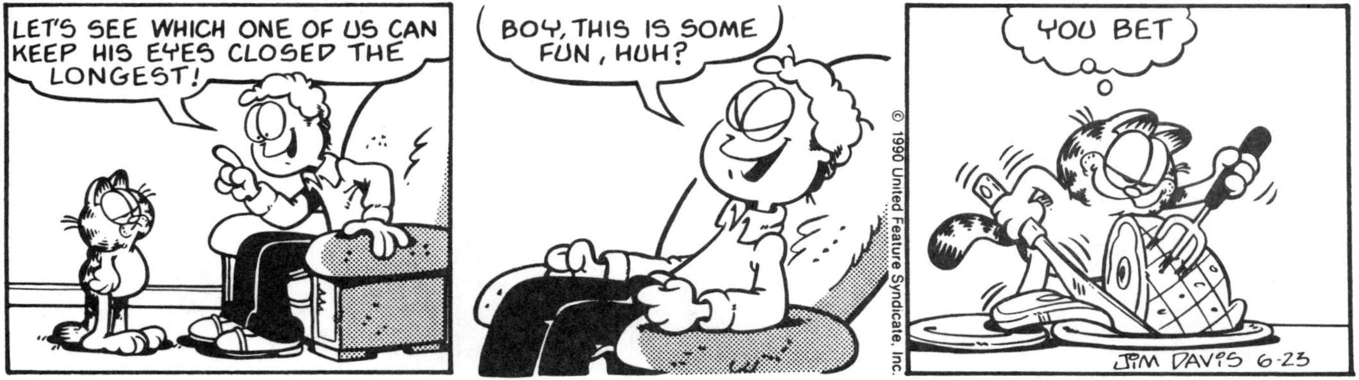
LET'S SEE WHICH ONE OF US CAN KEEP HIS EYES CLOSED THE LONGEST!
BOY, THIS IS SOME FUN, HUH?
© 1990 United Feature Syndicate, Inc.
YOU BET
JIM DAVIS 6-23

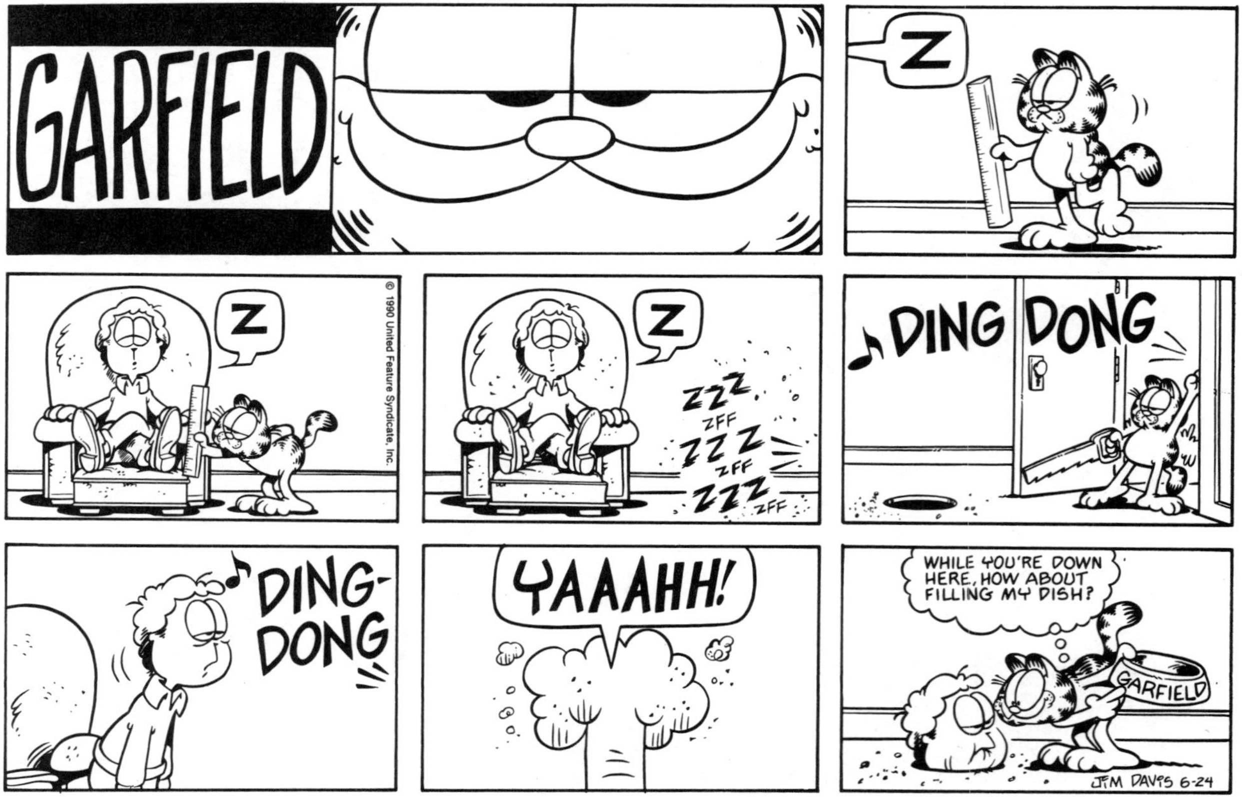
GARFIELD
Z
Z
© 1990 United Feature Syndicate, Inc.
Z
Z Z Z
ZFF
Z Z Z
ZFF
Z Z Z
ZFF
DING DONG
DING-
DONG
YAAAHH!
WHILE YOU'RE DOWN HERE, HOW ABOUT FILLING MY DISH?
GARFIELD
JIM DAVIS 6-24

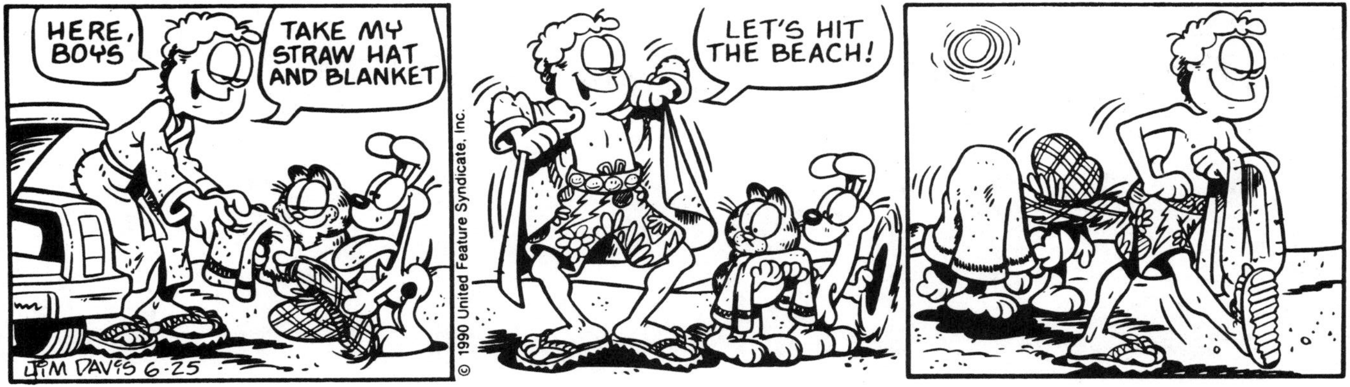
HERE, BOYS
TAKE MY STRAW HAT AND BLANKET
JIM DAVIS 6-25
© 1990 United Feature Syndicate, Inc.
LET'S HIT THE BEACH!

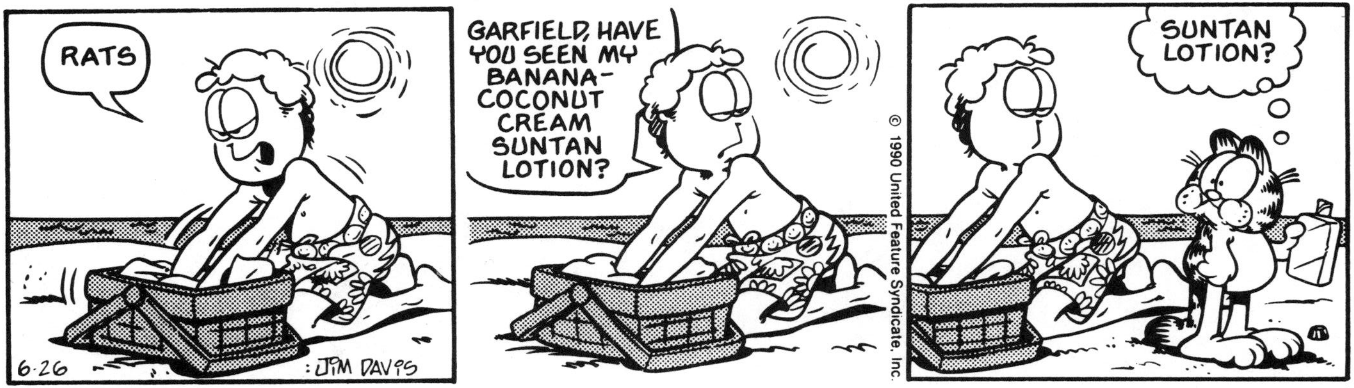
RATS
6-26
JIM DAVIS
GARFIELD, HAVE YOU SEEN MY BANANA-COCONUT CREAM SUNTAN LOTION?
© 1990 United Feature Syndicate, Inc.
SUNTAN LOTION?

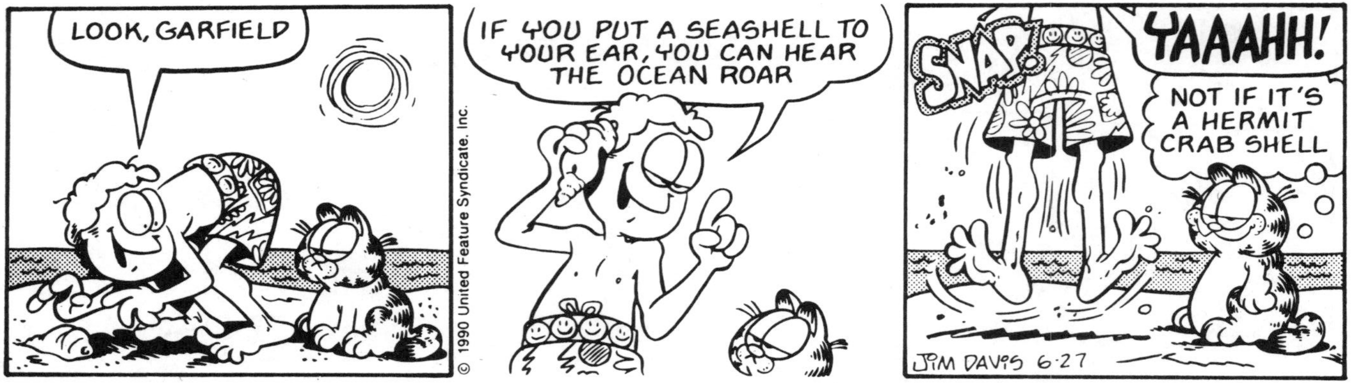
LOOK, GARFIELD
© 1990 United Feature Syndicate, Inc.
IF YOU PUT A SEASHELL TO YOUR EAR, YOU CAN HEAR THE OCEAN ROAR
SNAP!
YAAAHH!
NOT IF IT'S A HERMIT CRAB SHELL
JIM DAVIS 6·27

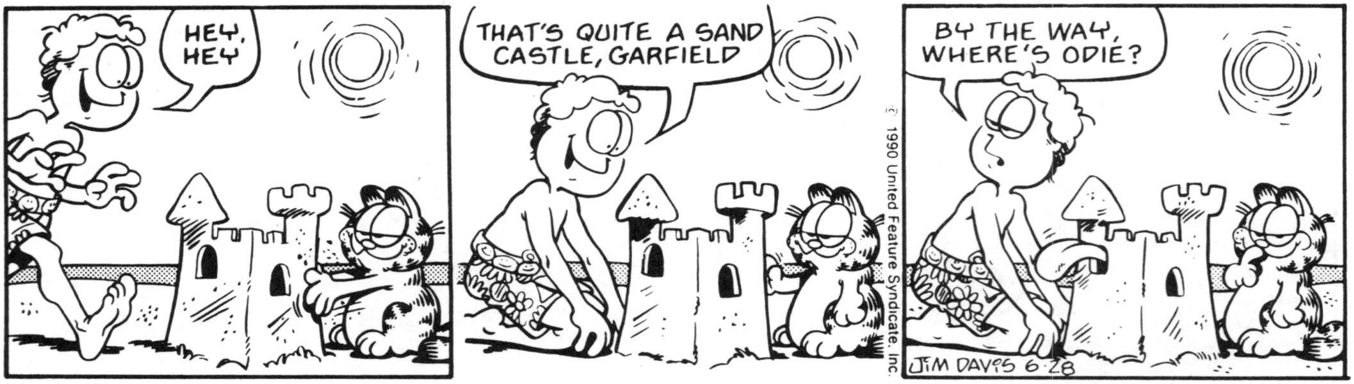
HEY, HEY
THAT'S QUITE A SAND CASTLE, GARFIELD
© 1990 United Feature Syndicate, Inc.
BY THE WAY, WHERE'S ODIE?
JIM DAVIS 6·28

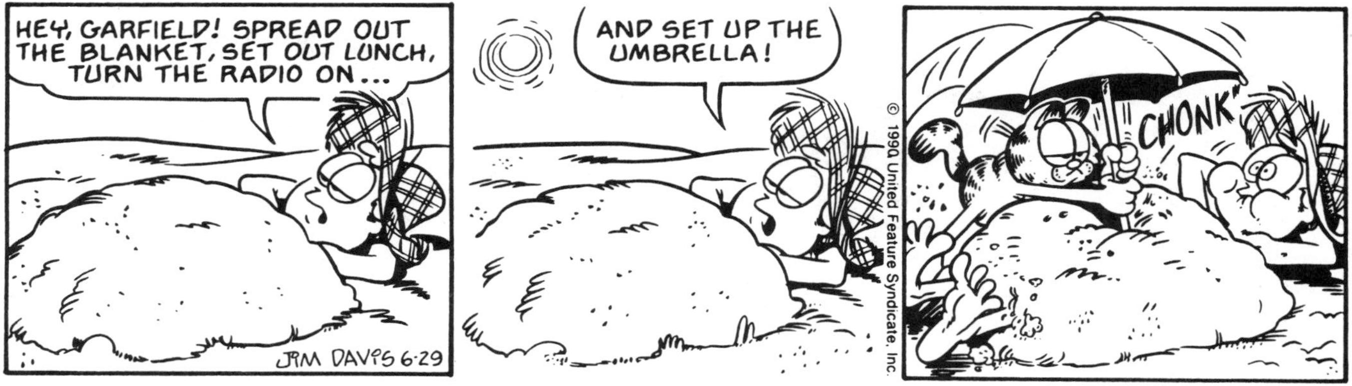
HEY, GARFIELD! SPREAD OUT THE BLANKET, SET OUT LUNCH, TURN THE RADIO ON...
JIM DAVIS 6-29
AND SET UP THE UMBRELLA!
CHONK

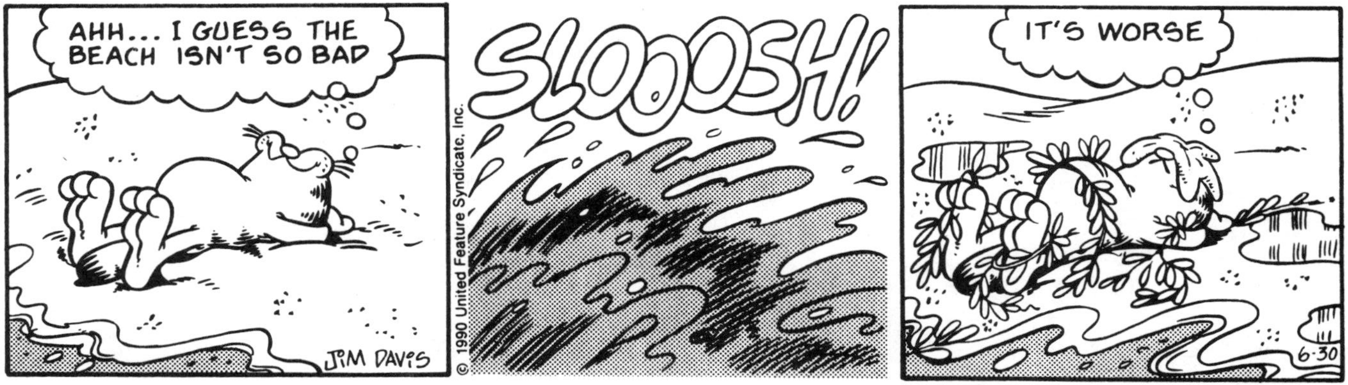
AHH... I GUESS THE BEACH ISN'T SO BAD
JIM DAVIS
SLOOOSH!
IT'S WORSE
6-30

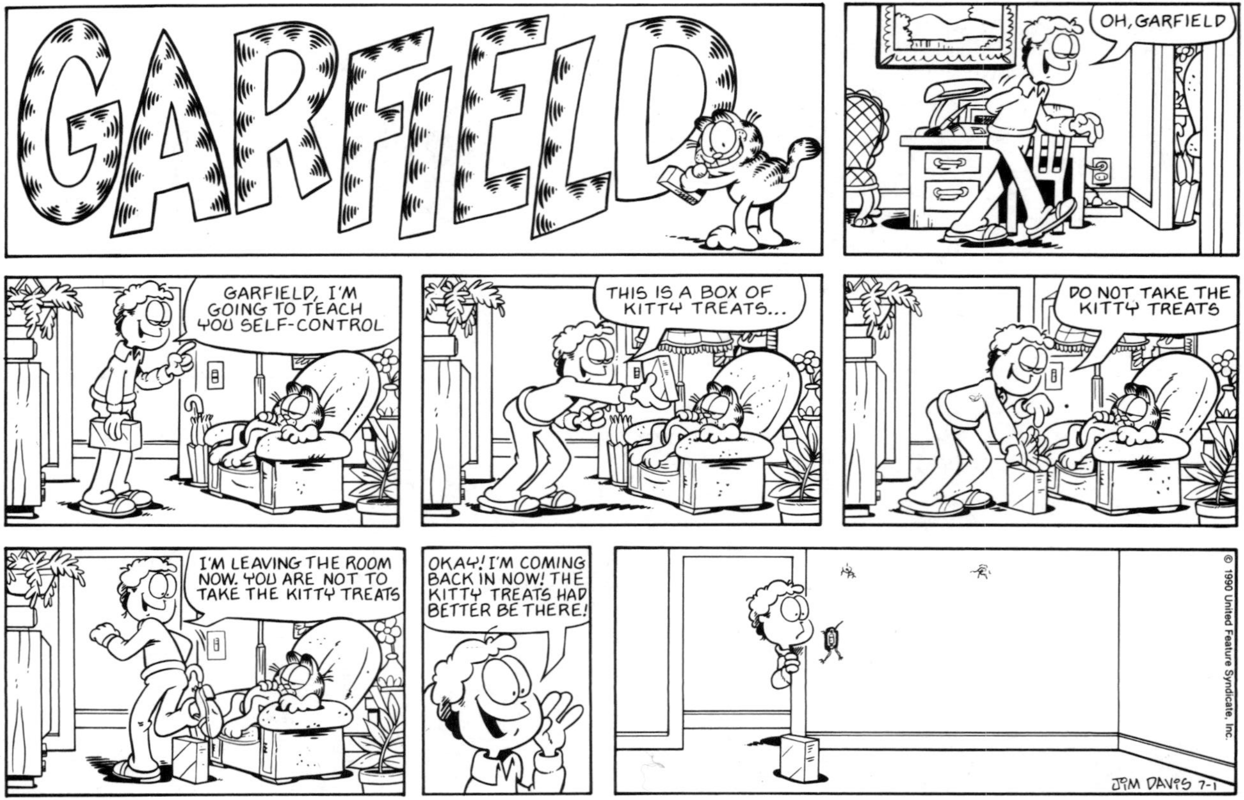
GARFIELD
OH, GARFIELD
GARFIELD, I'M GOING TO TEACH YOU SELF-CONTROL
THIS IS A BOX OF KITTY TREATS...
DO NOT TAKE THE KITTY TREATS
I'M LEAVING THE ROOM NOW. YOU ARE NOT TO TAKE THE KITTY TREATS
OKAY! I'M COMING BACK IN NOW! THE KITTY TREATS HAD BETTER BE THERE!
© 1990 United Feature Syndicate, Inc.
JIM DAVIS 7-1

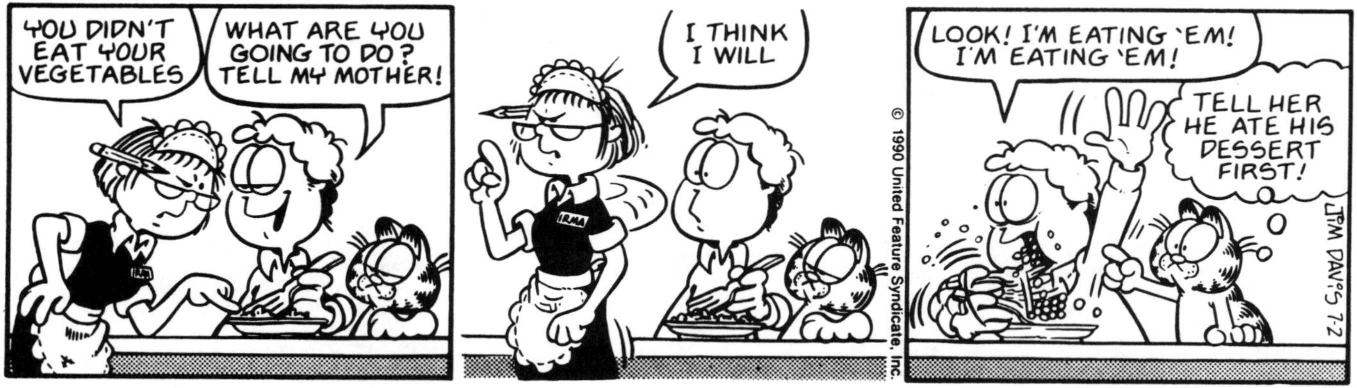
YOU DIDN'T EAT YOUR VEGETABLES
WHAT ARE YOU GOING TO DO? TELL MY MOTHER!
IRMA
I THINK I WILL
LOOK! I'M EATING 'EM! I'M EATING 'EM!
TELL HER HE ATE HIS DESSERT FIRST!
JIM DAVIS 7-2

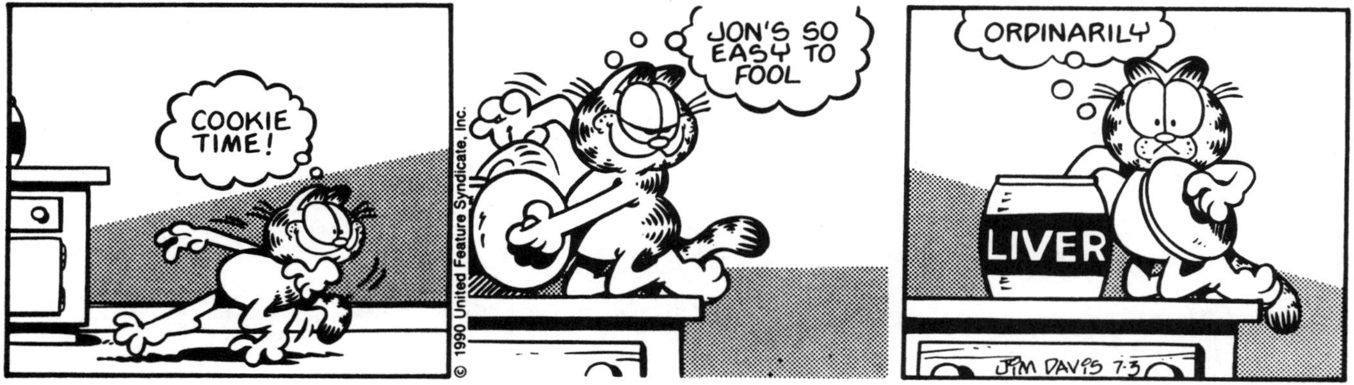
COOKIE TIME!
JON'S SO EASY TO FOOL
ORDINARILY
LIVER
JIM DAVIS 7-3

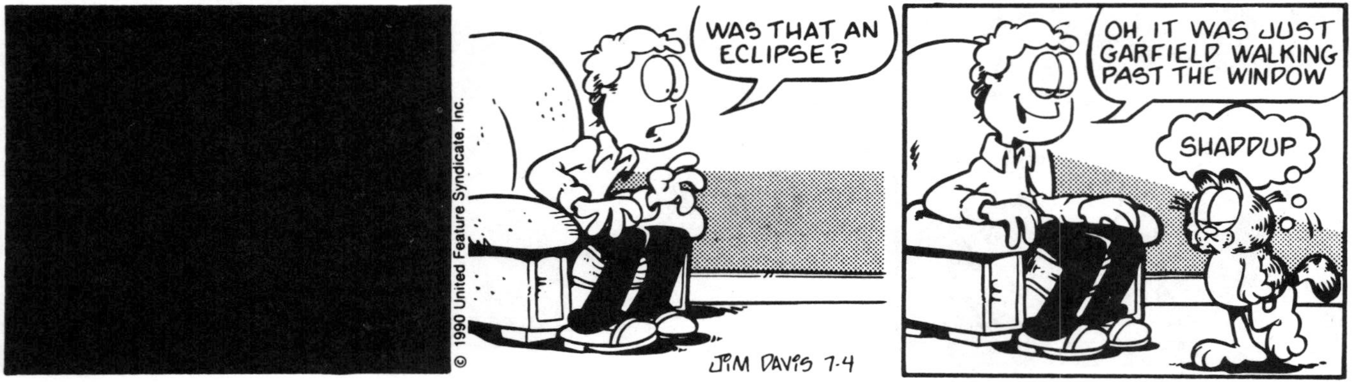
WAS THAT AN ECLIPSE?
© 1990 United Feature Syndicate, Inc.
JIM DAVIS 7-4
OH, IT WAS JUST GARFIELD WALKING PAST THE WINDOW
SHADDUP

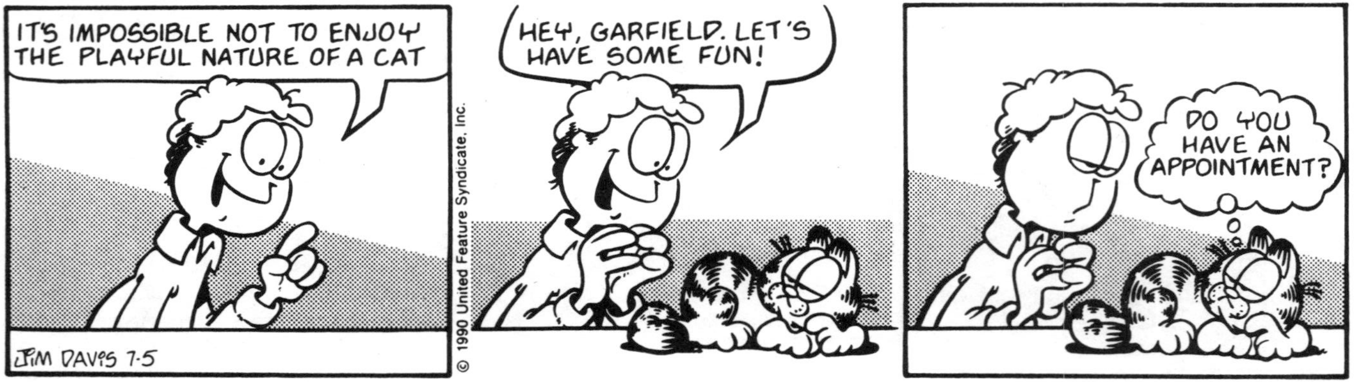
IT'S IMPOSSIBLE NOT TO ENJOY THE PLAYFUL NATURE OF A CAT
JIM DAVIS 7-5
© 1990 United Feature Syndicate, Inc.
HEY, GARFIELD. LET'S HAVE SOME FUN!
DO YOU HAVE AN APPOINTMENT?

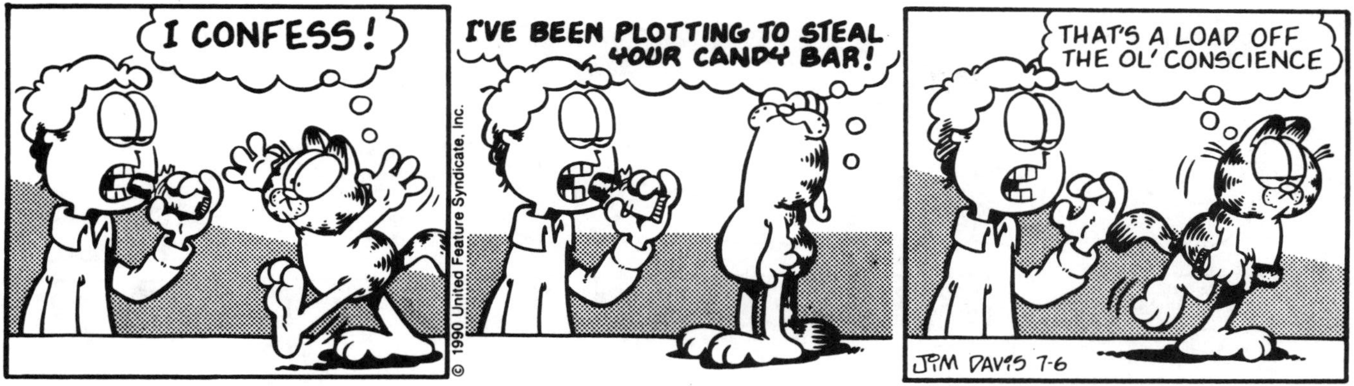
I CONFESS!
I'VE BEEN PLOTTING TO STEAL YOUR CANDY BAR!
THAT'S A LOAD OFF THE OL' CONSCIENCE
JIM DAVIS 7-6

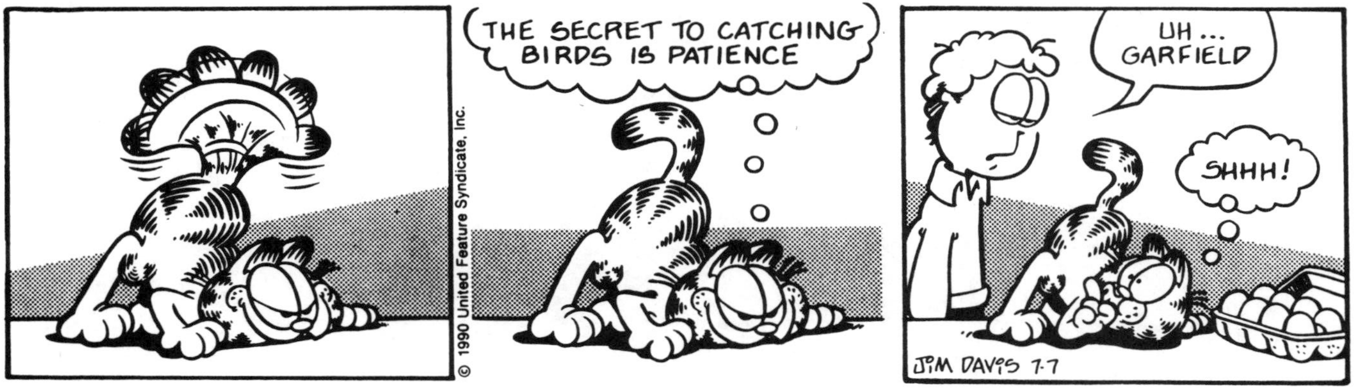
THE SECRET TO CATCHING BIRDS IS PATIENCE
UH... GARFIELD
SHHH!
JIM DAVIS 7-7

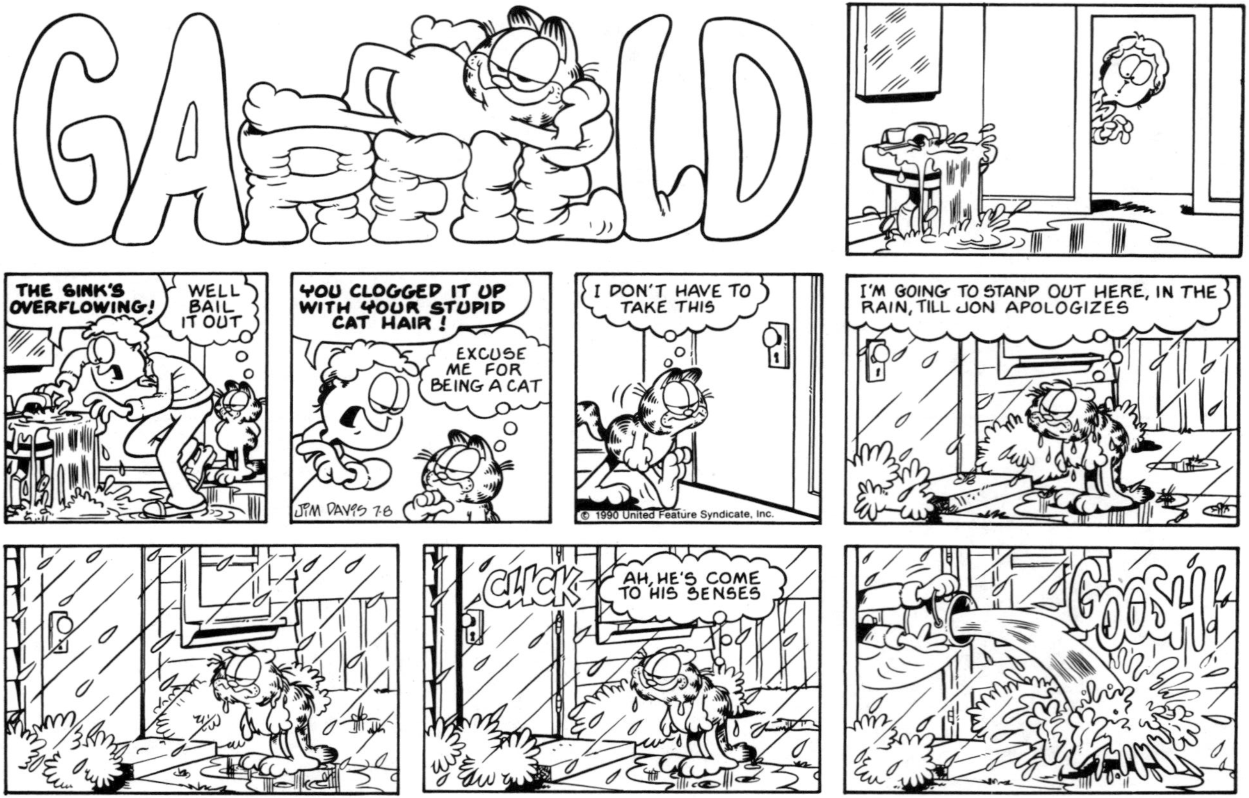
GARFIELD
THE SINK'S OVERFLOWING!
WELL BAIL IT OUT
YOU CLOGGED IT UP WITH YOUR STUPID CAT HAIR!
EXCUSE ME FOR BEING A CAT
JIM DAVIS 7-8
I DON'T HAVE TO TAKE THIS
© 1990 United Feature Syndicate, Inc.
I'M GOING TO STAND OUT HERE, IN THE RAIN, TILL JON APOLOGIZES
CLICK
AH, HE'S COME TO HIS SENSES
GOOSH!

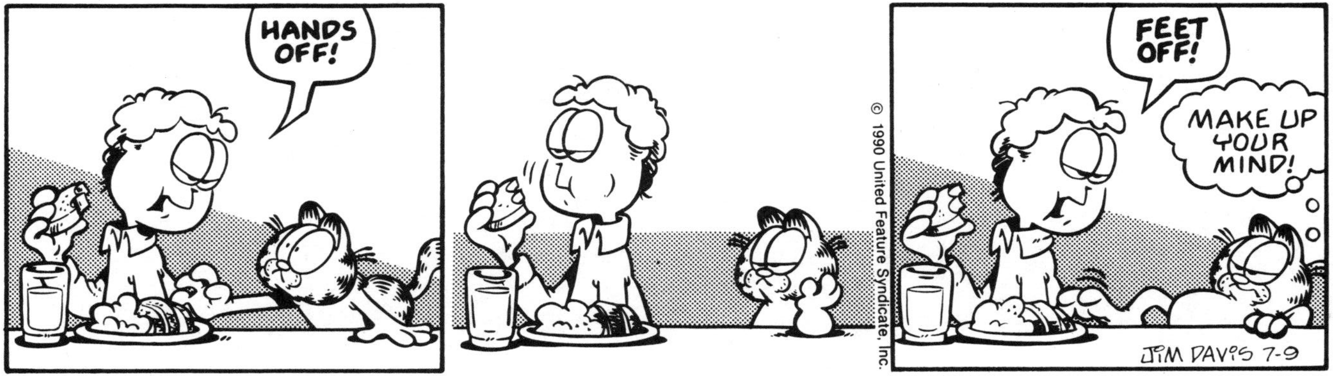
HANDS OFF!
FEET OFF!
MAKE UP YOUR MIND!
JIM DAVIS 7-9
© 1990 United Feature Syndicate, Inc.

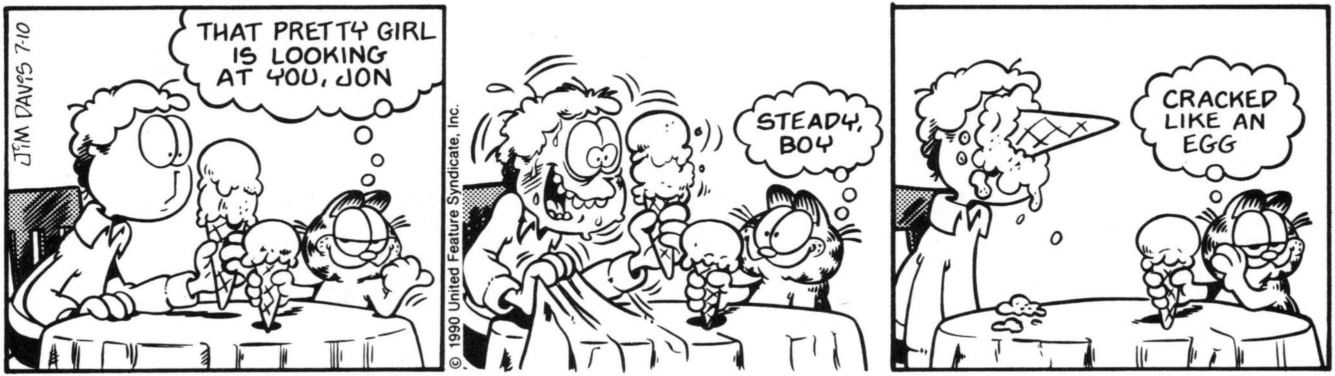
JIM DAVIS 7-10
THAT PRETTY GIRL IS LOOKING AT YOU, JON
© 1990 United Feature Syndicate, Inc.
STEADY, BOY
CRACKED LIKE AN EGG

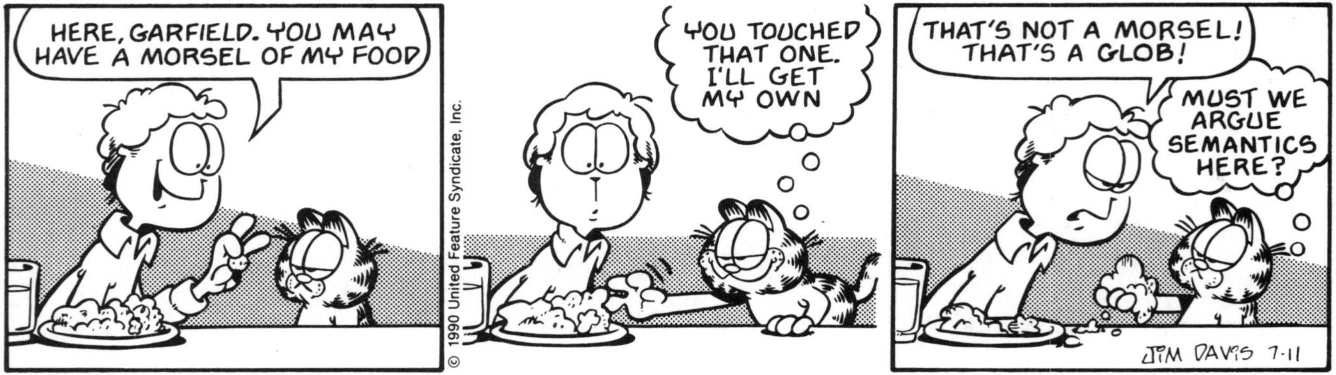
HERE, GARFIELD. YOU MAY HAVE A MORSEL OF MY FOOD
YOU TOUCHED THAT ONE. I'LL GET MY OWN
THAT'S NOT A MORSEL! THAT'S A GLOB!
MUST WE ARGUE SEMANTICS HERE?
JIM DAVIS 7-11
© 1990 United Feature Syndicate, Inc.

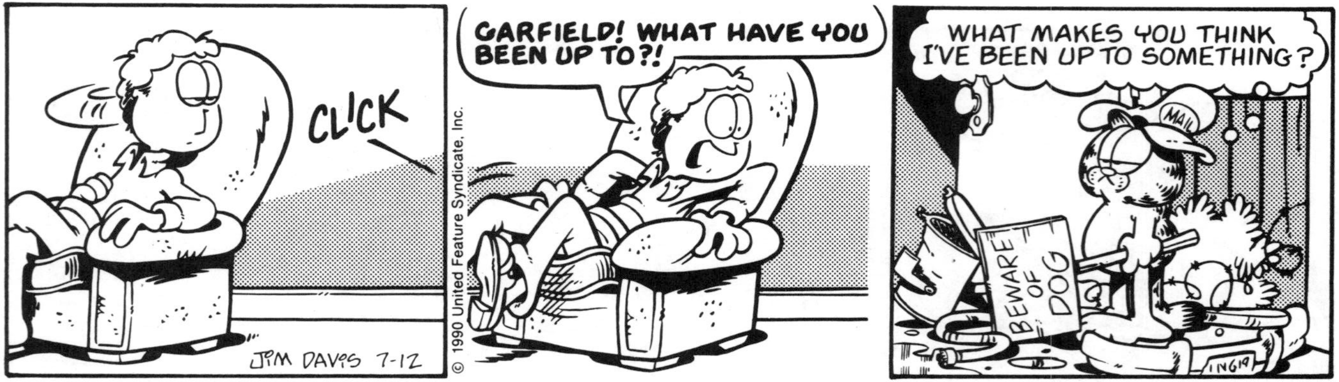
CLICK
JIM DAVIS 7-12
GARFIELD! WHAT HAVE YOU BEEN UP TO?!
WHAT MAKES YOU THINK I'VE BEEN UP TO SOMETHING?
MAIL
BEWARE OF DOG
© 1990 United Feature Syndicate, Inc.

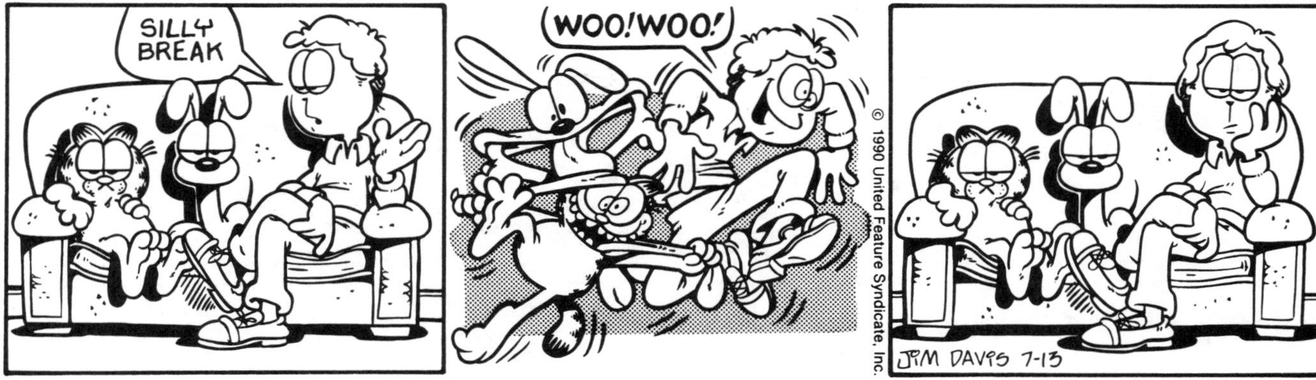
SILLY BREAK
WOO! WOO!
© 1990 United Feature Syndicate, Inc.
JIM DAVIS 7-13

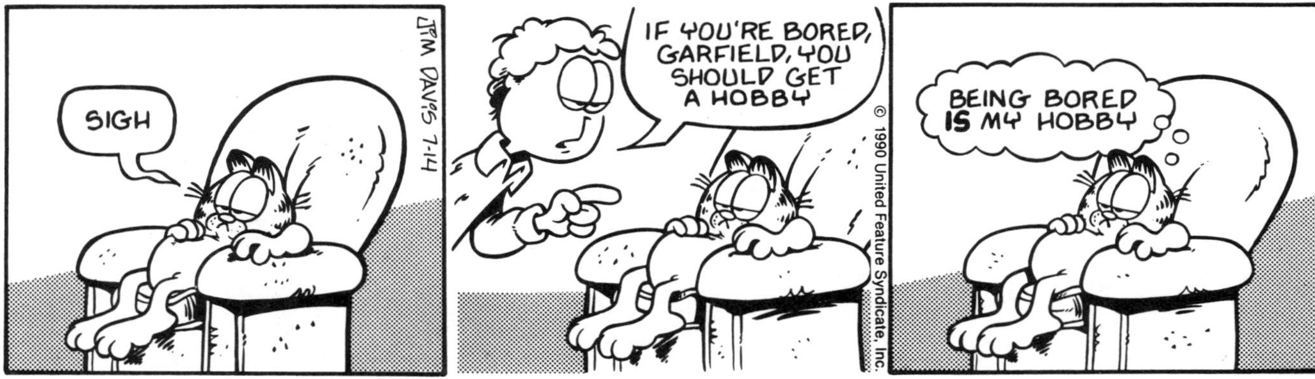
SIGH
JIM DAVIS 7-14
IF YOU'RE BORED, GARFIELD, YOU SHOULD GET A HOBBY
© 1990 United Feature Syndicate, Inc.
BEING BORED **IS** MY HOBBY

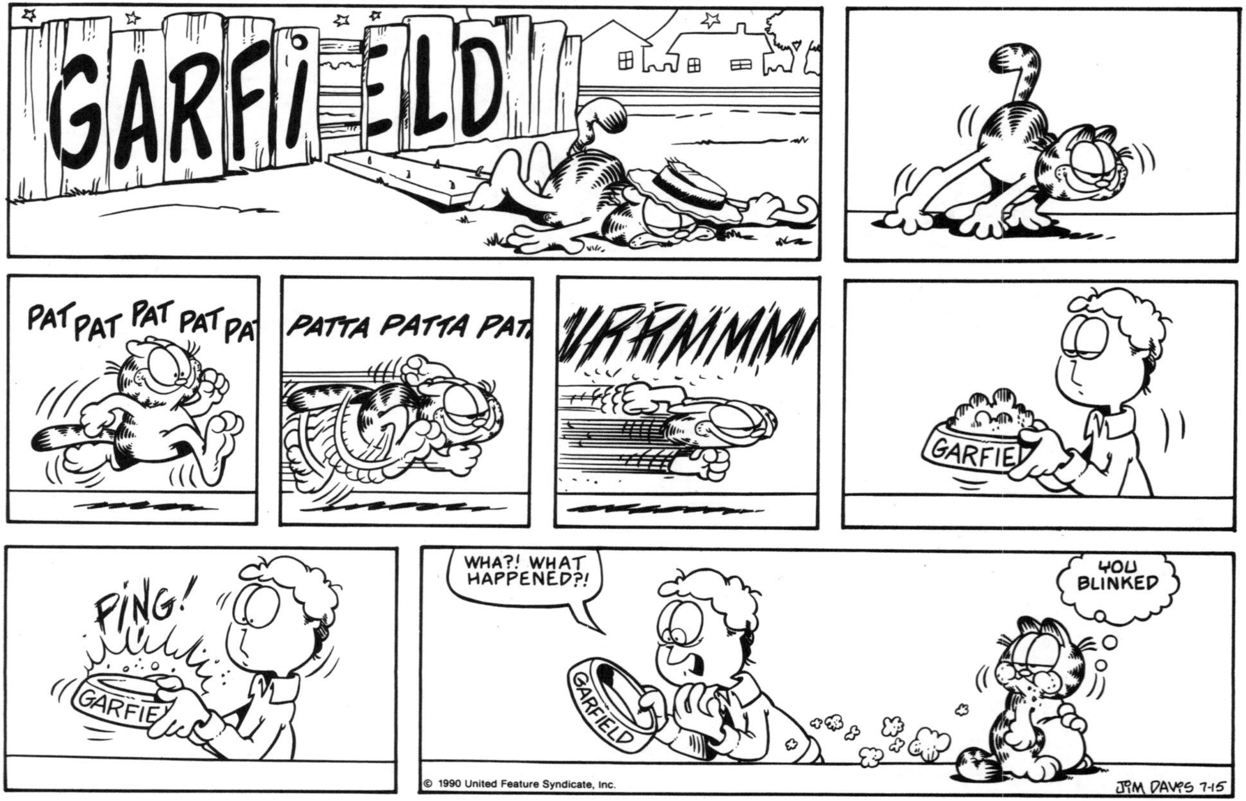
GARFIELD
PAT PAT PAT PAT PAT
PATTA PATTA PAT
VRRMMM
GARFIE
PING!
GARFIE
WHA?! WHAT HAPPENED?!
GARFIELD
YOU BLINKED
© 1990 United Feature Syndicate, Inc.
JIM DAVIS 7-15

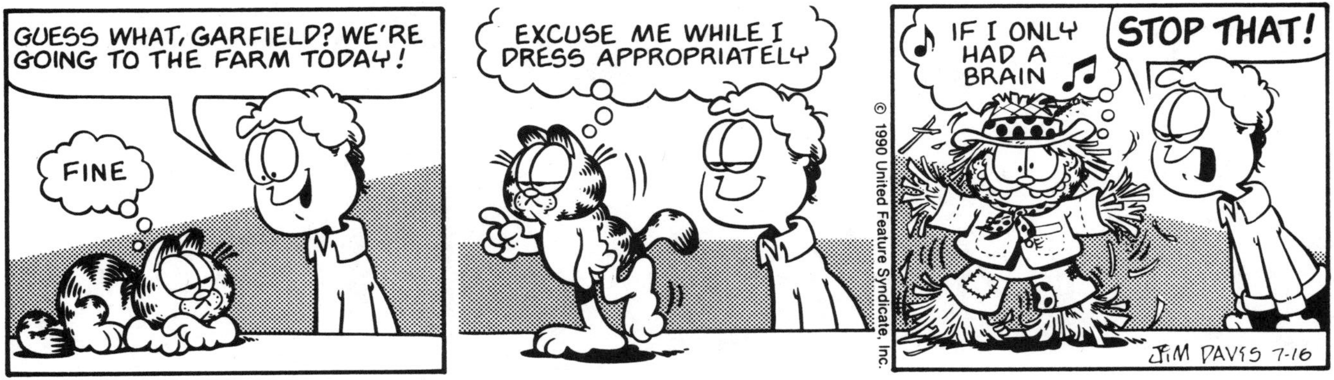
GUESS WHAT, GARFIELD? WE'RE GOING TO THE FARM TODAY!
FINE
EXCUSE ME WHILE I DRESS APPROPRIATELY
IF I ONLY HAD A BRAIN
STOP THAT!
JIM DAVIS 7-16
© 1990 United Feature Syndicate, Inc.

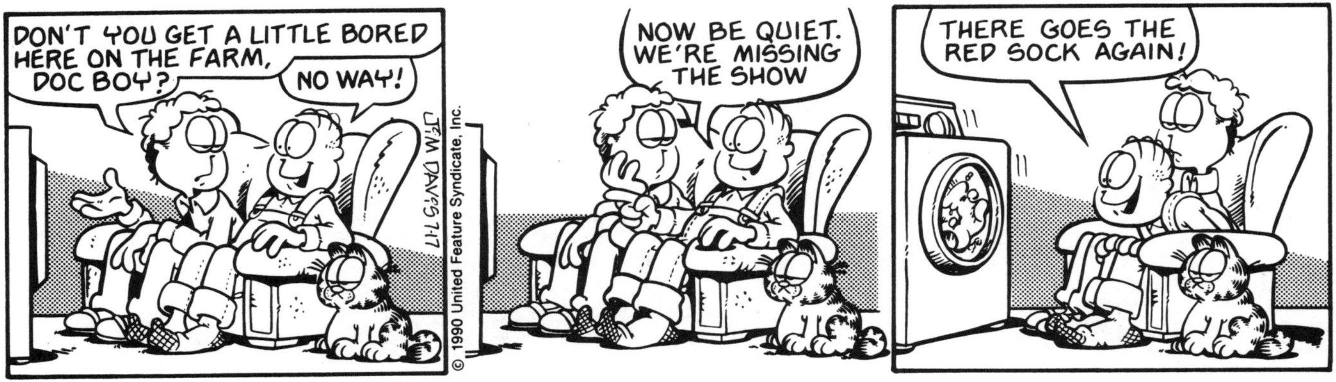
DON'T YOU GET A LITTLE BORED HERE ON THE FARM, DOC BOY?
NO WAY!
JIM DAVIS 7-17
© 1990 United Feature Syndicate, Inc.
NOW BE QUIET. WE'RE MISSING THE SHOW
THERE GOES THE RED SOCK AGAIN!

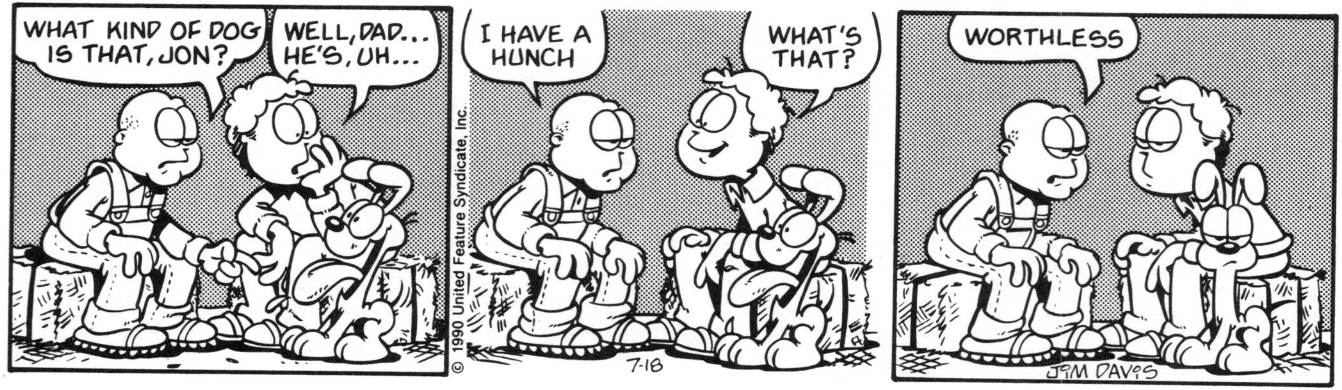
WHAT KIND OF DOG IS THAT, JON?
WELL, DAD... HE'S, UH...
I HAVE A HUNCH
WHAT'S THAT?
WORTHLESS
© 1990 United Feature Syndicate, Inc.
7-18
JIM DAVIS

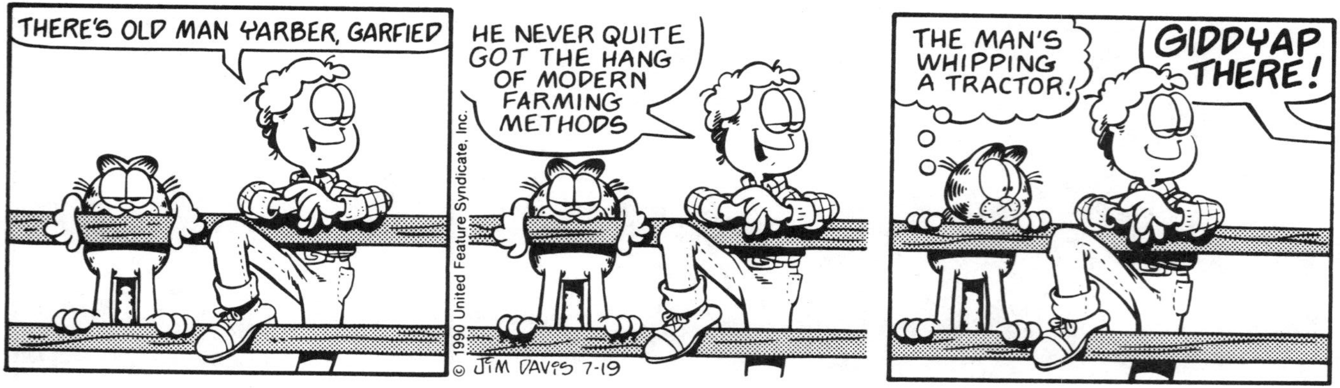
THERE'S OLD MAN YARBER, GARFIED
HE NEVER QUITE GOT THE HANG OF MODERN FARMING METHODS
THE MAN'S WHIPPING A TRACTOR!
GIDDYAP THERE!
© 1990 United Feature Syndicate, Inc.
JIM DAVIS 7-19

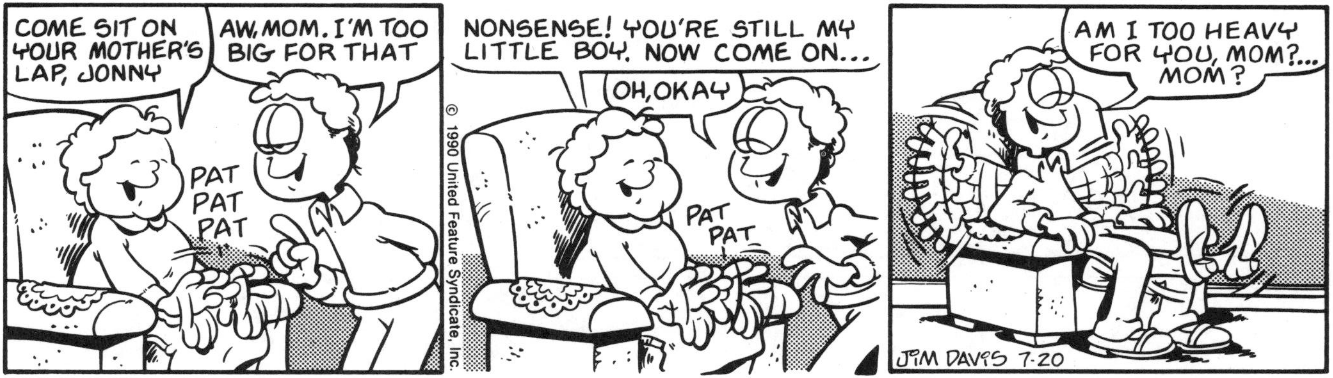
COME SIT ON YOUR MOTHER'S LAP, JONNY
AW, MOM. I'M TOO BIG FOR THAT
PAT PAT PAT
NONSENSE! YOU'RE STILL MY LITTLE BOY. NOW COME ON...
OH, OKAY
PAT PAT
AM I TOO HEAVY FOR YOU, MOM?... MOM?
JIM DAVIS 7-20

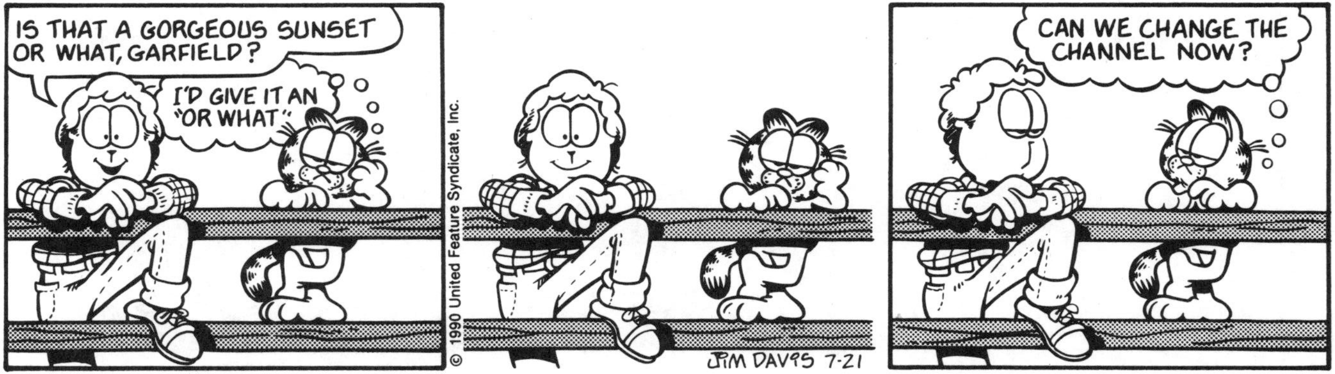
IS THAT A GORGEOUS SUNSET OR WHAT, GARFIELD?
I'D GIVE IT AN "OR WHAT"
JIM DAVIS 7-21
CAN WE CHANGE THE CHANNEL NOW?

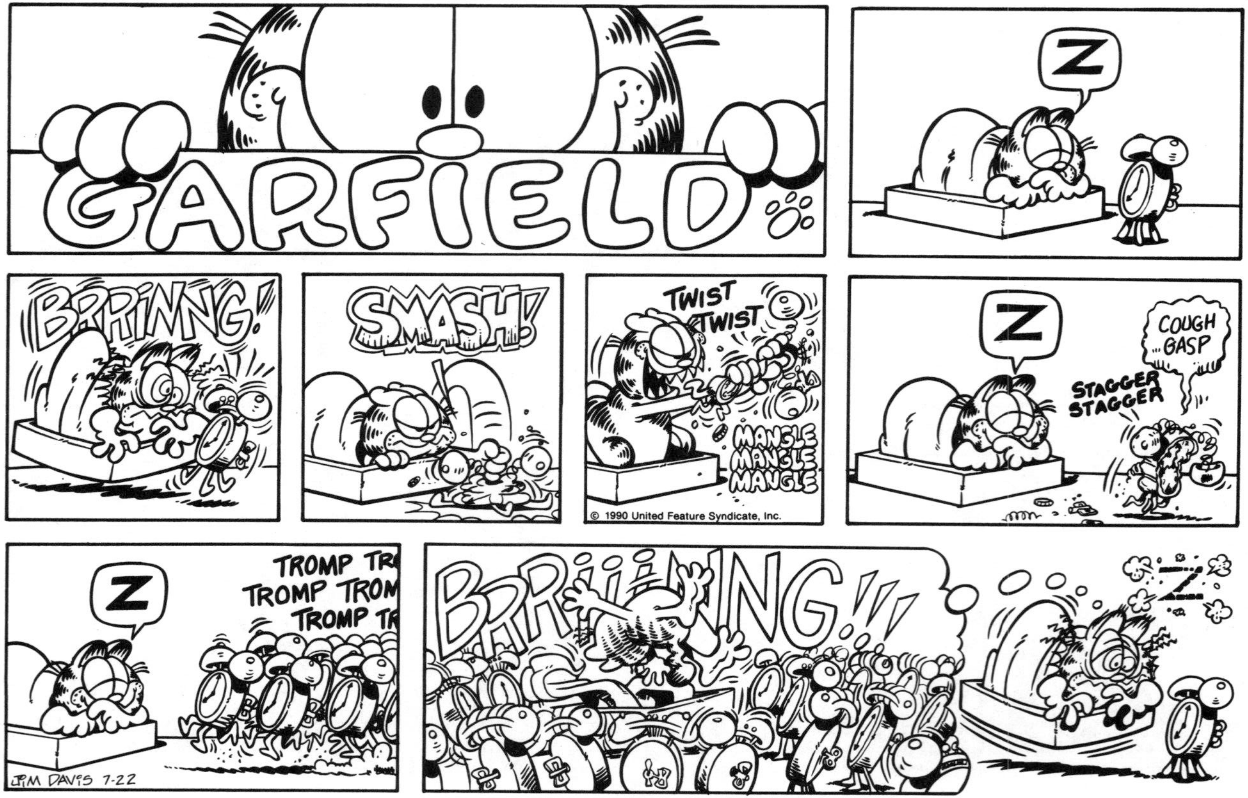
GARFIELD
Z
BRRINNG!
SMASH!
TWIST
TWIST
MANGLE
MANGLE
MANGLE
© 1990 United Feature Syndicate, Inc.
Z
STAGGER
STAGGER
COUGH
...GASP
Z
TROMP TR
TROMP TROM
TROMP TR
JIM DAVIS 7-22
BRRIIING!!!
Z

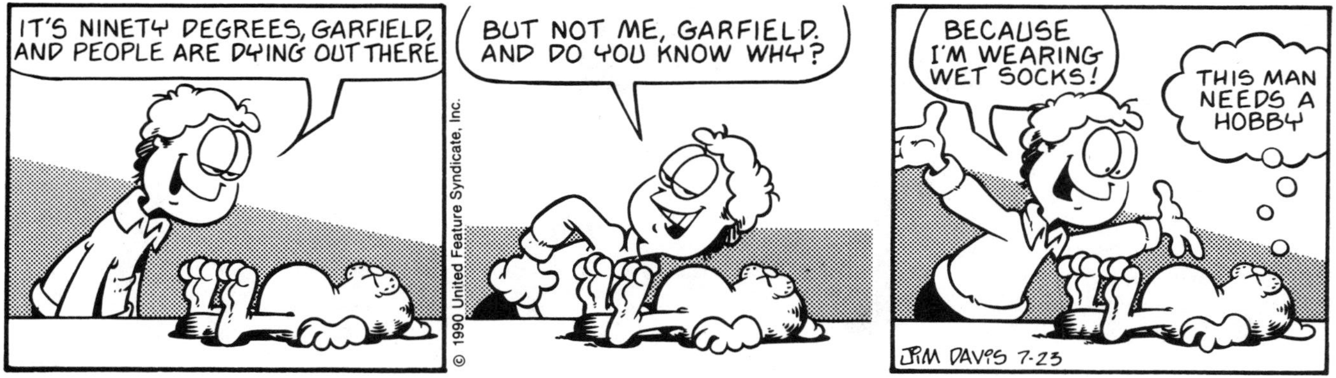
IT'S NINETY DEGREES, GARFIELD, AND PEOPLE ARE DYING OUT THERE
© 1990 United Feature Syndicate, Inc.
BUT NOT ME, GARFIELD. AND DO YOU KNOW WHY?
BECAUSE I'M WEARING WET SOCKS!
THIS MAN NEEDS A HOBBY
JIM DAVIS 7-23

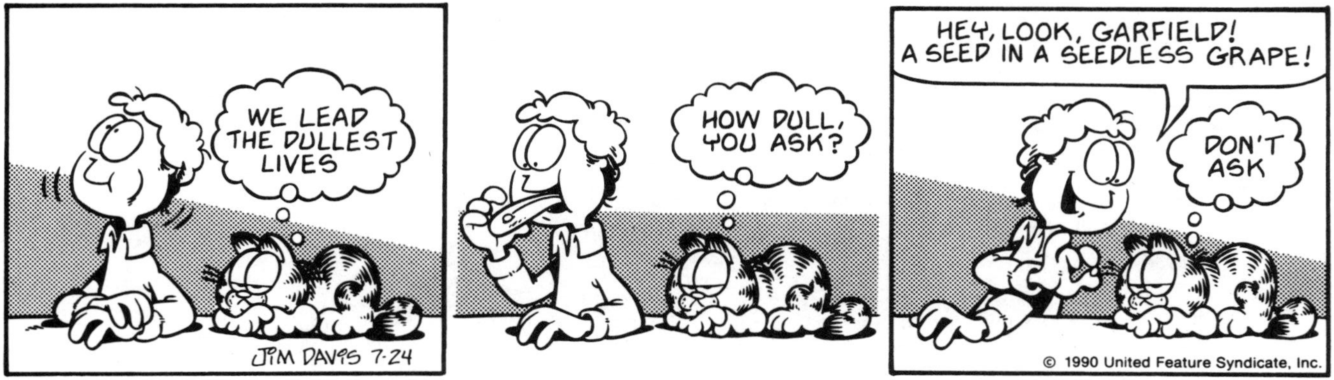
WE LEAD THE DULLEST LIVES
JIM DAVIS 7-24
HOW DULL, YOU ASK?
HEY, LOOK, GARFIELD! A SEED IN A SEEDLESS GRAPE!
DON'T ASK
© 1990 United Feature Syndicate, Inc.

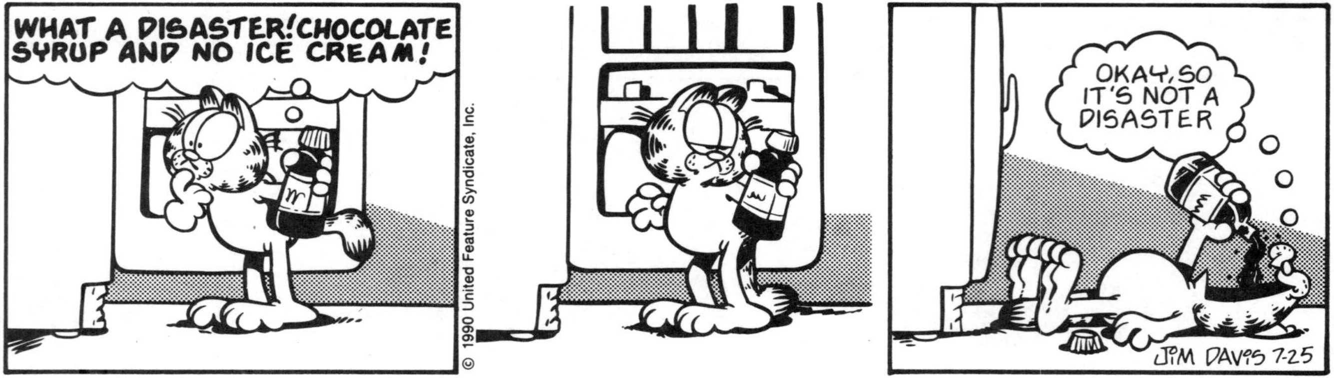
WHAT A DISASTER! CHOCOLATE SYRUP AND NO ICE CREAM!
OKAY, SO IT'S NOT A DISASTER
JIM DAVIS 7-25

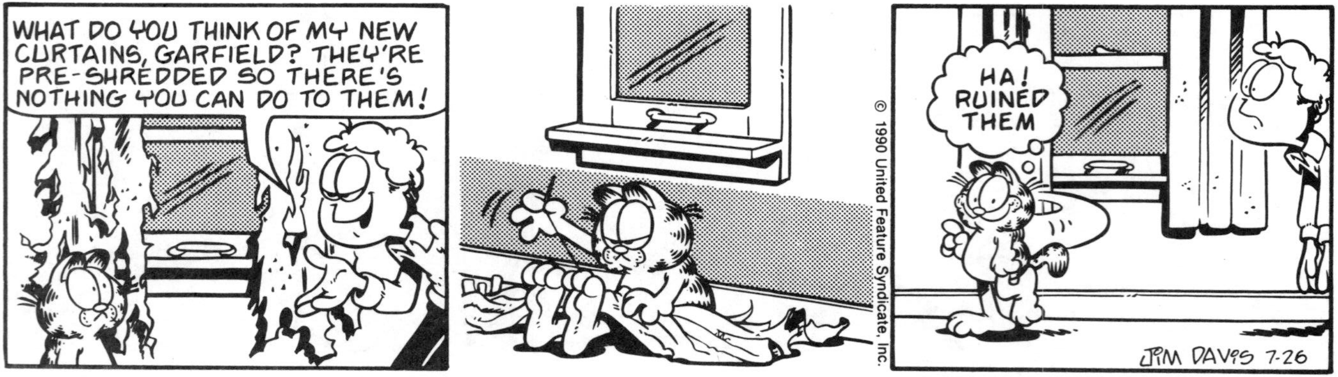
WHAT DO YOU THINK OF MY NEW CURTAINS, GARFIELD? THEY'RE PRE-SHREDDED SO THERE'S NOTHING YOU CAN DO TO THEM!
HA! RUINED THEM
JIM DAVIS 7-26

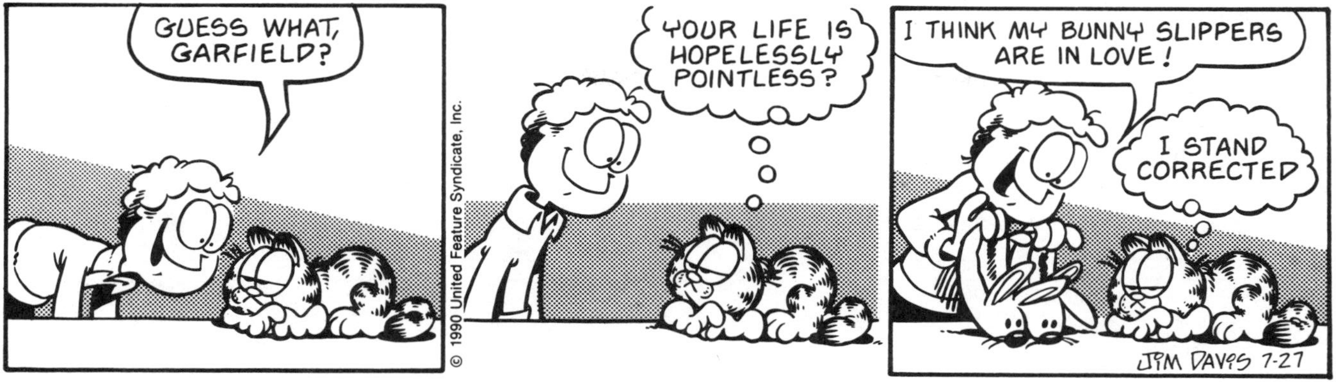
GUESS WHAT, GARFIELD?
YOUR LIFE IS HOPELESSLY POINTLESS?
I THINK MY BUNNY SLIPPERS ARE IN LOVE!
I STAND CORRECTED
JIM DAVIS 7-27
© 1990 United Feature Syndicate, Inc.

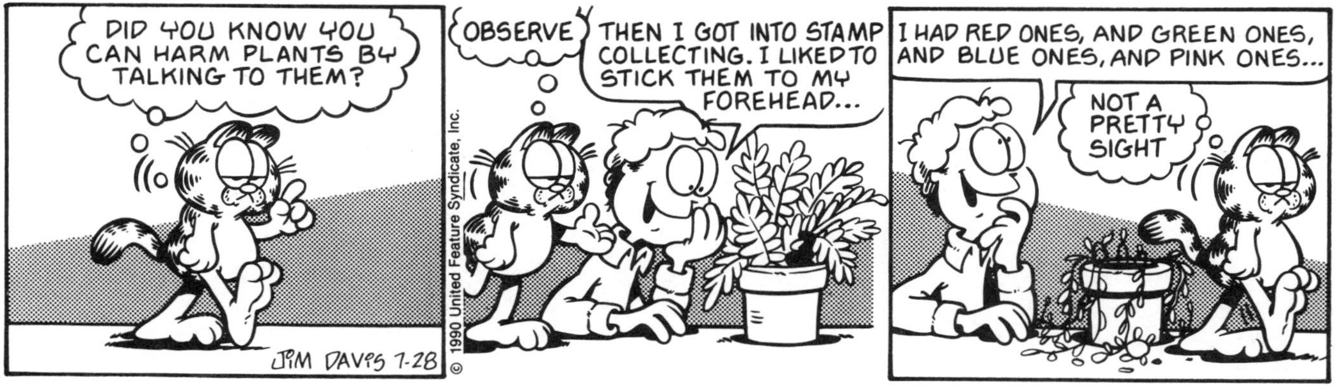
DID YOU KNOW YOU CAN HARM PLANTS BY TALKING TO THEM?
JIM DAVIS 7-28
OBSERVE
THEN I GOT INTO STAMP COLLECTING. I LIKED TO STICK THEM TO MY FOREHEAD...
I HAD RED ONES, AND GREEN ONES, AND BLUE ONES, AND PINK ONES...
NOT A PRETTY SIGHT
© 1990 United Feature Syndicate, Inc.

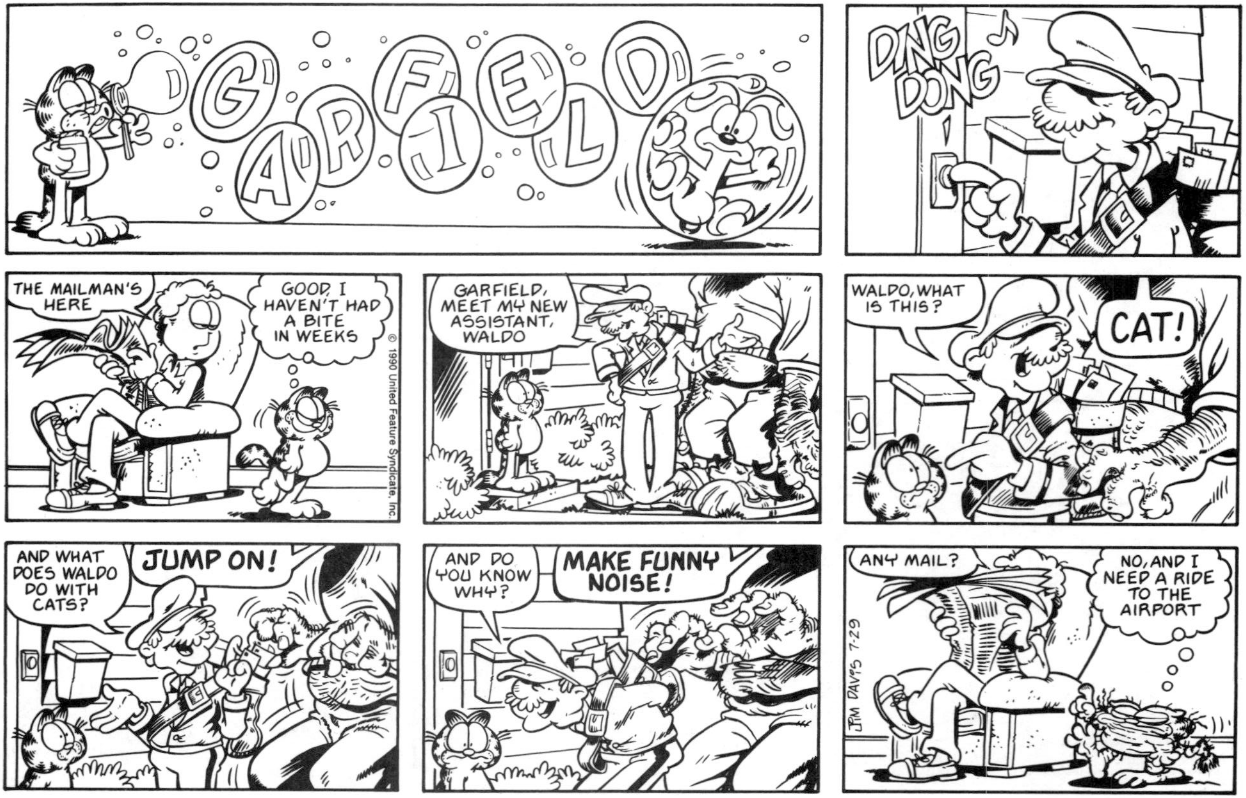
GARFIELD
DING DONG
THE MAILMAN'S HERE
GOOD, I HAVEN'T HAD A BITE IN WEEKS
© 1990 United Feature Syndicate, Inc.
GARFIELD, MEET MY NEW ASSISTANT, WALDO
WALDO, WHAT IS THIS?
CAT!
AND WHAT DOES WALDO DO WITH CATS?
JUMP ON!
AND DO YOU KNOW WHY?
MAKE FUNNY NOISE!
ANY MAIL?
NO, AND I NEED A RIDE TO THE AIRPORT
JIM DAVIS 7-29

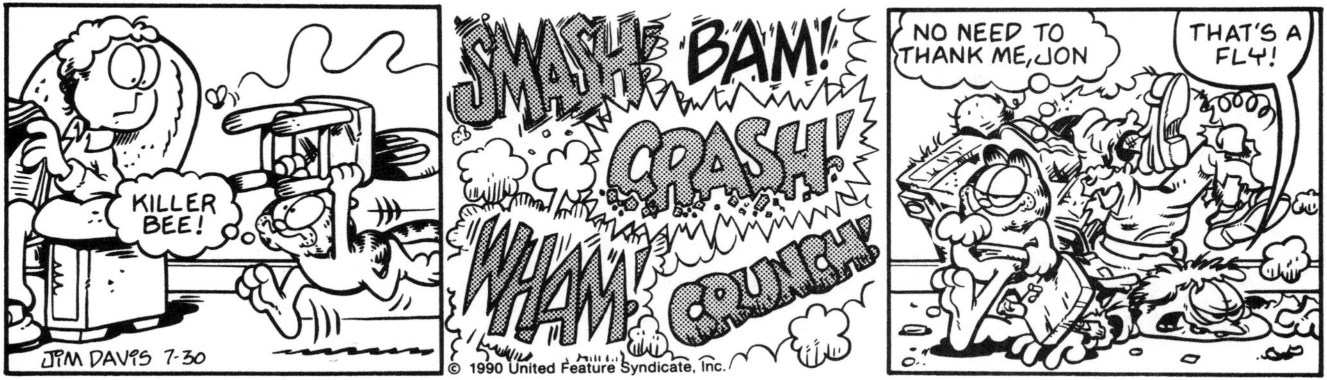
KILLER BEE!
JIM DAVIS 7-30
SMASH! BAM!
CRASH!
WHAM! CRUNCH!
© 1990 United Feature Syndicate, Inc.
NO NEED TO THANK ME, JON
THAT'S A FLY!

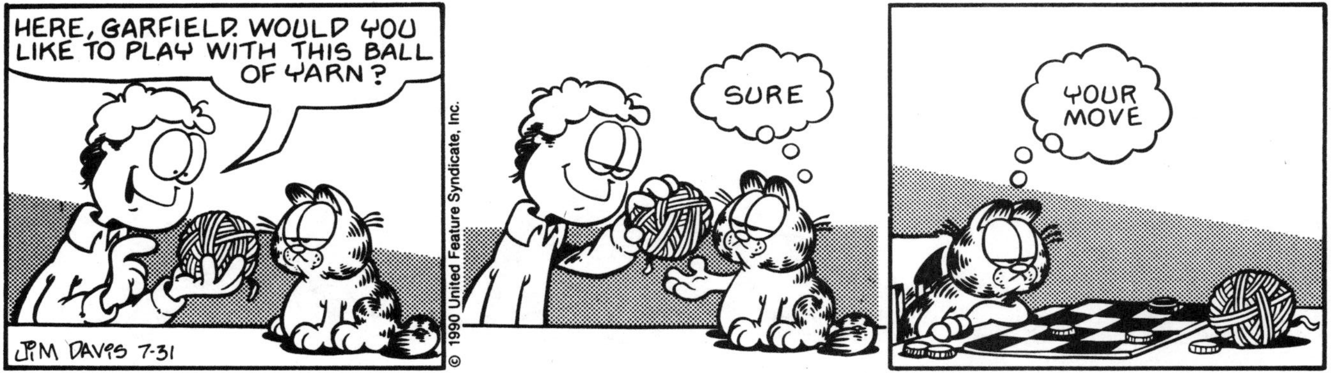
HERE, GARFIELD. WOULD YOU LIKE TO PLAY WITH THIS BALL OF YARN?
JIM DAVIS 7-31
© 1990 United Feature Syndicate, Inc.
SURE
YOUR MOVE

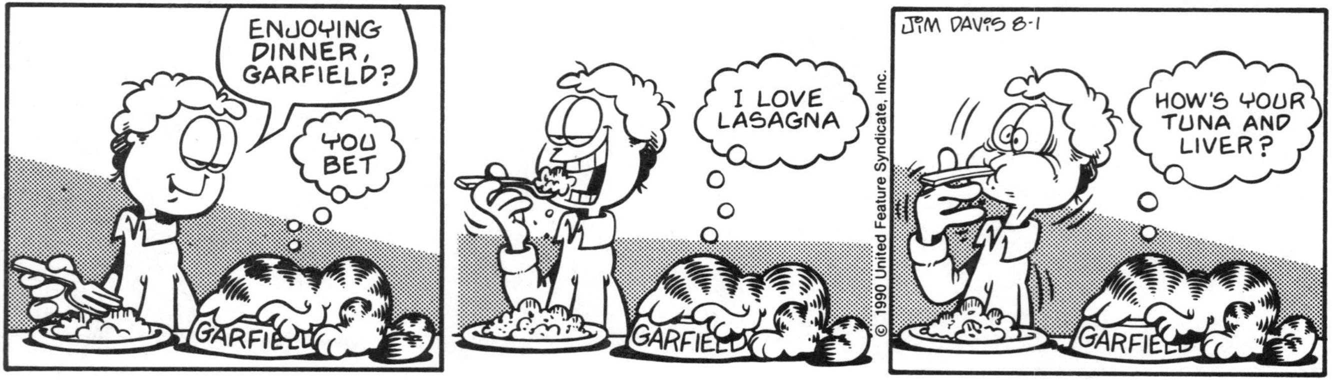
ENJOYING DINNER, GARFIELD?
YOU BET
GARFIELD
I LOVE LASAGNA
GARFIELD
© 1990 United Feature Syndicate, Inc.
JIM DAVIS 8-1
HOW'S YOUR TUNA AND LIVER?
GARFIELD

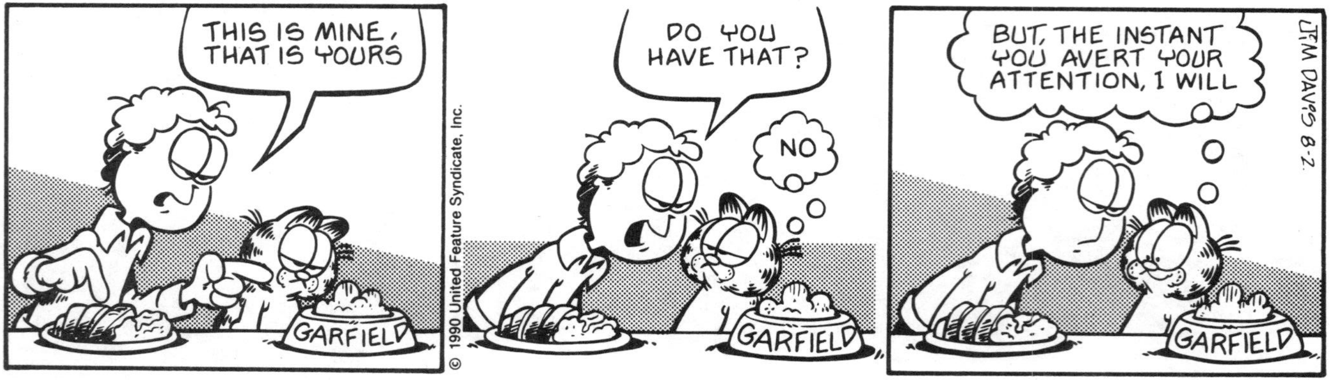
THIS IS MINE, THAT IS YOURS
GARFIELD
© 1990 United Feature Syndicate, Inc.
DO YOU HAVE THAT?
NO
GARFIELD
BUT, THE INSTANT YOU AVERT YOUR ATTENTION, I WILL
JIM DAVIS 8-2
GARFIELD

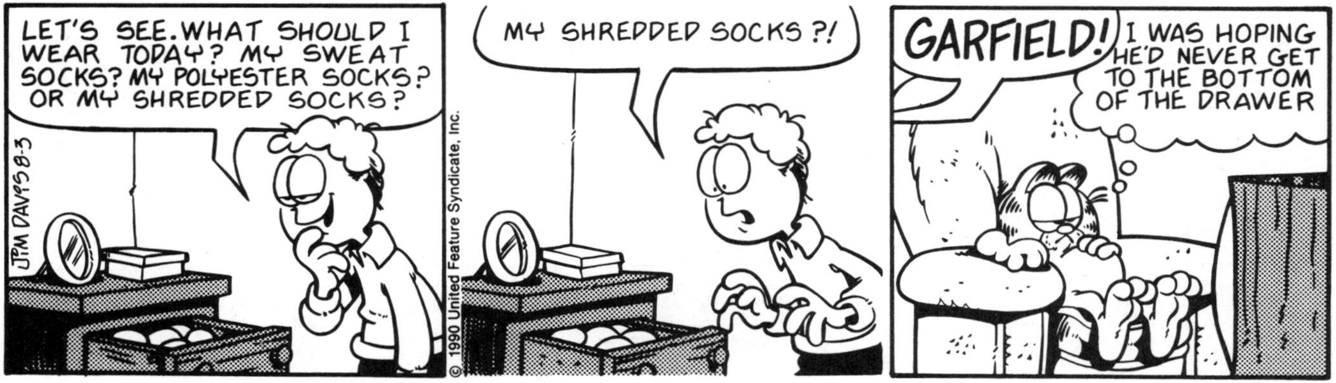
LET'S SEE. WHAT SHOULD I WEAR TODAY? MY SWEAT SOCKS? MY POLYESTER SOCKS? OR MY SHREDDED SOCKS?
JIM DAVIS 8-3
© 1990 United Feature Syndicate, Inc.
MY SHREDDED SOCKS ?!
GARFIELD!
I WAS HOPING HE'D NEVER GET TO THE BOTTOM OF THE DRAWER

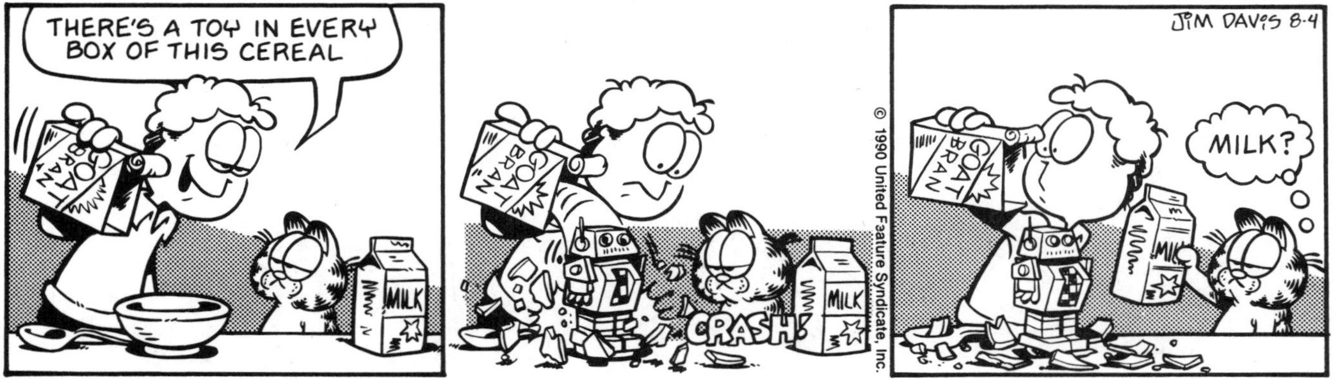
THERE'S A TOY IN EVERY BOX OF THIS CEREAL
GOAT BRAN
MILK
CRASH!
© 1990 United Feature Syndicate, Inc.
JIM DAVIS 8-4
MILK?

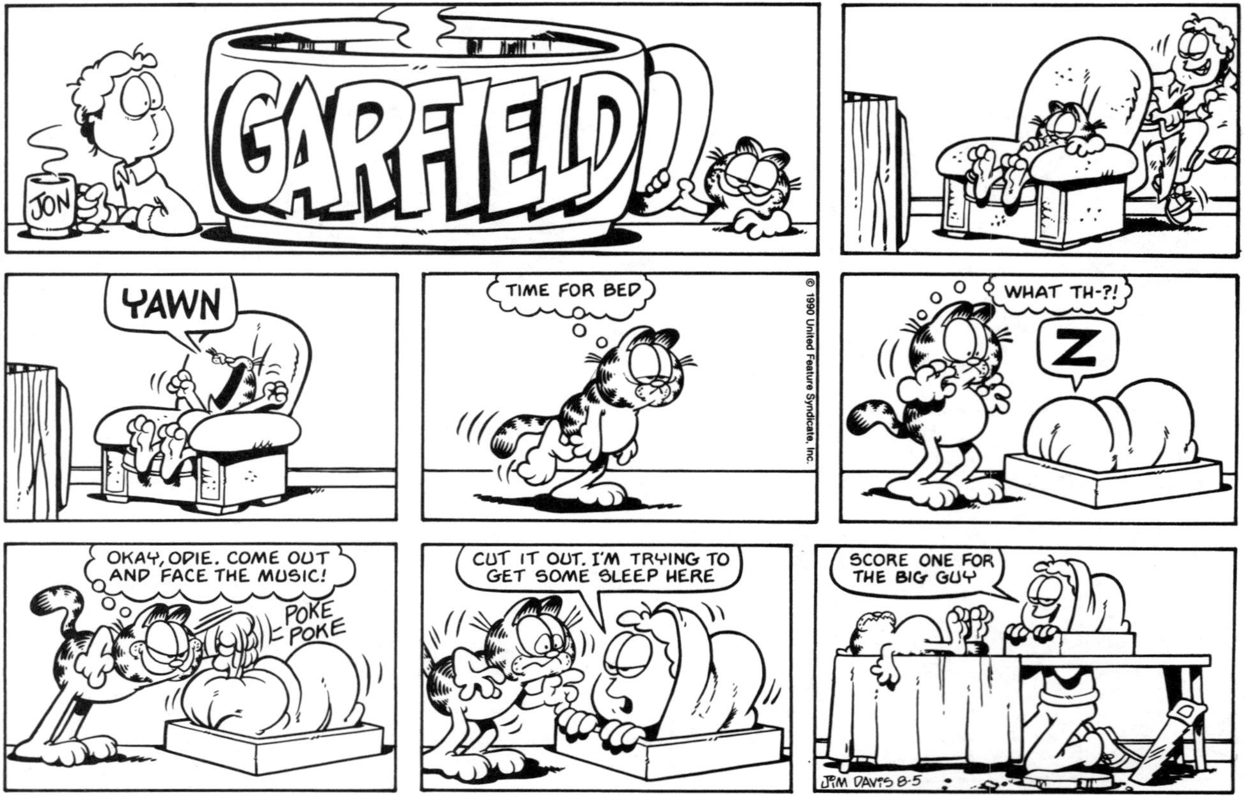
JON
GARFIELD
YAWN
TIME FOR BED
WHAT TH-?!
Z
OKAY, ODIE. COME OUT AND FACE THE MUSIC!
POKE POKE
CUT IT OUT. I'M TRYING TO GET SOME SLEEP HERE
SCORE ONE FOR THE BIG GUY
JIM DAVIS 8-5

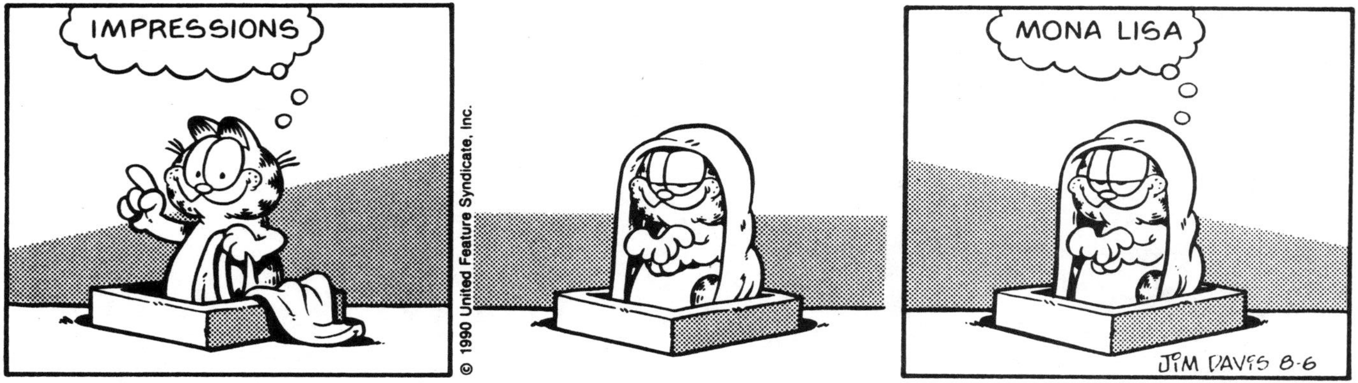
IMPRESSIONS
© 1990 United Feature Syndicate, Inc.
MONA LISA
JIM DAVIS 8-6

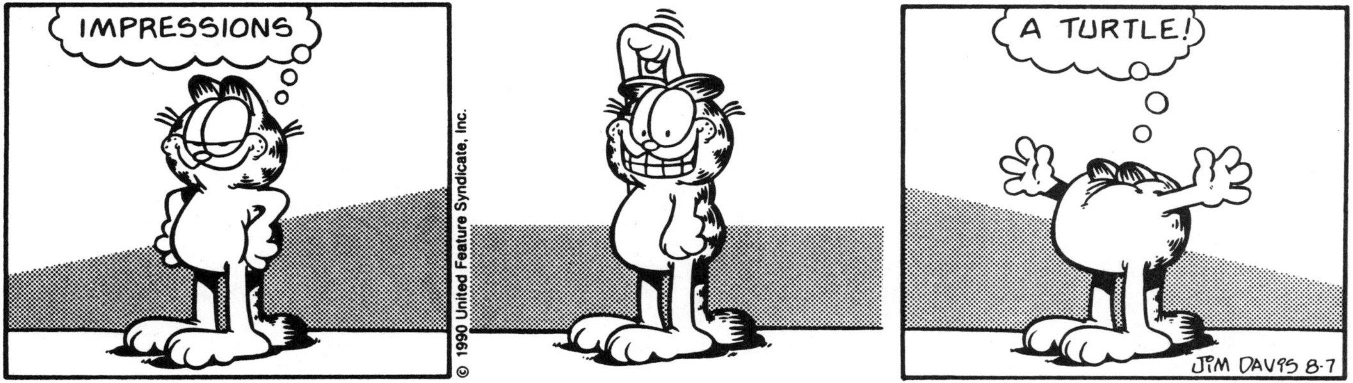
IMPRESSIONS
© 1990 United Feature Syndicate, Inc.
A TURTLE!
JIM DAVIS 8-7

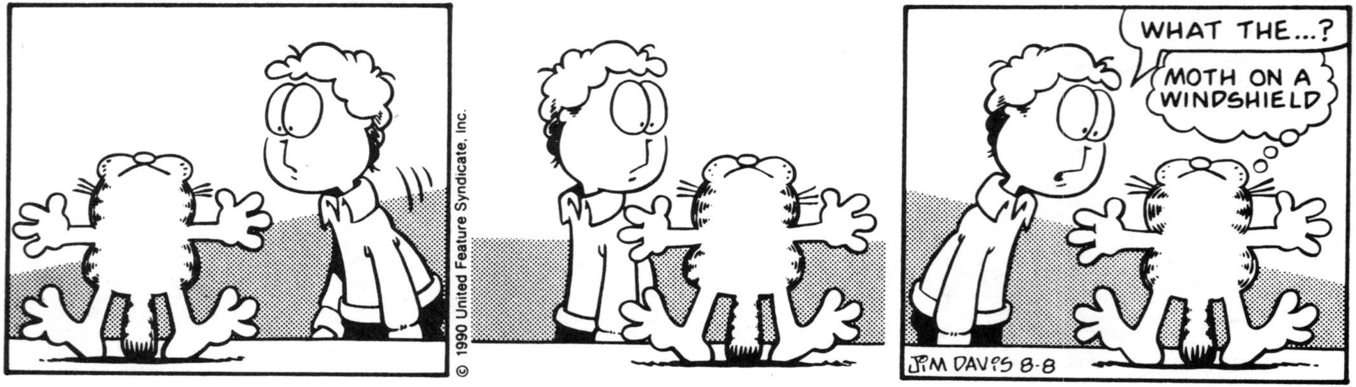
WHAT THE...?
MOTH ON A WINDSHIELD
JIM DAVIS 8-8

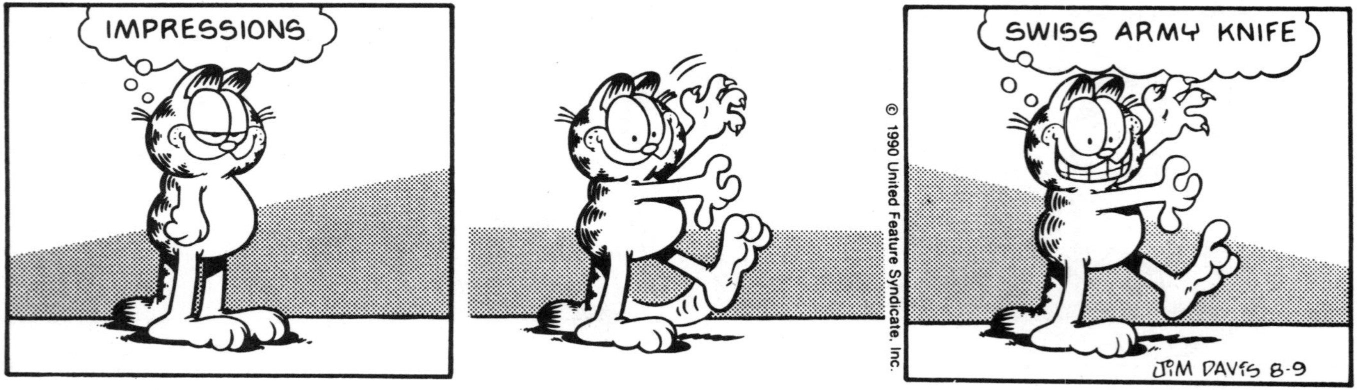
IMPRESSIONS
SWISS ARMY KNIFE
JIM DAVIS 8-9

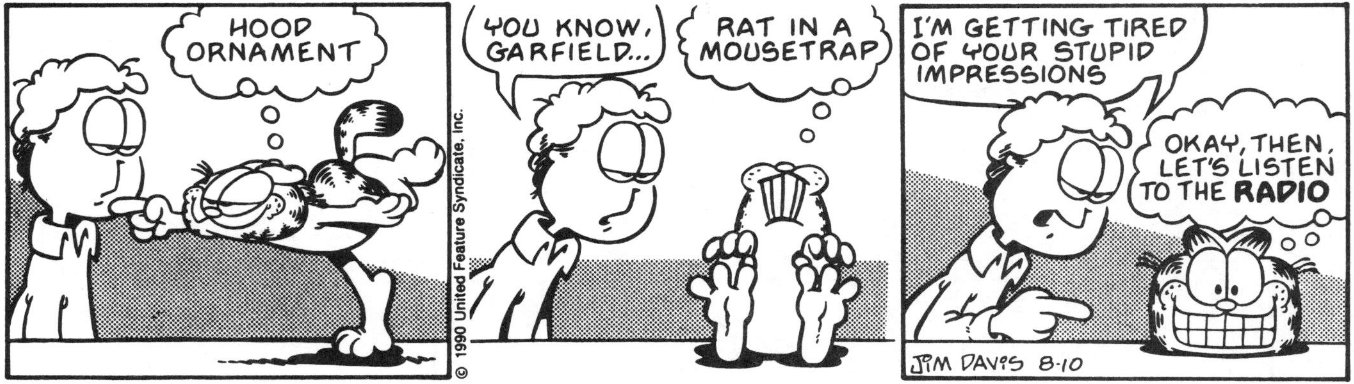
HOOD ORNAMENT
YOU KNOW, GARFIELD...
RAT IN A MOUSETRAP
I'M GETTING TIRED OF YOUR STUPID IMPRESSIONS
OKAY, THEN, LET'S LISTEN TO THE **RADIO**
JIM DAVIS 8-10

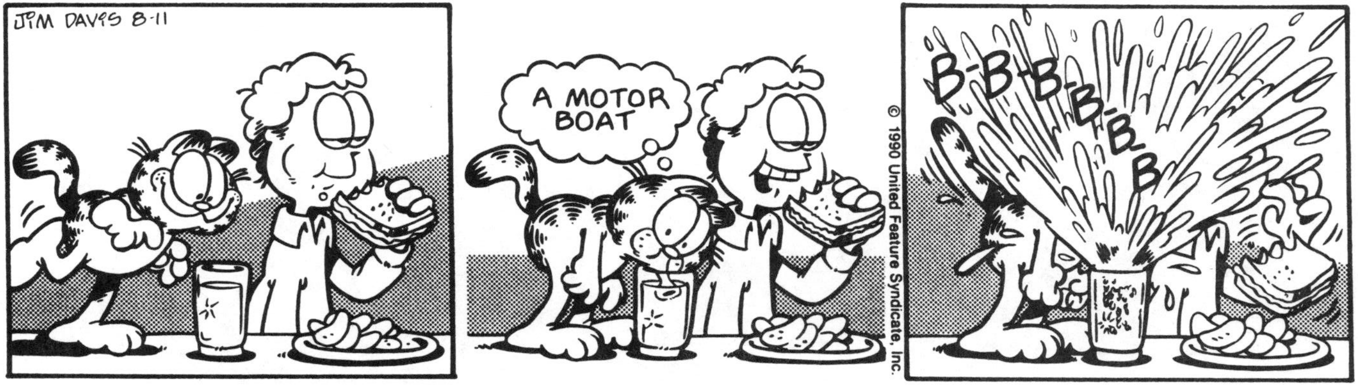
JIM DAVIS 8-11
A MOTOR BOAT
B-B-B-B-B-B

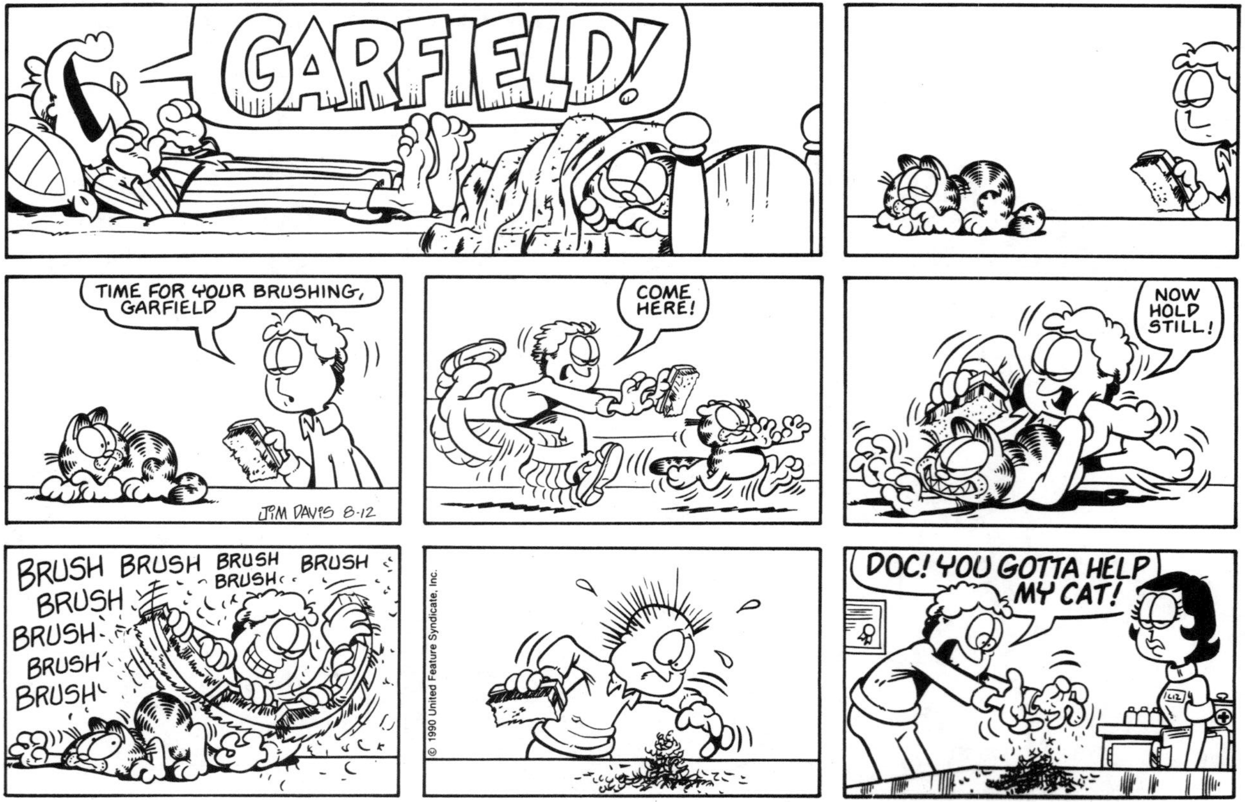
GARFIELD!
TIME FOR YOUR BRUSHING, GARFIELD
JIM DAVIS 8-12
COME HERE!
NOW HOLD STILL!
BRUSH BRUSH BRUSH BRUSH BRUSH BRUSH BRUSH BRUSH BRUSH
© 1990 United Feature Syndicate, Inc.
DOC! YOU GOTTA HELP MY CAT!

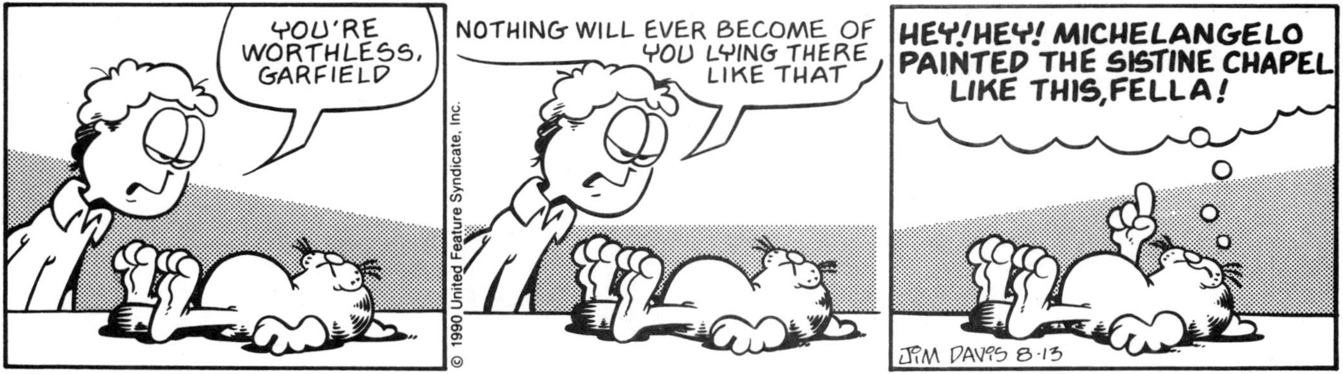
YOU'RE WORTHLESS, GARFIELD
NOTHING WILL EVER BECOME OF YOU LYING THERE LIKE THAT
HEY! HEY! MICHELANGELO PAINTED THE SISTINE CHAPEL LIKE THIS, FELLA!
JIM DAVIS 8-13
© 1990 United Feature Syndicate, Inc.

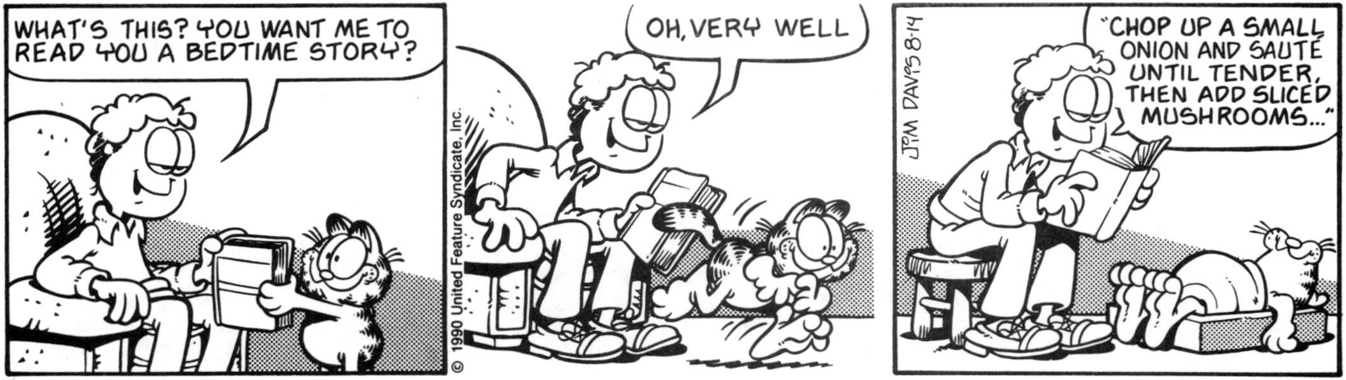
WHAT'S THIS? YOU WANT ME TO READ YOU A BEDTIME STORY?
OH, VERY WELL
"CHOP UP A SMALL ONION AND SAUTÉ UNTIL TENDER, THEN ADD SLICED MUSHROOMS..."
JIM DAVIS 8-14
© 1990 United Feature Syndicate, Inc.

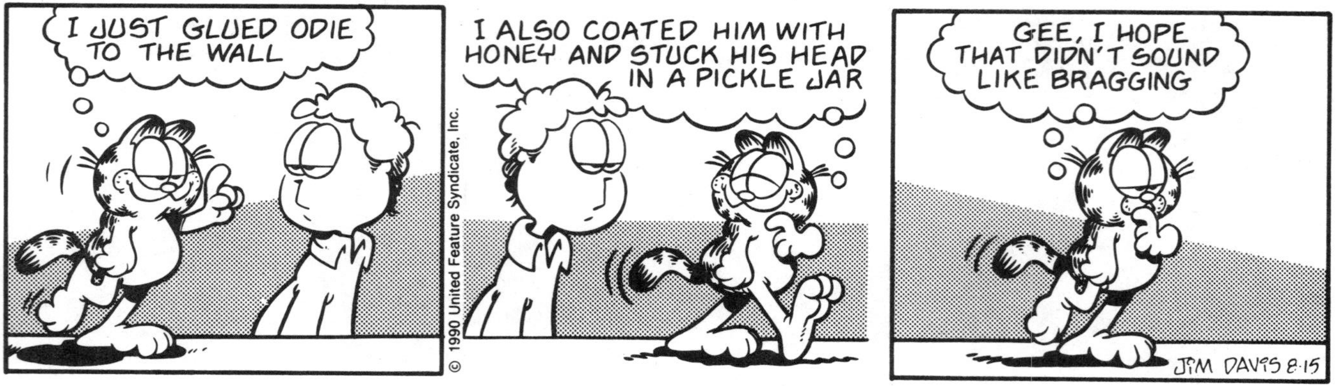
I JUST GLUED ODIE TO THE WALL
I ALSO COATED HIM WITH HONEY AND STUCK HIS HEAD IN A PICKLE JAR
GEE, I HOPE THAT DIDN'T SOUND LIKE BRAGGING
JIM DAVIS 8-15
© 1990 United Feature Syndicate, Inc.

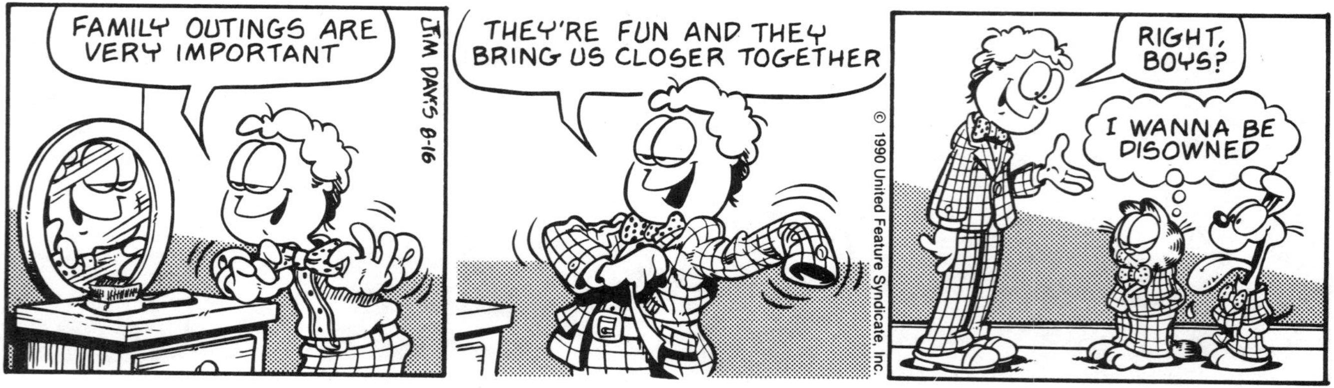
FAMILY OUTINGS ARE VERY IMPORTANT
JIM DAVIS 8-16
THEY'RE FUN AND THEY BRING US CLOSER TOGETHER
RIGHT, BOYS?
I WANNA BE DISOWNED
© 1990 United Feature Syndicate, Inc.

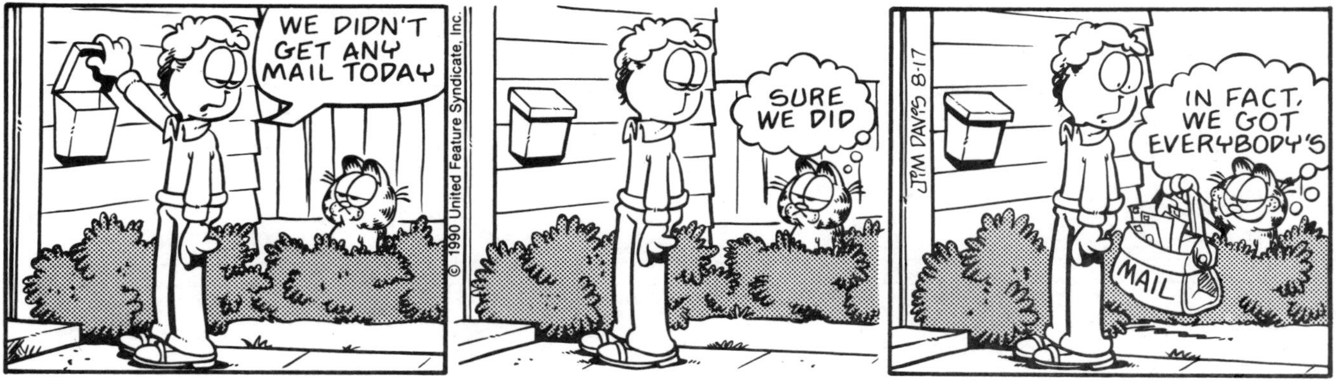
WE DIDN'T GET ANY MAIL TODAY
SURE WE DID
IN FACT, WE GOT EVERYBODY'S
MAIL
JIM DAVIS 8-17

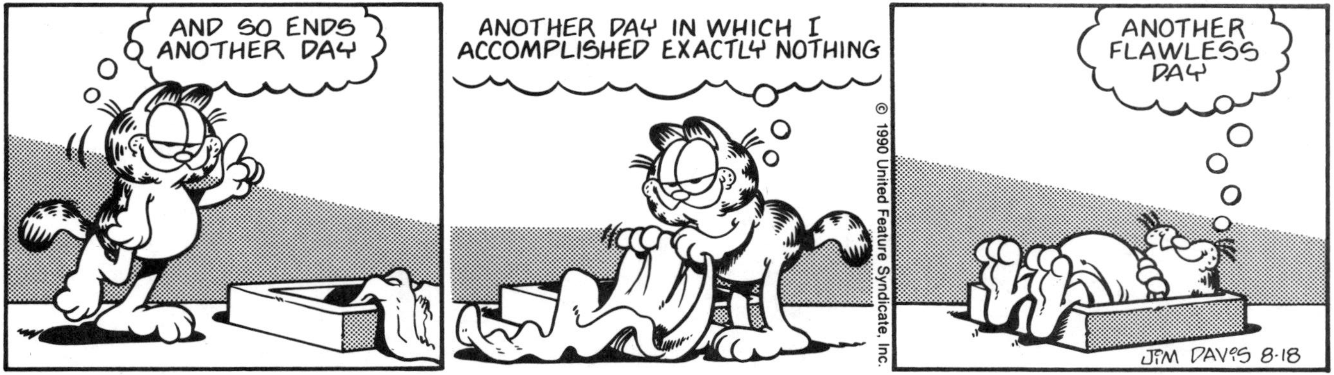
AND SO ENDS ANOTHER DAY
ANOTHER DAY IN WHICH I ACCOMPLISHED EXACTLY NOTHING
ANOTHER FLAWLESS DAY
JIM DAVIS 8-18

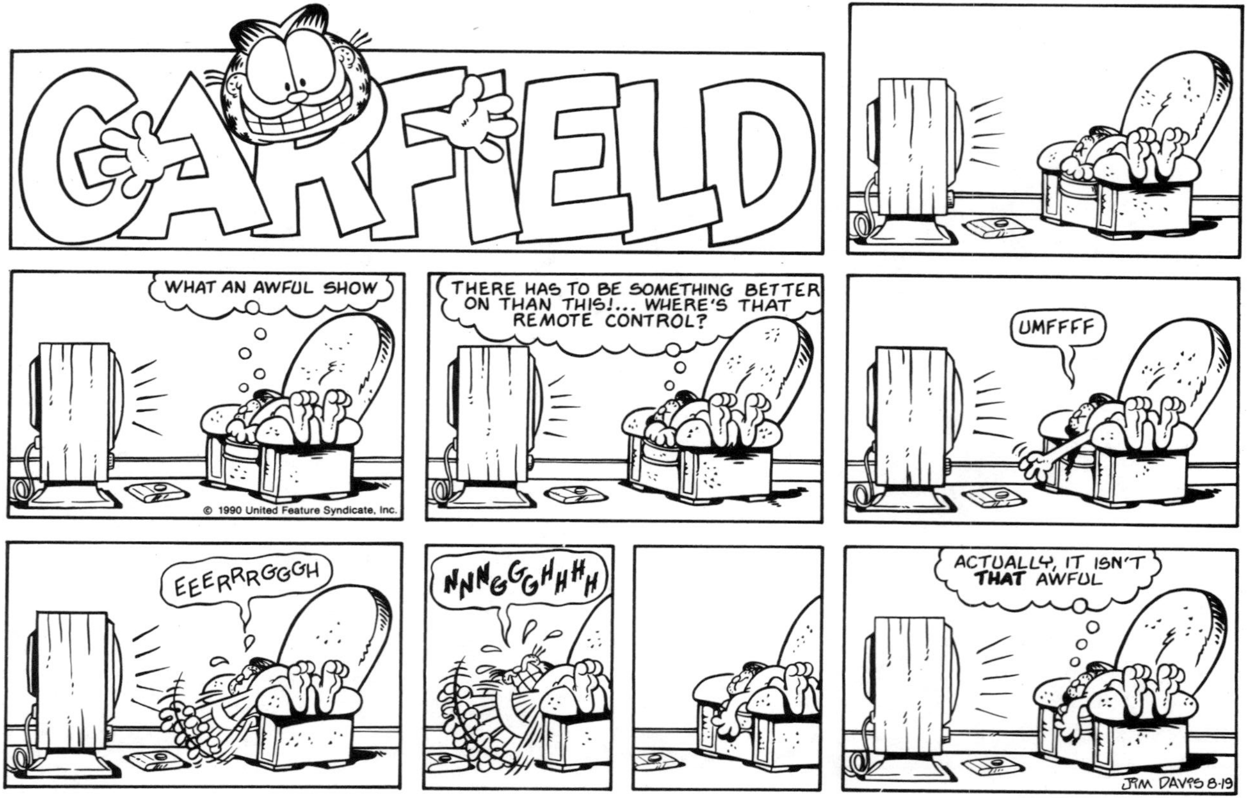
GARFIELD
WHAT AN AWFUL SHOW
© 1990 United Feature Syndicate, Inc.
THERE HAS TO BE SOMETHING BETTER ON THAN THIS!... WHERE'S THAT REMOTE CONTROL?
UMFFFF
EEERRRGGGH
NNNGGGHHHH
ACTUALLY, IT ISN'T **THAT** AWFUL
JIM DAVIS 8·19

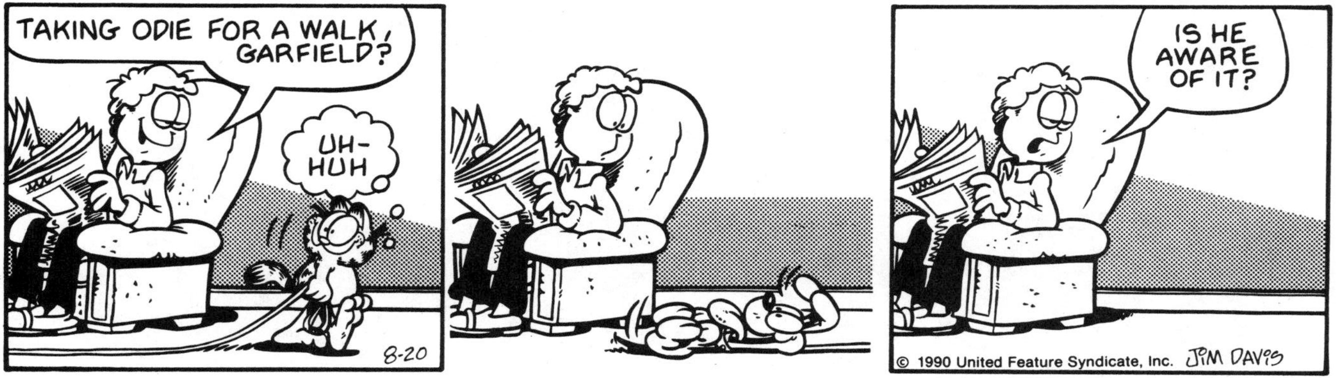
TAKING ODIE FOR A WALK, GARFIELD?
UH-HUH
8-20
IS HE AWARE OF IT?
© 1990 United Feature Syndicate, Inc.
JIM DAVIS

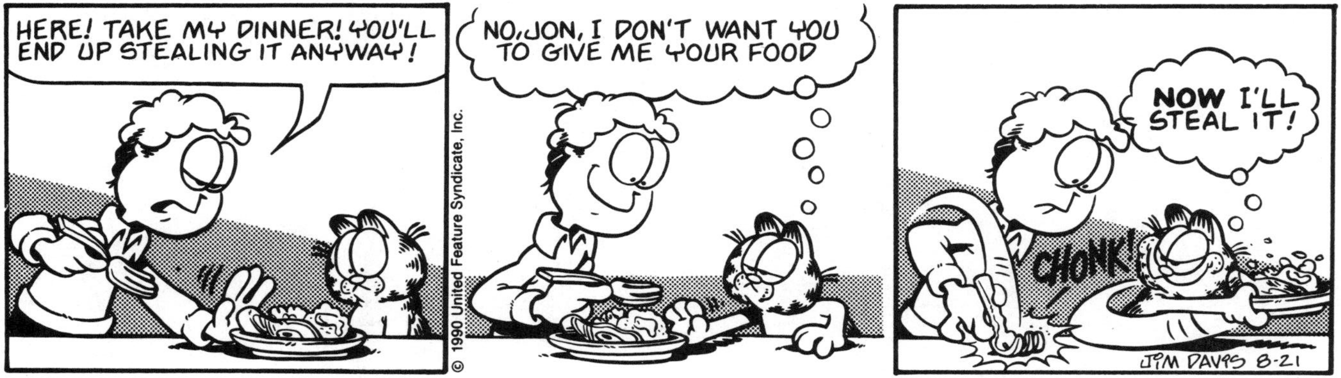
HERE! TAKE MY DINNER! YOU'LL END UP STEALING IT ANYWAY!
© 1990 United Feature Syndicate, Inc.
NO, JON, I DON'T WANT YOU TO GIVE ME YOUR FOOD
NOW I'LL STEAL IT!
CHONK!
JIM DAVIS 8-21

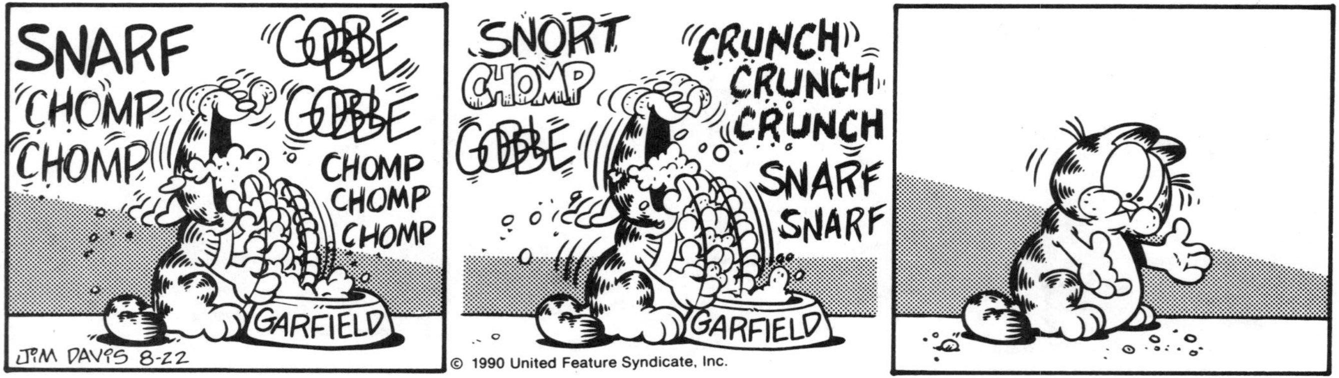
SNARF
CHOMP
CHOMP
GOBBLE
GOBBLE
CHOMP
CHOMP
CHOMP
GARFIELD
JIM DAVIS 8-22
SNORT
CHOMP
GOBBLE
CRUNCH
CRUNCH
CRUNCH
SNARF
SNARF
GARFIELD

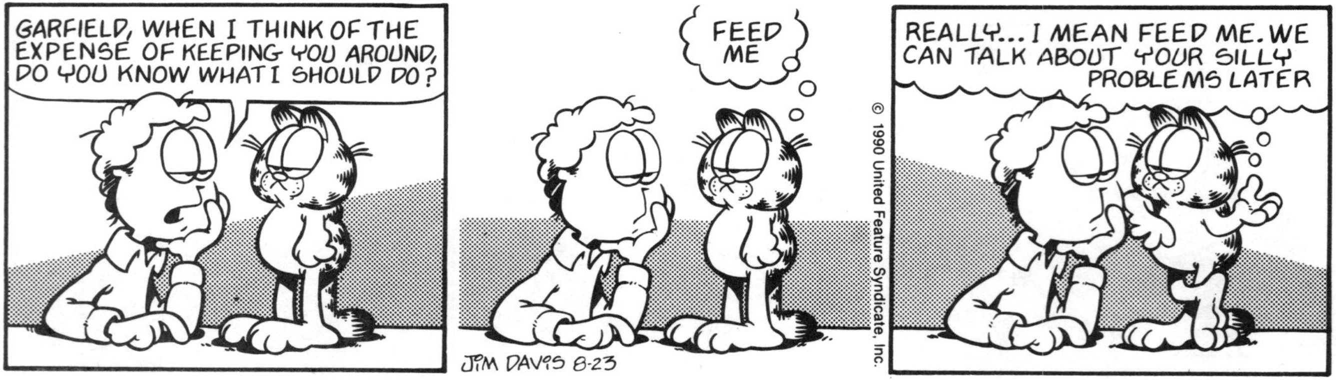
GARFIELD, WHEN I THINK OF THE EXPENSE OF KEEPING YOU AROUND, DO YOU KNOW WHAT I SHOULD DO?
FEED ME
JIM DAVIS 8-23
REALLY... I MEAN FEED ME. WE CAN TALK ABOUT YOUR SILLY PROBLEMS LATER

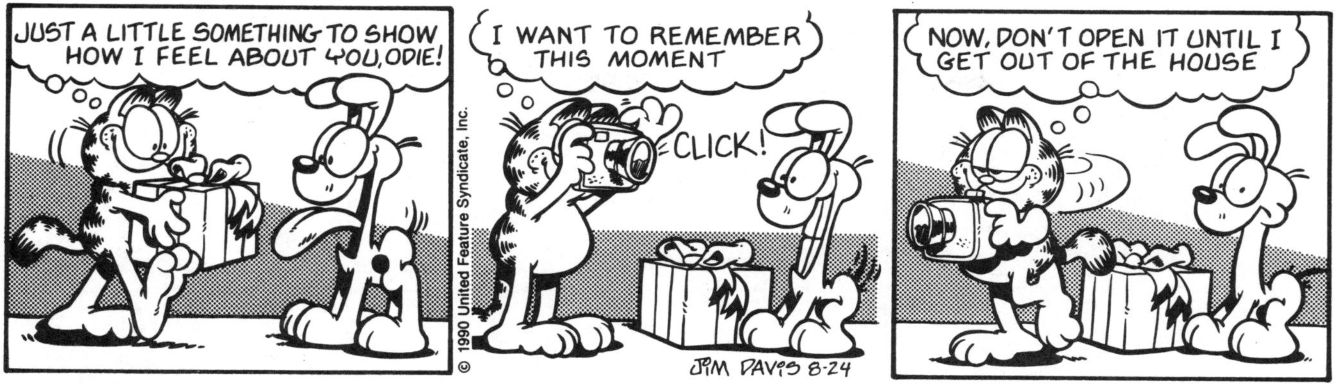
JUST A LITTLE SOMETHING TO SHOW HOW I FEEL ABOUT YOU, ODIE!
I WANT TO REMEMBER THIS MOMENT
CLICK!
NOW, DON'T OPEN IT UNTIL I GET OUT OF THE HOUSE
JIM DAVIS 8-24

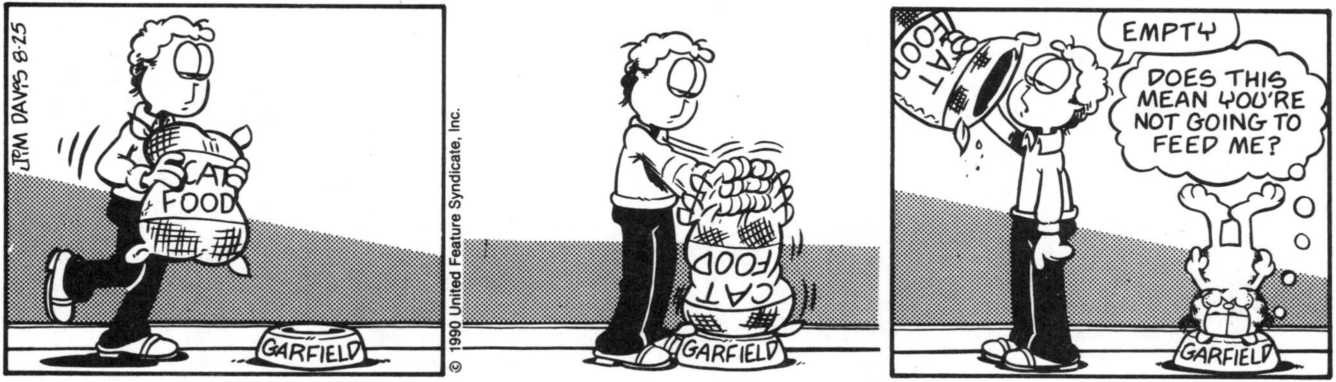
JIM DAVIS 8-25
CAT FOOD
GARFIELD
CAT FOOD
GARFIELD
CAT FOOD
EMPTY
DOES THIS MEAN YOU'RE NOT GOING TO FEED ME?
GARFIELD

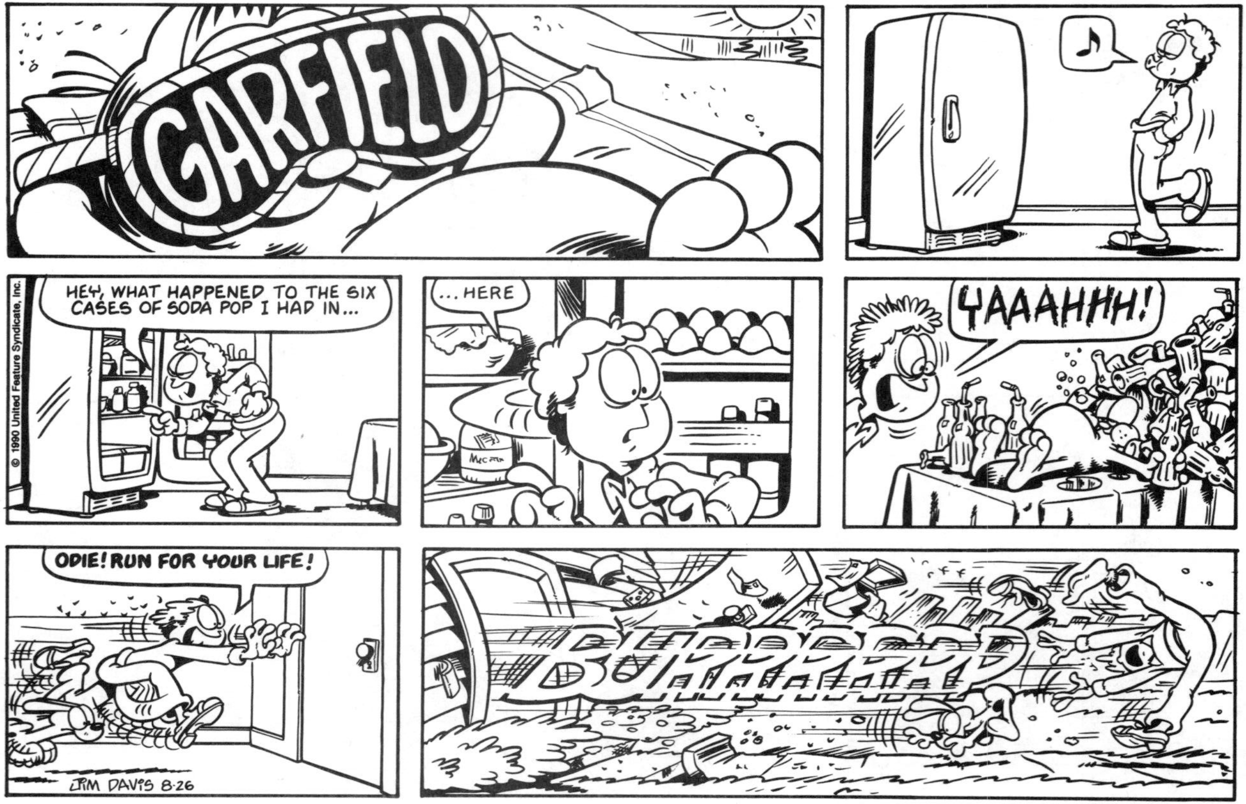
GARFIELD
♪
HEY, WHAT HAPPENED TO THE SIX CASES OF SODA POP I HAD IN...
... HERE
YAAAHHH!
ODIE! RUN FOR YOUR LIFE!
JIM DAVIS 8-26
© 1990 United Feature Syndicate, Inc.

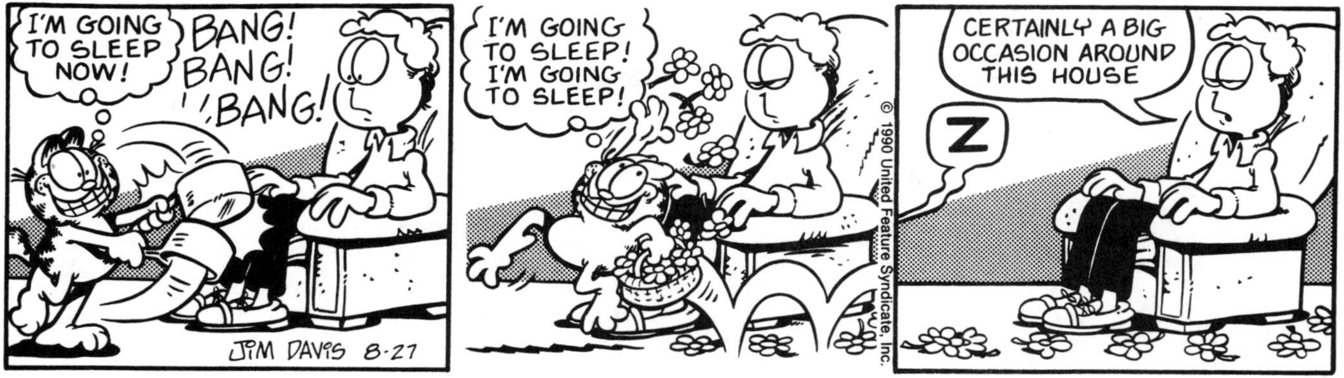
I'M GOING TO SLEEP NOW!
BANG! BANG! BANG!
JIM DAVIS 8-27
I'M GOING TO SLEEP! I'M GOING TO SLEEP!
© 1990 United Feature Syndicate, Inc.
CERTAINLY A BIG OCCASION AROUND THIS HOUSE
Z

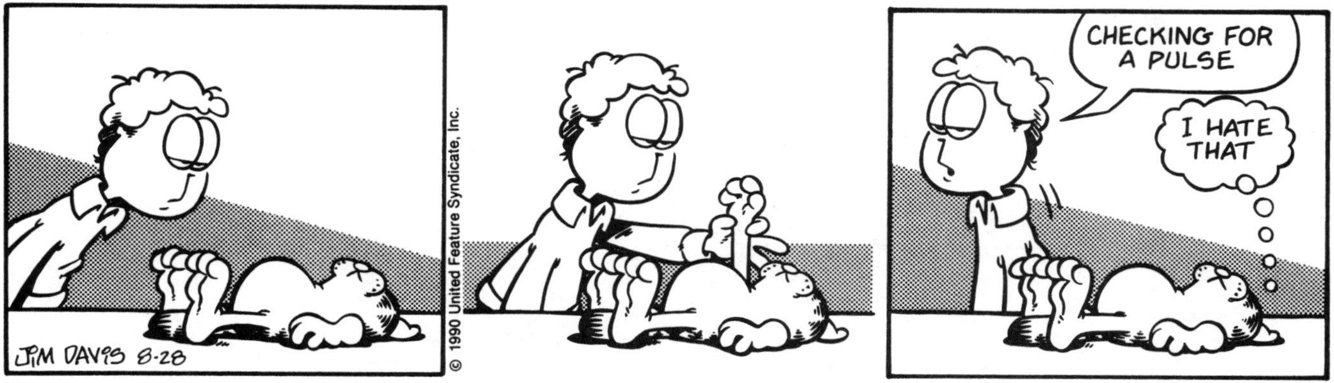
JIM DAVIS 8-28
© 1990 United Feature Syndicate, Inc.
CHECKING FOR A PULSE
I HATE THAT

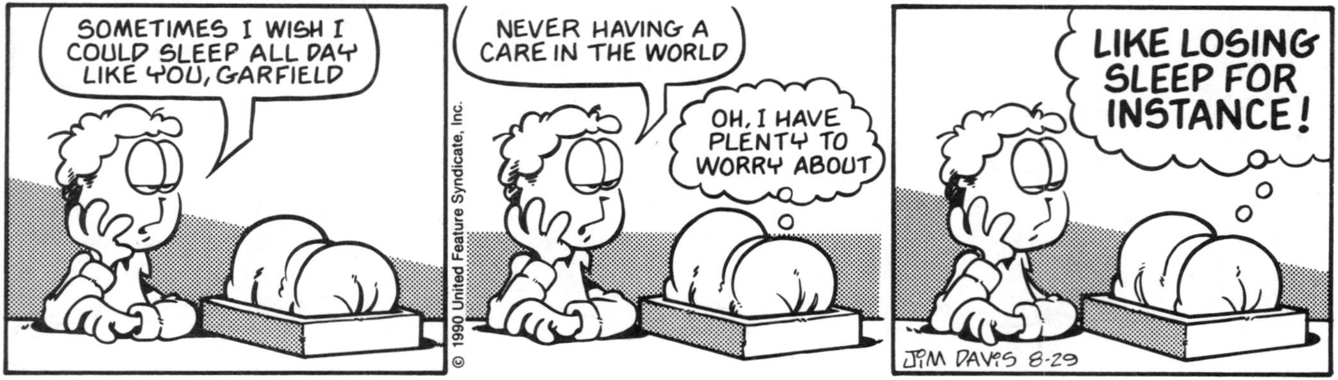
SOMETIMES I WISH I COULD SLEEP ALL DAY LIKE YOU, GARFIELD
© 1990 United Feature Syndicate, Inc.
NEVER HAVING A CARE IN THE WORLD
OH, I HAVE PLENTY TO WORRY ABOUT
LIKE LOSING SLEEP FOR INSTANCE!
JIM DAVIS 8-29

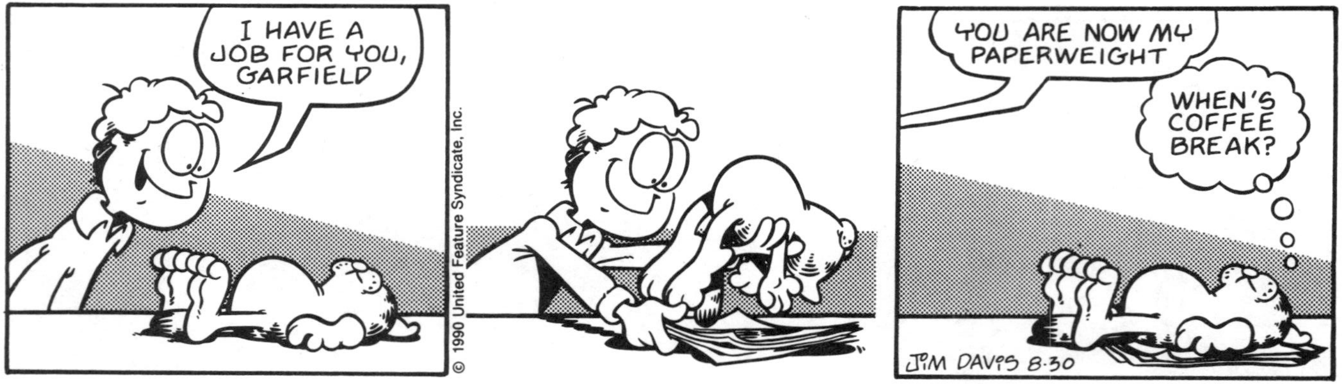
I HAVE A JOB FOR YOU, GARFIELD
© 1990 United Feature Syndicate, Inc.
YOU ARE NOW MY PAPERWEIGHT
WHEN'S COFFEE BREAK?
JIM DAVIS 8-30

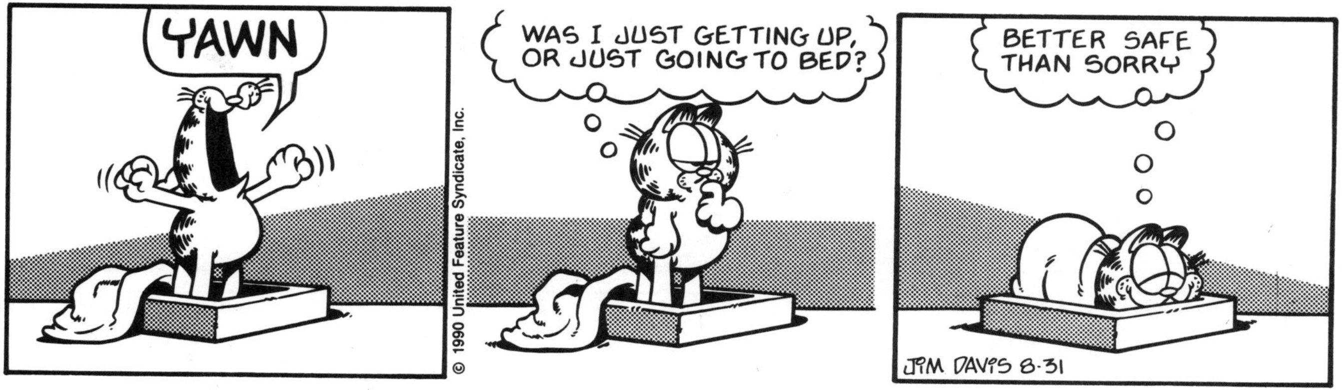
YAWN
WAS I JUST GETTING UP, OR JUST GOING TO BED?
BETTER SAFE THAN SORRY
JIM DAVIS 8-31

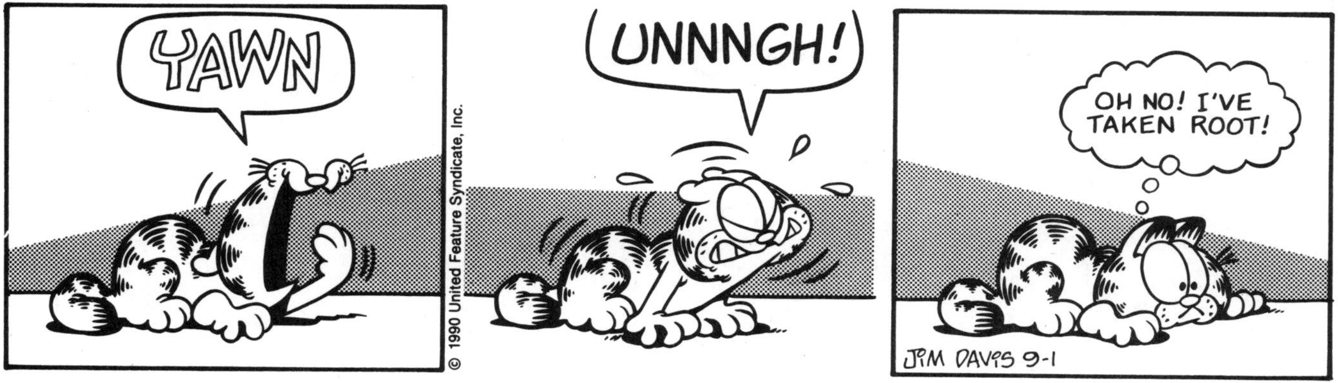
YAWN
UNNNGH!
OH NO! I'VE TAKEN ROOT!
JIM DAVIS 9-1

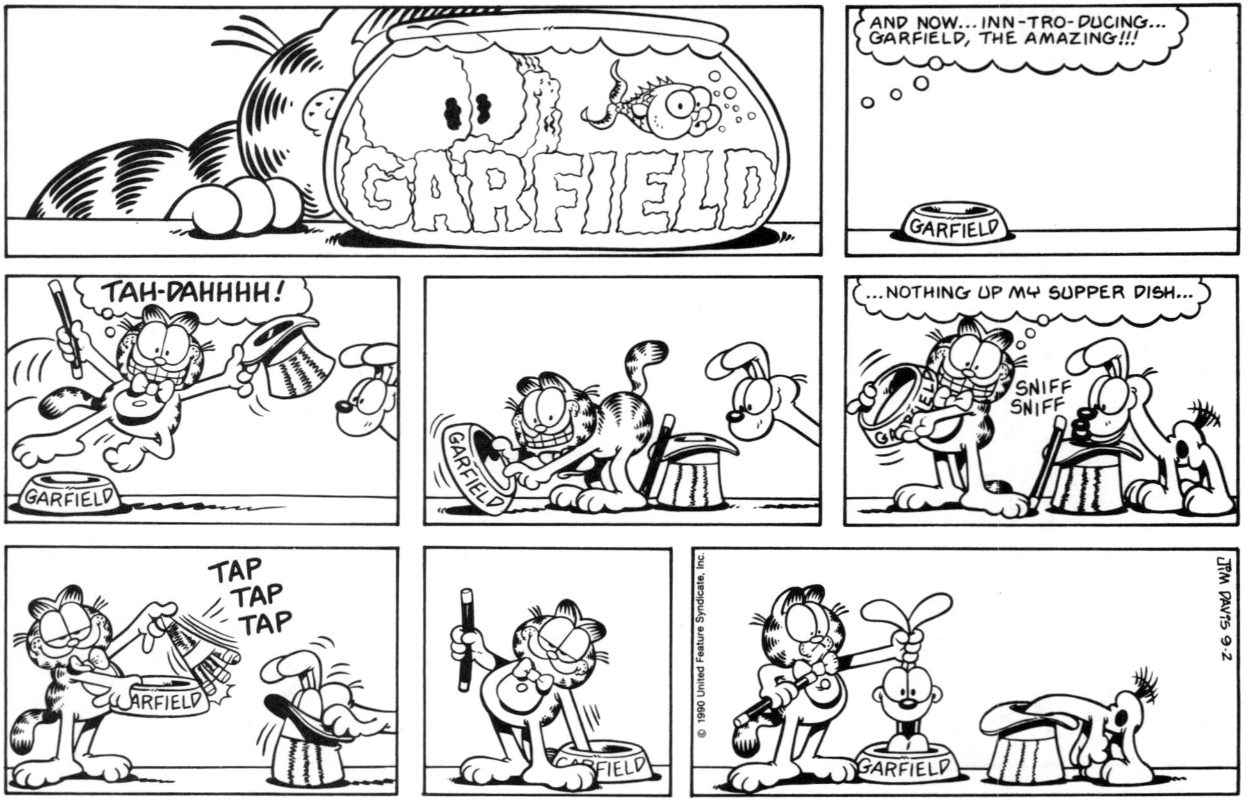
GARFIELD
AND NOW... INN-TRO-DUCING... GARFIELD, THE AMAZING!!!
GARFIELD
TAH-DAHHHH!
GARFIELD
GARFIELD
...NOTHING UP MY SUPPER DISH...
SNIFF
SNIFF
TAP
TAP
TAP
JIM DAVIS 9-2
© 1990 United Feature Syndicate, Inc.
GARFIELD

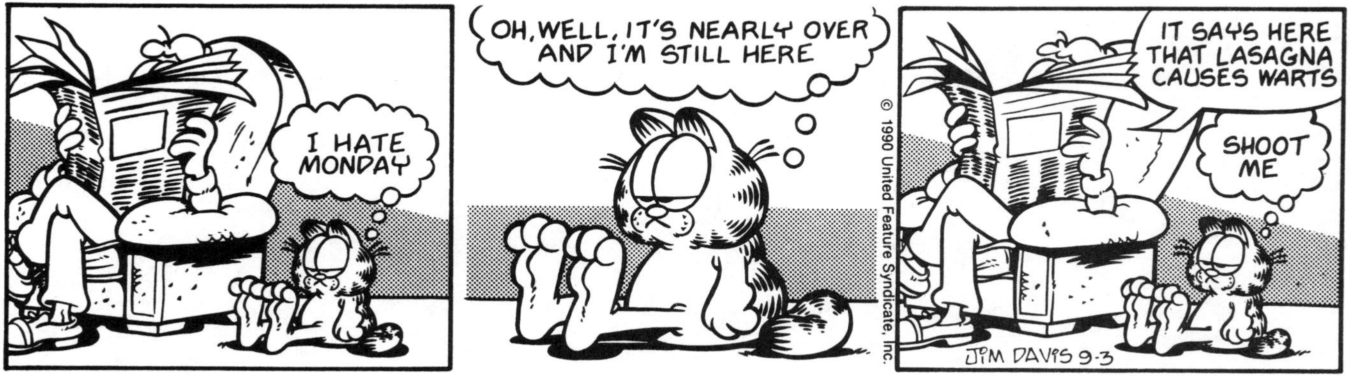

I HATE MONDAY
OH, WELL, IT'S NEARLY OVER AND I'M STILL HERE
IT SAYS HERE THAT LASAGNA CAUSES WARTS
SHOOT ME
JIM DAVIS 9-3
© 1990 United Feature Syndicate, Inc.

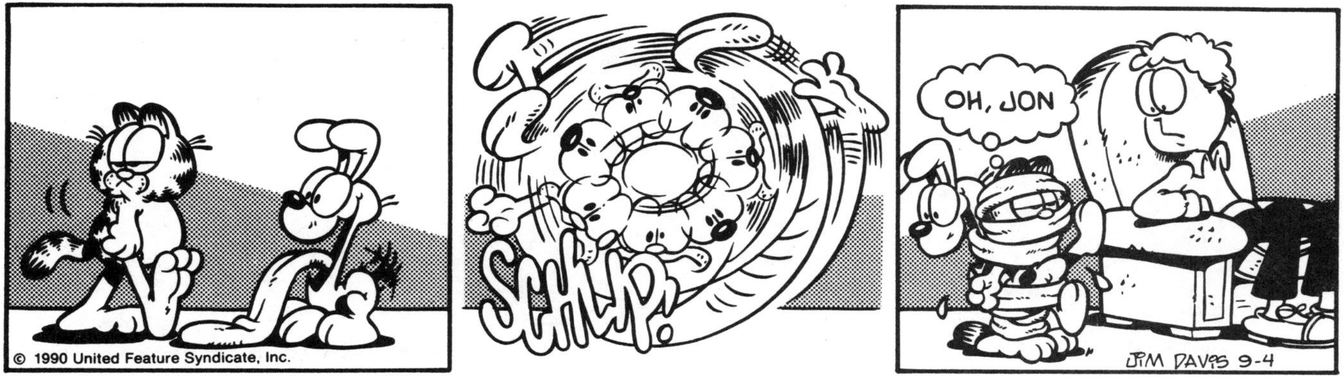

SCHLUP!
OH, JON
JIM DAVIS 9-4
© 1990 United Feature Syndicate, Inc.

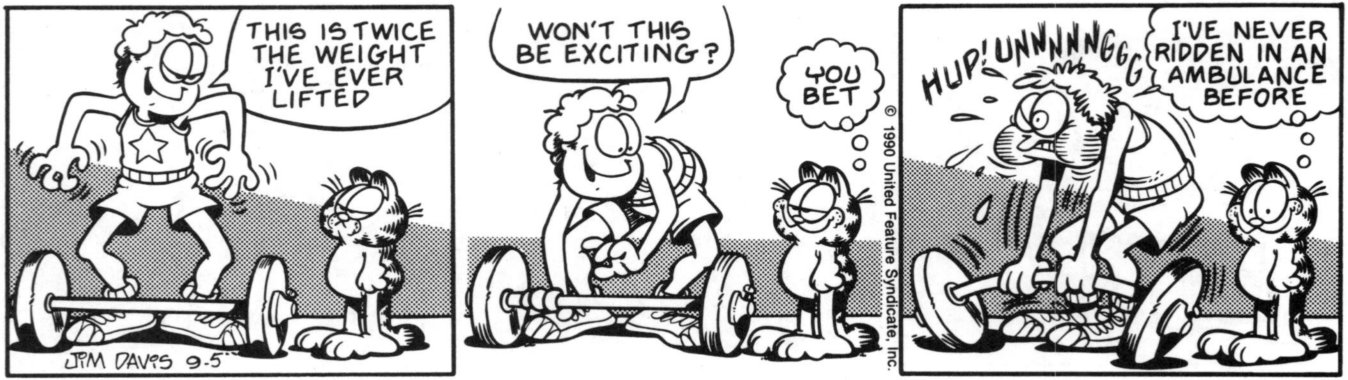
THIS IS TWICE THE WEIGHT I'VE EVER LIFTED
JIM DAVIS 9-5
WON'T THIS BE EXCITING?
YOU BET
© 1990 United Feature Syndicate, Inc.
HUP! UNNNNNGGG
I'VE NEVER RIDDEN IN AN AMBULANCE BEFORE

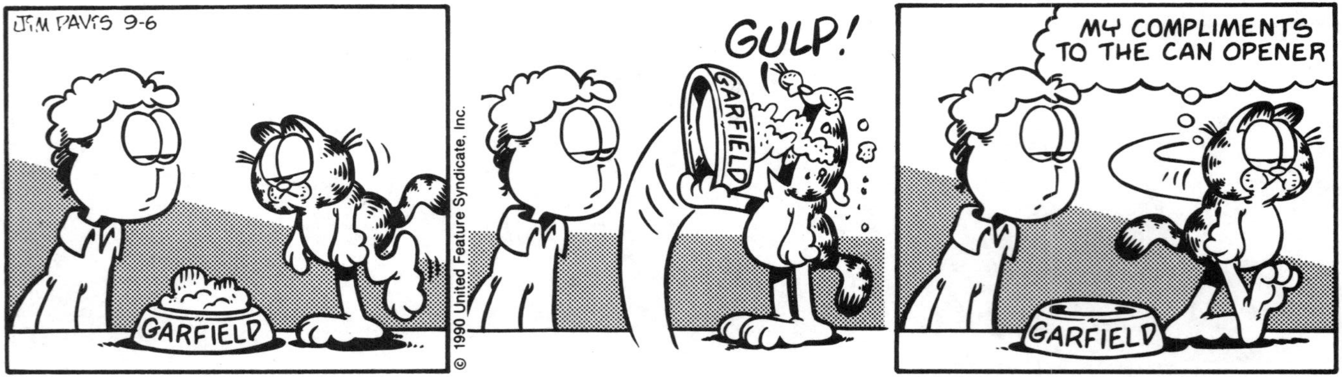
JIM DAVIS 9-6
GARFIELD
© 1990 United Feature Syndicate, Inc.
GULP!
GARFIELD
MY COMPLIMENTS TO THE CAN OPENER
GARFIELD

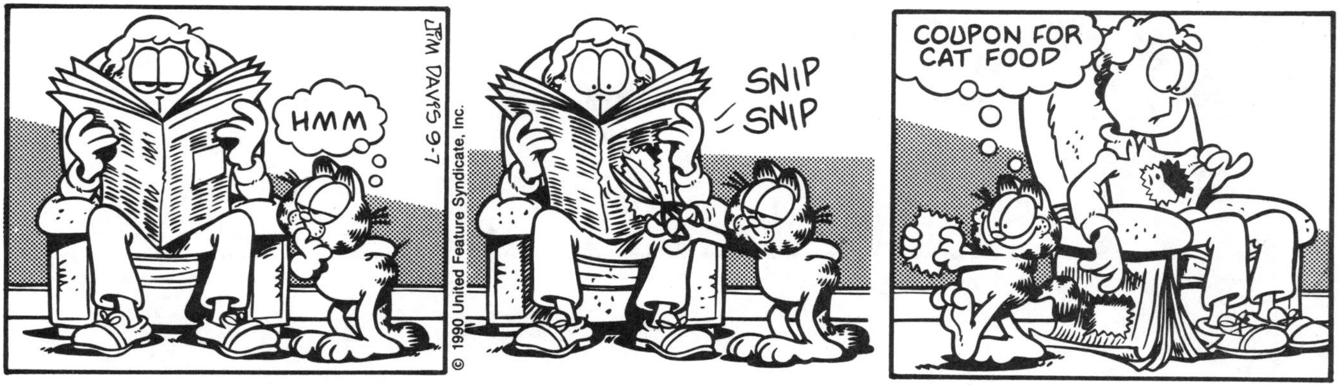
HMM
JIM DAVIS 9-7
© 1990 United Feature Syndicate, Inc.
SNIP
SNIP
COUPON FOR CAT FOOD

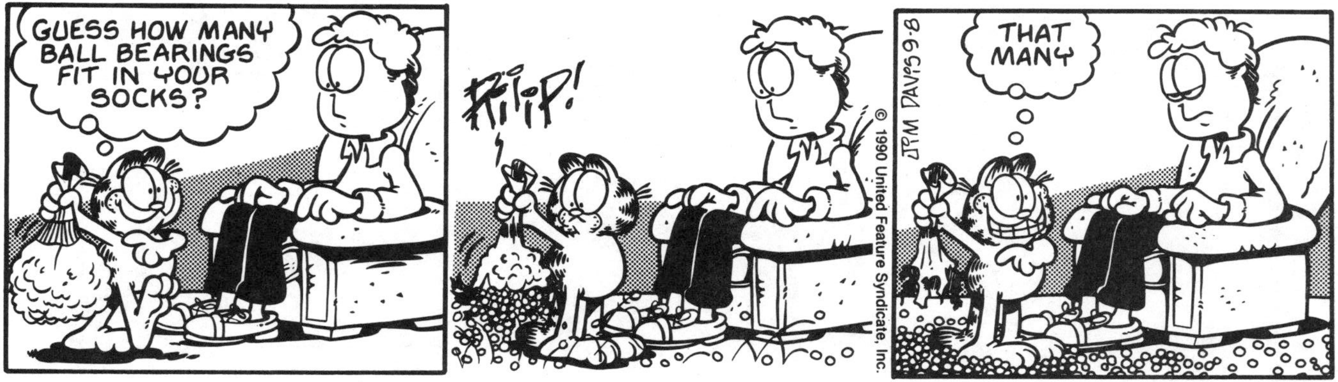
GUESS HOW MANY BALL BEARINGS FIT IN YOUR SOCKS?
RIIIP!
© 1990 United Feature Syndicate, Inc.
JIM DAVIS 9-8
THAT MANY

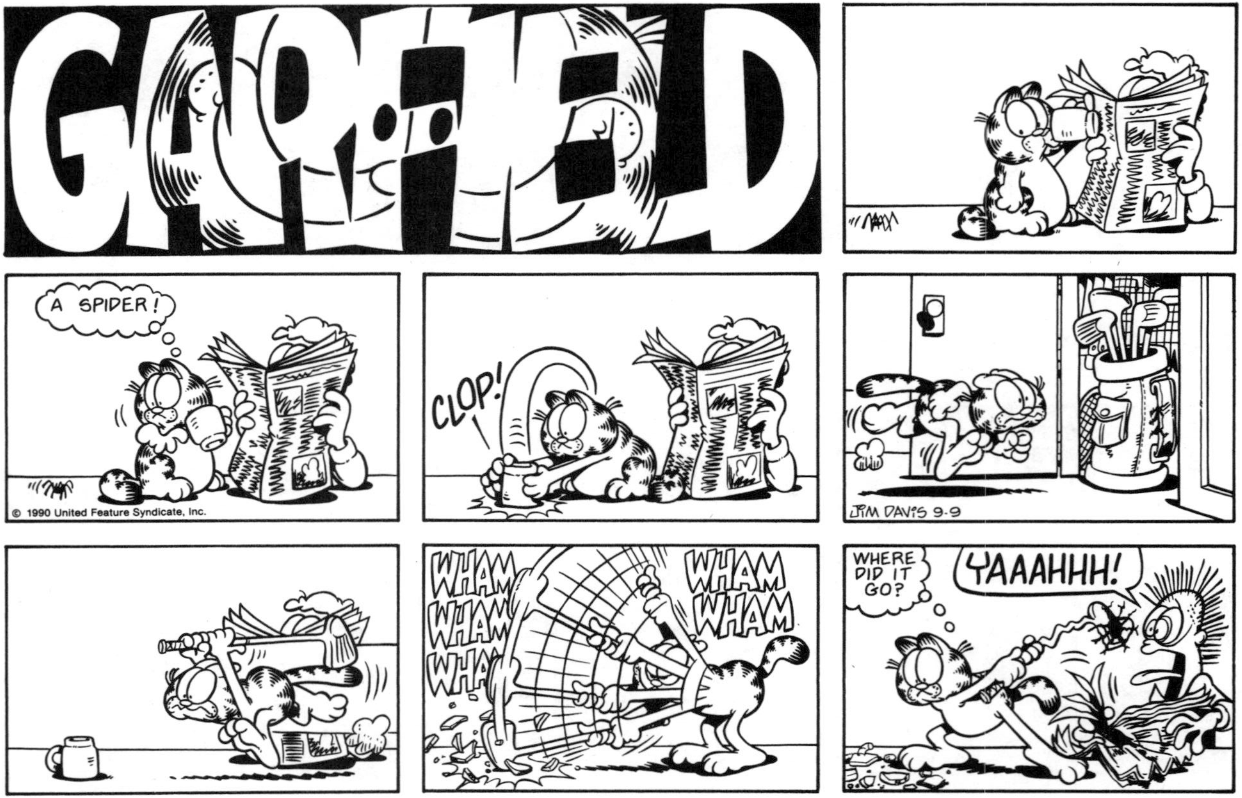
GARFIELD
A SPIDER!
© 1990 United Feature Syndicate, Inc.
CLOP!
JIM DAVIS 9-9
WHAM
WHAM
WHAM
WHAM
WHAM
WHAM
WHERE DID IT GO?
YAAAHHH!

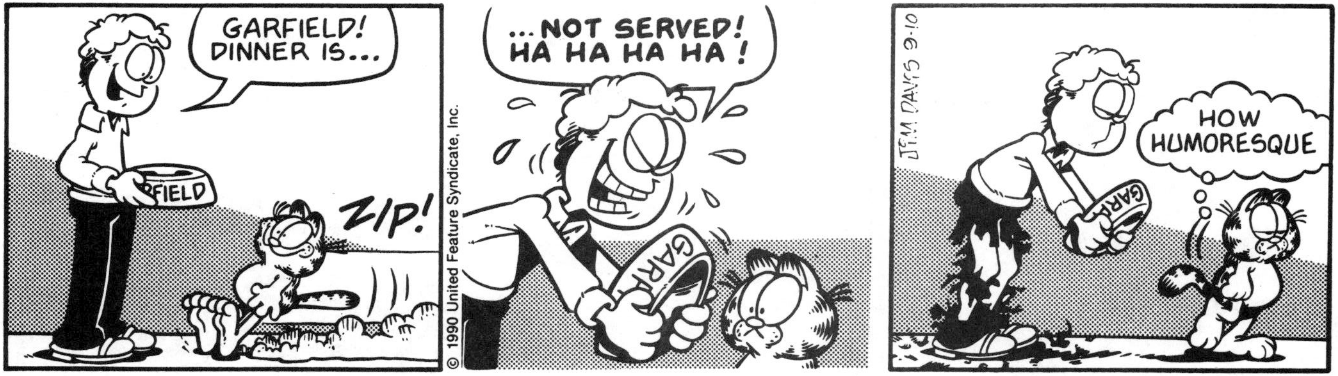
GARFIELD! DINNER IS...
FIELD
ZIP!
© 1990 United Feature Syndicate, Inc.
...NOT SERVED! HA HA HA HA!
GARF
JIM DAVIS 9-10
GARF
HOW HUMORESQUE

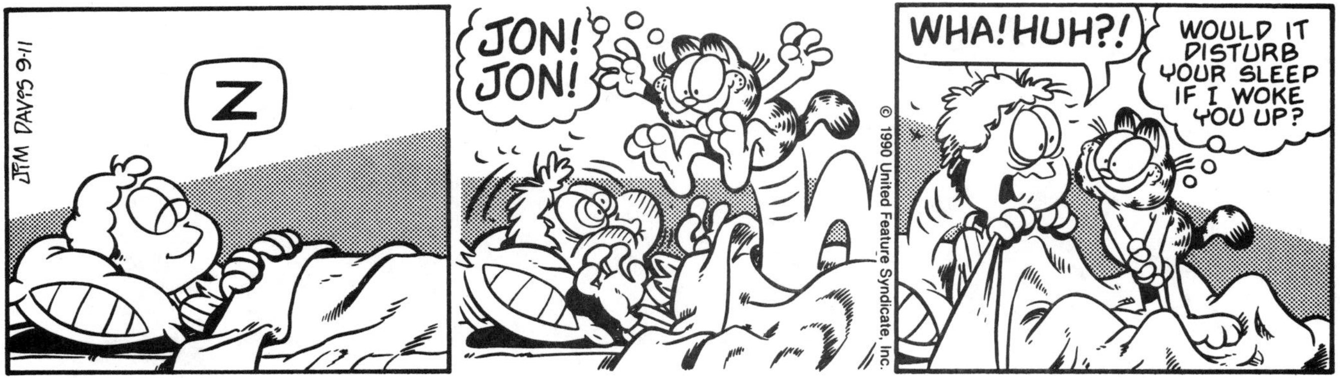
JIM DAVIS 9-11
Z
JON! JON!
© 1990 United Feature Syndicate, Inc.
WHA! HUH?!
WOULD IT DISTURB YOUR SLEEP IF I WOKE YOU UP?

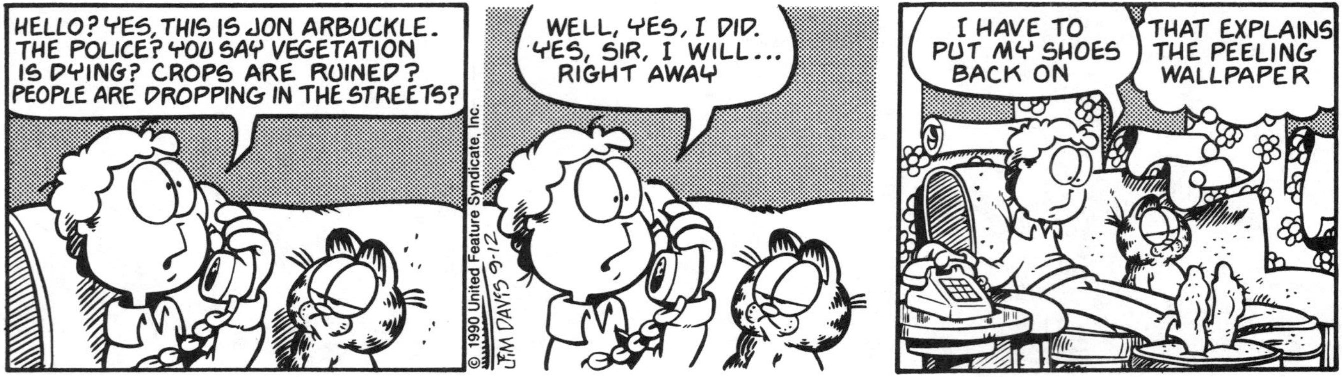
HELLO? YES, THIS IS JON ARBUCKLE. THE POLICE? YOU SAY VEGETATION IS DYING? CROPS ARE RUINED? PEOPLE ARE DROPPING IN THE STREETS?
WELL, YES, I DID. YES, SIR, I WILL... RIGHT AWAY
I HAVE TO PUT MY SHOES BACK ON
THAT EXPLAINS THE PEELING WALLPAPER
JIM DAVIS 9-12

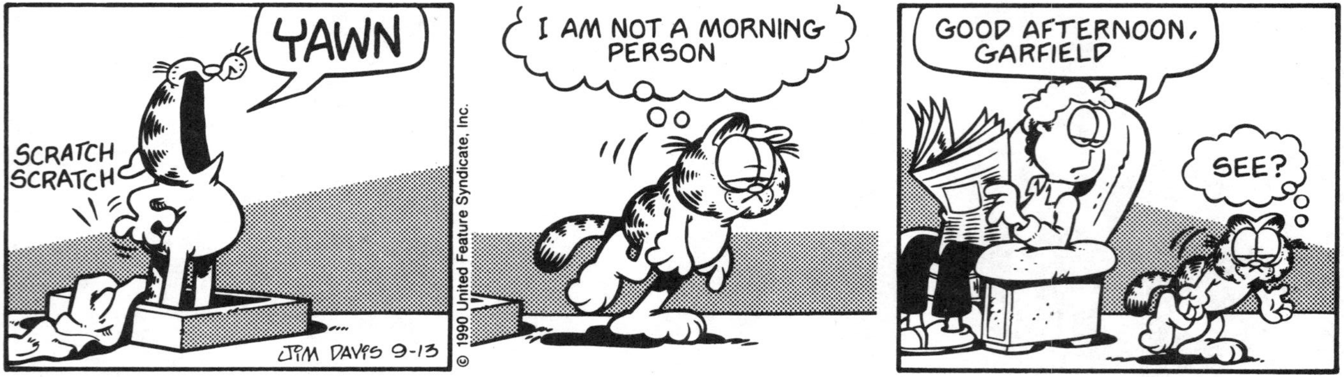
SCRATCH SCRATCH
YAWN
I AM NOT A MORNING PERSON
GOOD AFTERNOON, GARFIELD
SEE?
JIM DAVIS 9-13

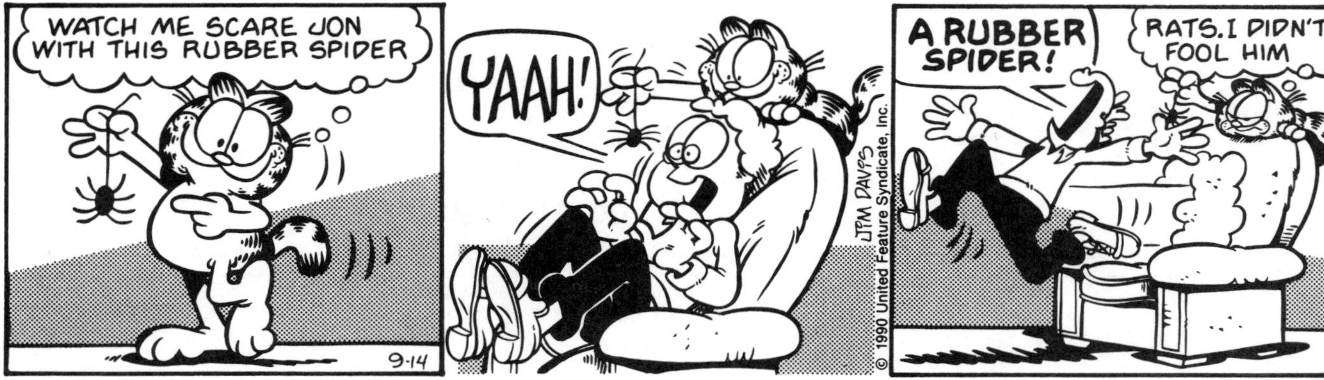
WATCH ME SCARE JON WITH THIS RUBBER SPIDER
9-14
YAAH!
JIM DAVIS
A RUBBER SPIDER!
RATS. I DIDN'T FOOL HIM

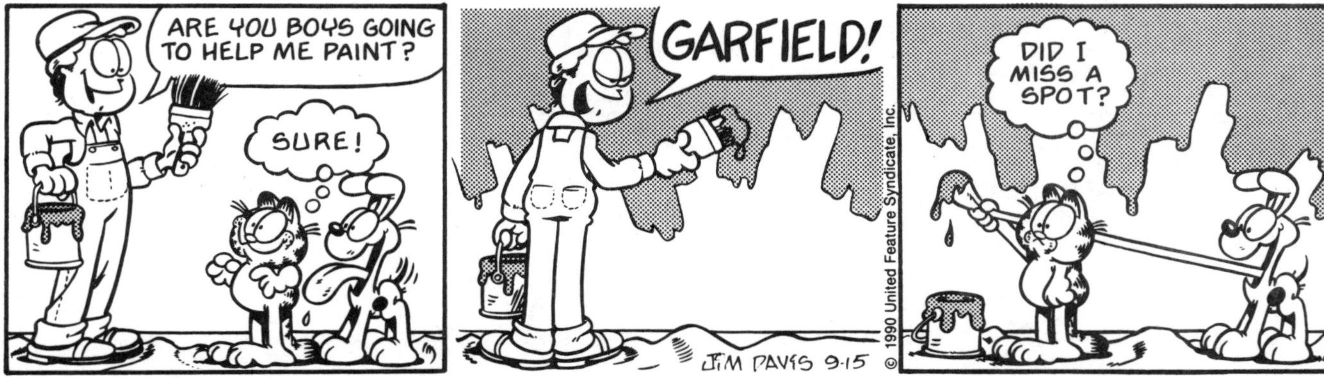
ARE YOU BOYS GOING TO HELP ME PAINT?
SURE!
GARFIELD!
JIM DAVIS 9-15
DID I MISS A SPOT?

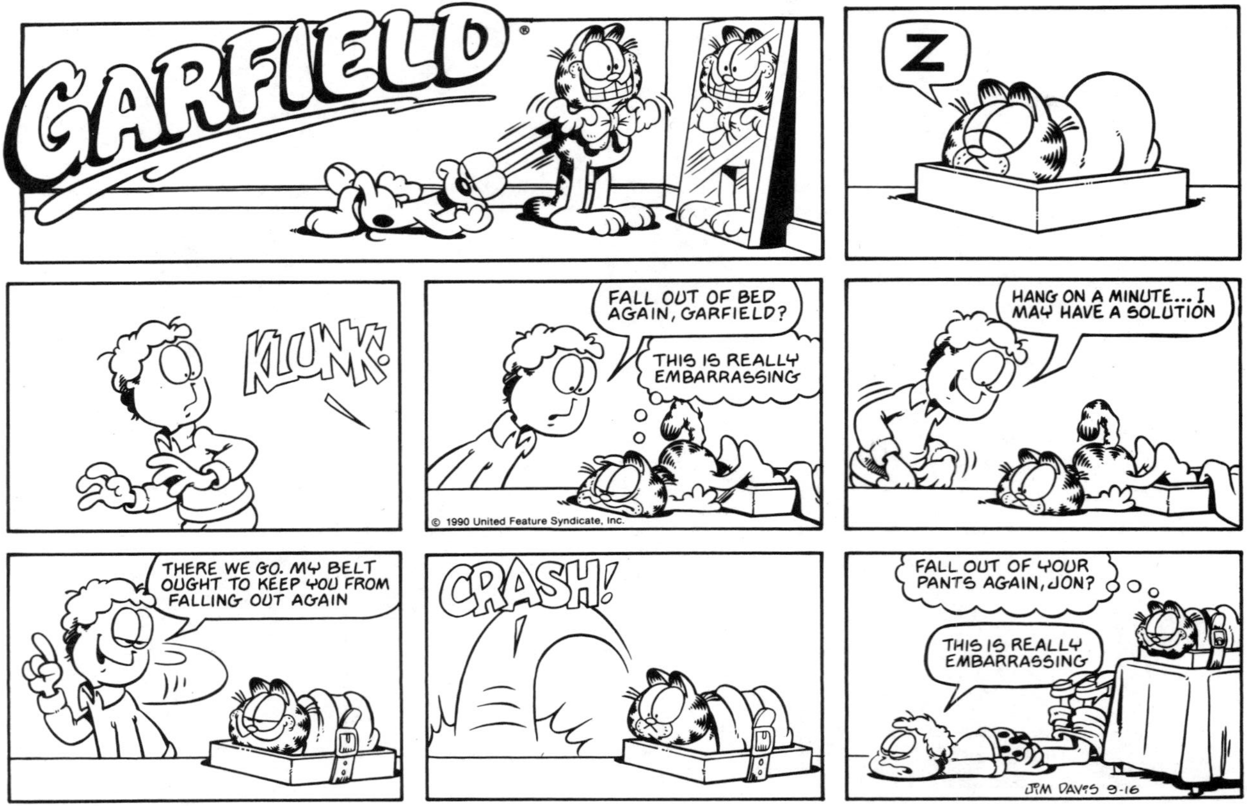
GARFIELD
Z
KLUNK!
FALL OUT OF BED AGAIN, GARFIELD?
THIS IS REALLY EMBARRASSING
HANG ON A MINUTE... I MAY HAVE A SOLUTION
THERE WE GO. MY BELT OUGHT TO KEEP YOU FROM FALLING OUT AGAIN
CRASH!
FALL OUT OF YOUR PANTS AGAIN, JON?
THIS IS REALLY EMBARRASSING
JIM DAVIS 9-16
© 1990 United Feature Syndicate, Inc.

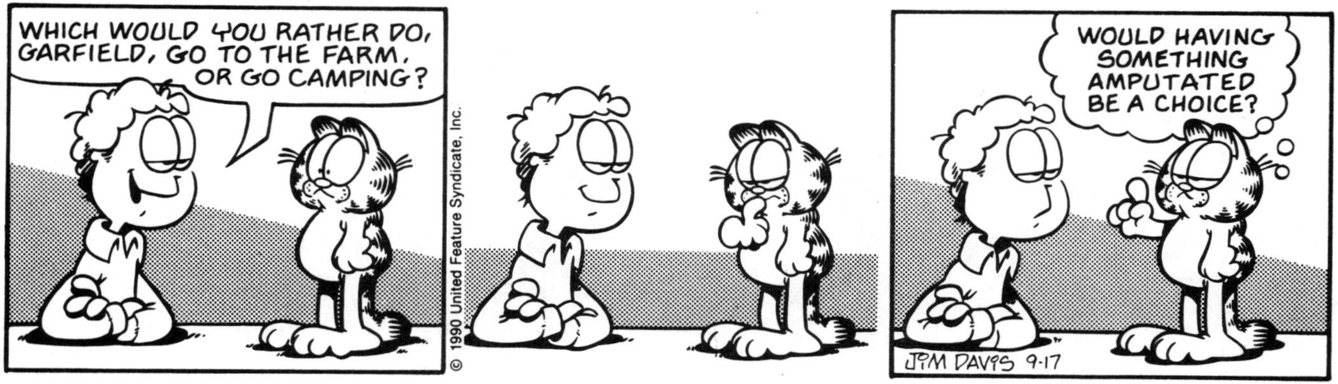
WHICH WOULD YOU RATHER DO, GARFIELD, GO TO THE FARM, OR GO CAMPING?
© 1990 United Feature Syndicate, Inc.
WOULD HAVING SOMETHING AMPUTATED BE A CHOICE?
JIM DAVIS 9-17

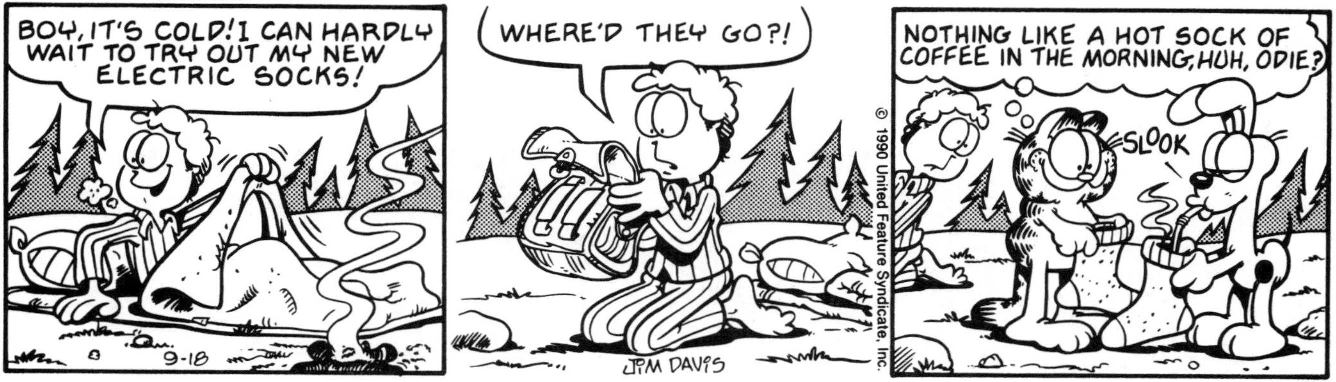
BOY, IT'S COLD! I CAN HARDLY WAIT TO TRY OUT MY NEW ELECTRIC SOCKS!
9-18
WHERE'D THEY GO?!
JIM DAVIS
© 1990 United Feature Syndicate, Inc.
NOTHING LIKE A HOT SOCK OF COFFEE IN THE MORNING, HUH, ODIE?
SLOOK

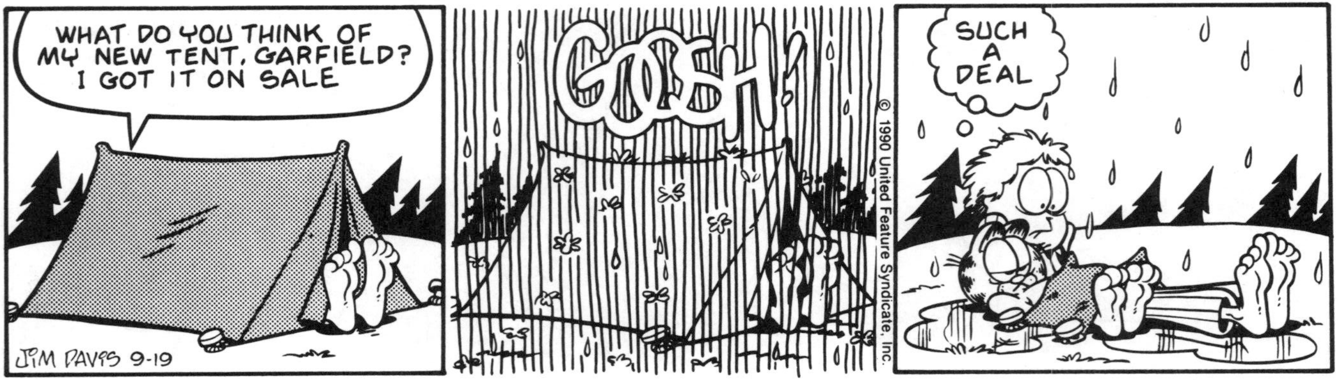
WHAT DO YOU THINK OF MY NEW TENT, GARFIELD? I GOT IT ON SALE
GOOSH!
SUCH A DEAL
JIM DAVIS 9-19
© 1990 United Feature Syndicate, Inc.

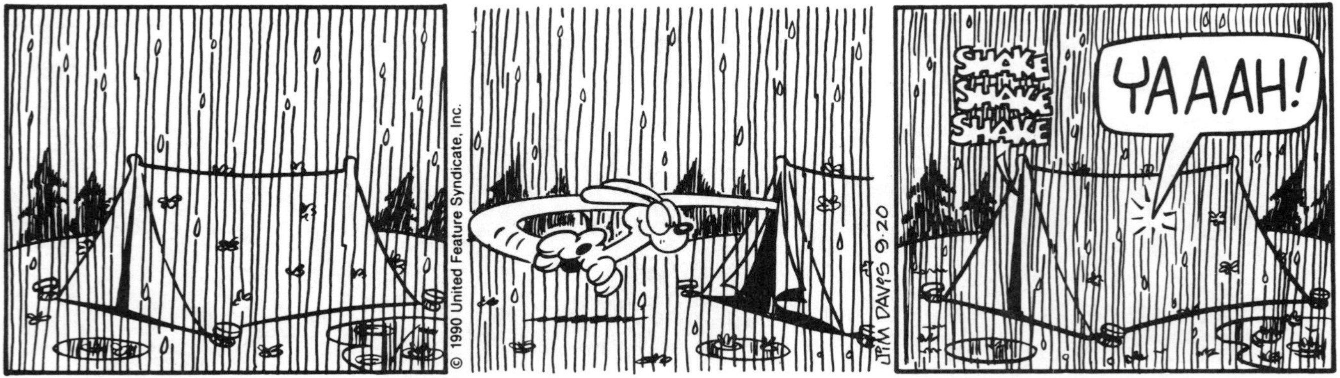
SHAKE SHAKE SHAKE
YAAAH!
JIM DAVIS 9-20
© 1990 United Feature Syndicate, Inc.

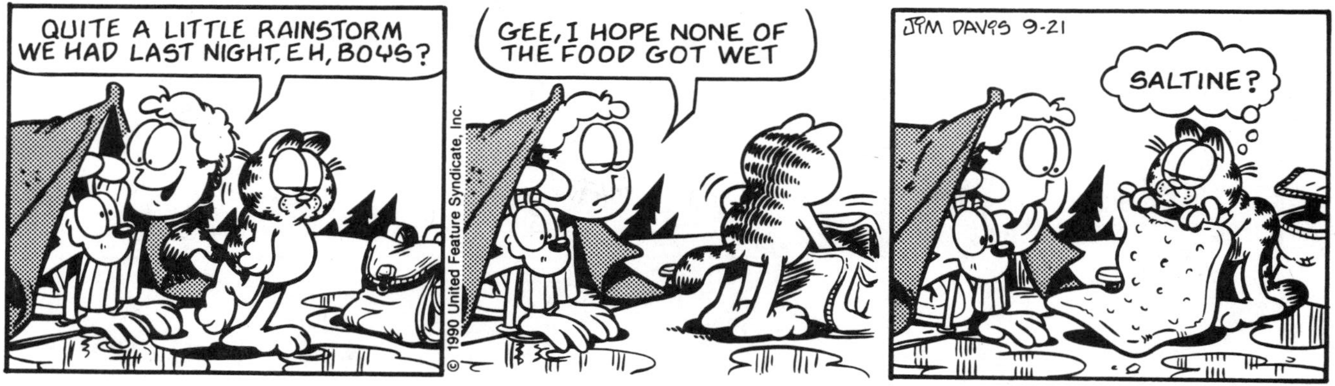
QUITE A LITTLE RAINSTORM WE HAD LAST NIGHT, EH, BOYS?
GEE, I HOPE NONE OF THE FOOD GOT WET
JIM DAVIS 9-21
SALTINE?
© 1990 United Feature Syndicate, Inc.

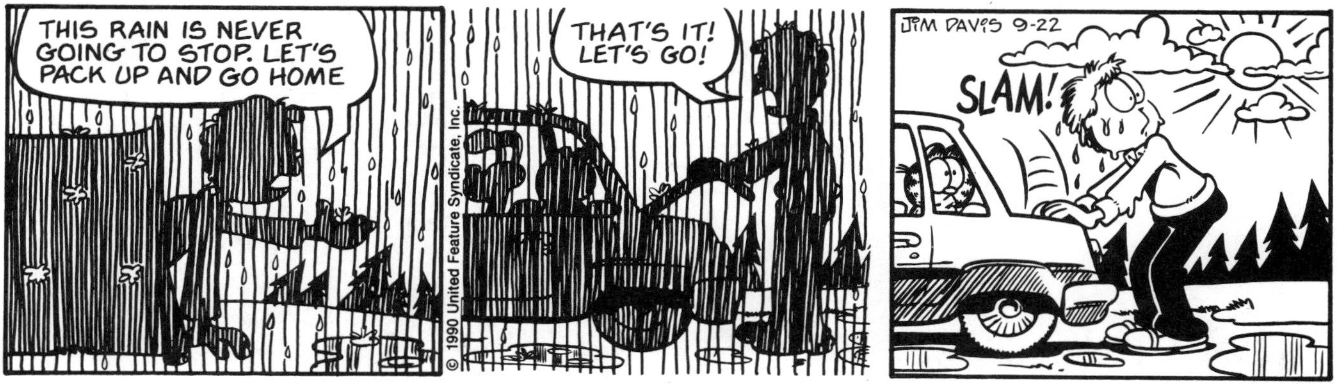
THIS RAIN IS NEVER GOING TO STOP. LET'S PACK UP AND GO HOME
THAT'S IT! LET'S GO!
JIM DAVIS 9-22
SLAM!
© 1990 United Feature Syndicate, Inc.

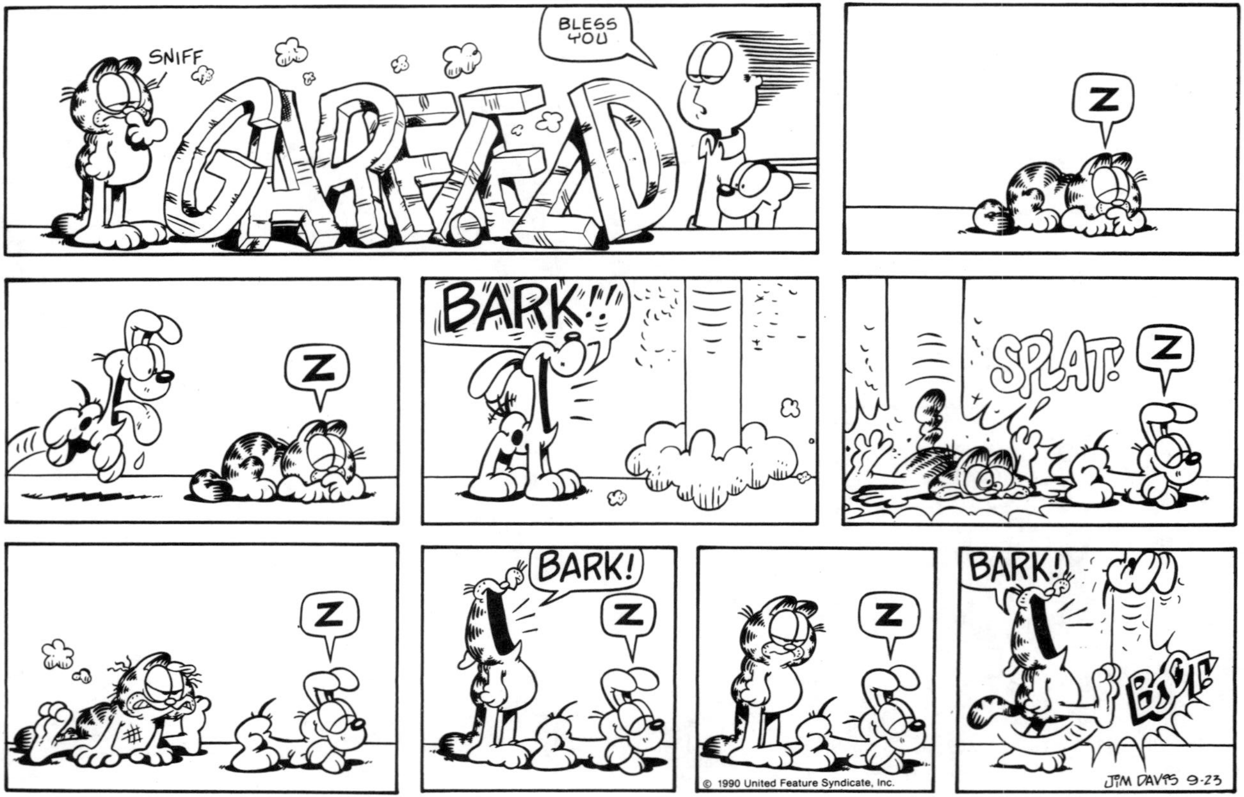
SNIFF
GARFIELD
BLESS YOU
Z
Z
BARK!!!
SPLAT!
Z
Z
BARK!
Z
Z
BARK!
BOOT!
© 1990 United Feature Syndicate, Inc.
JIM DAVIS 9-23

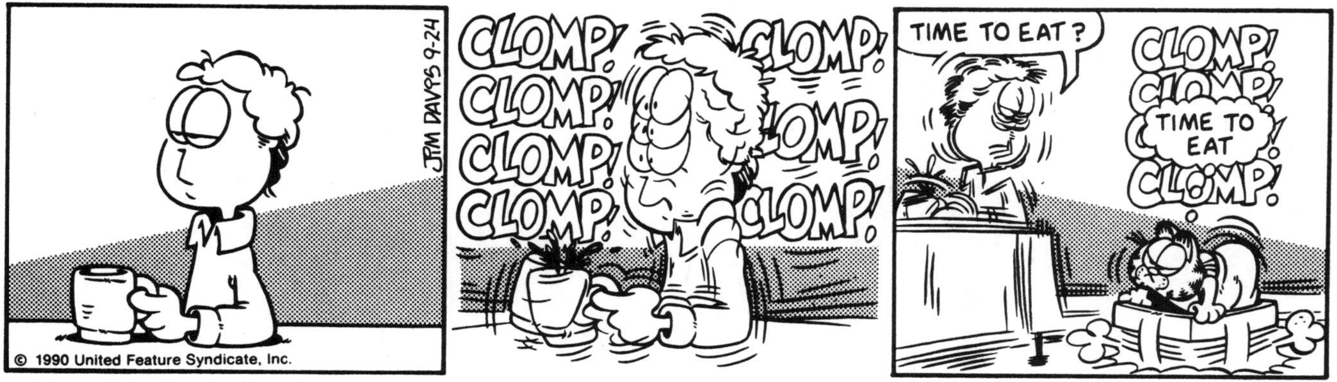
JIM DAVIS 9-24
© 1990 United Feature Syndicate, Inc.
CLOMP! CLOMP! CLOMP! CLOMP!
CLOMP! CLOMP! CLOMP!
TIME TO EAT?
CLOMP! CLOMP! CLOMP!
TIME TO EAT

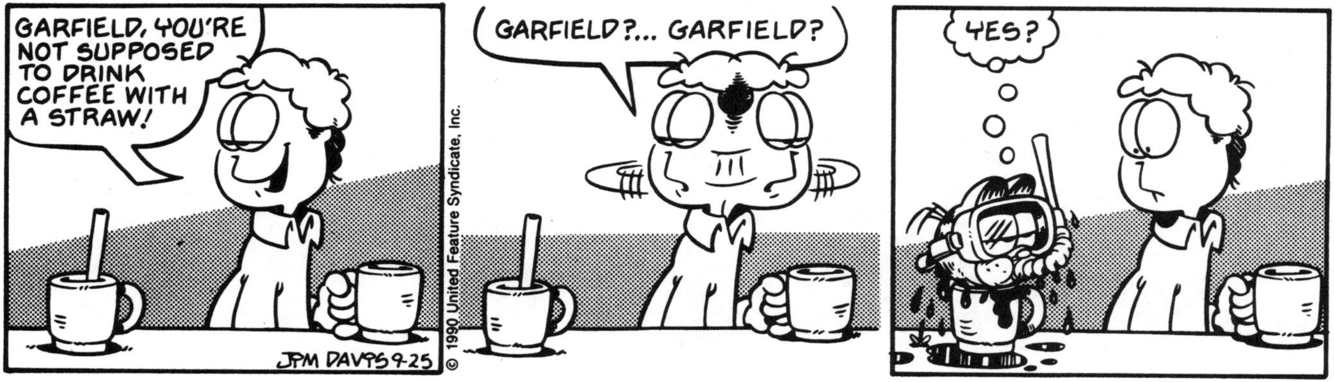
GARFIELD, YOU'RE NOT SUPPOSED TO DRINK COFFEE WITH A STRAW!
JIM DAVIS 9-25
© 1990 United Feature Syndicate, Inc.
GARFIELD?... GARFIELD?
YES?

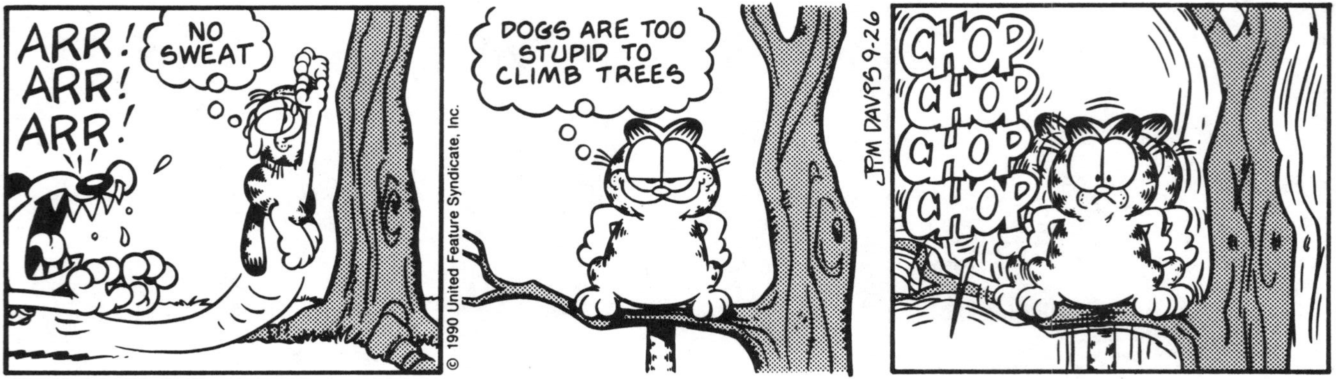
ARR! ARR! ARR!
NO SWEAT
© 1990 United Feature Syndicate, Inc.
DOGS ARE TOO STUPID TO CLIMB TREES
JIM DAVIS 9-26
CHOP CHOP CHOP CHOP

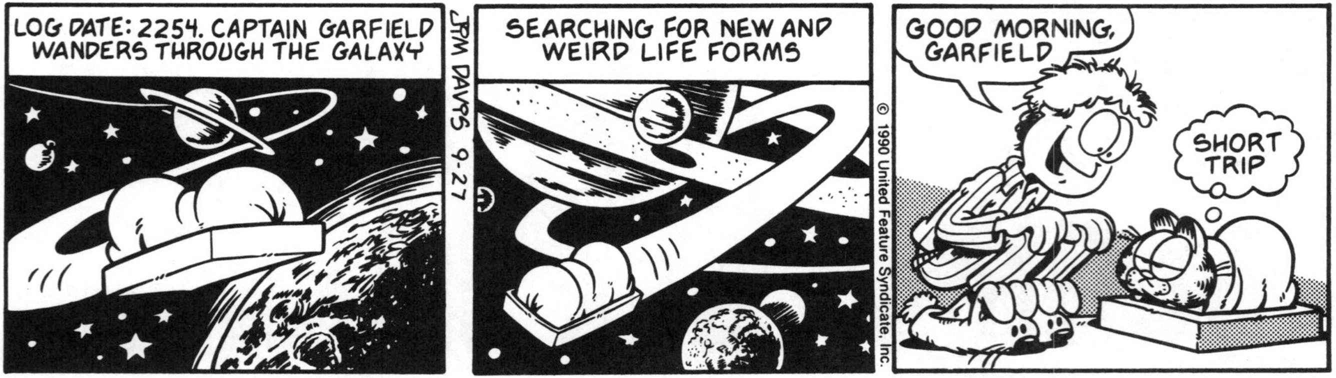
LOG DATE: 2254. CAPTAIN GARFIELD WANDERS THROUGH THE GALAXY
JIM DAVIS 9-27
SEARCHING FOR NEW AND WEIRD LIFE FORMS
© 1990 United Feature Syndicate, Inc.
GOOD MORNING, GARFIELD
SHORT TRIP

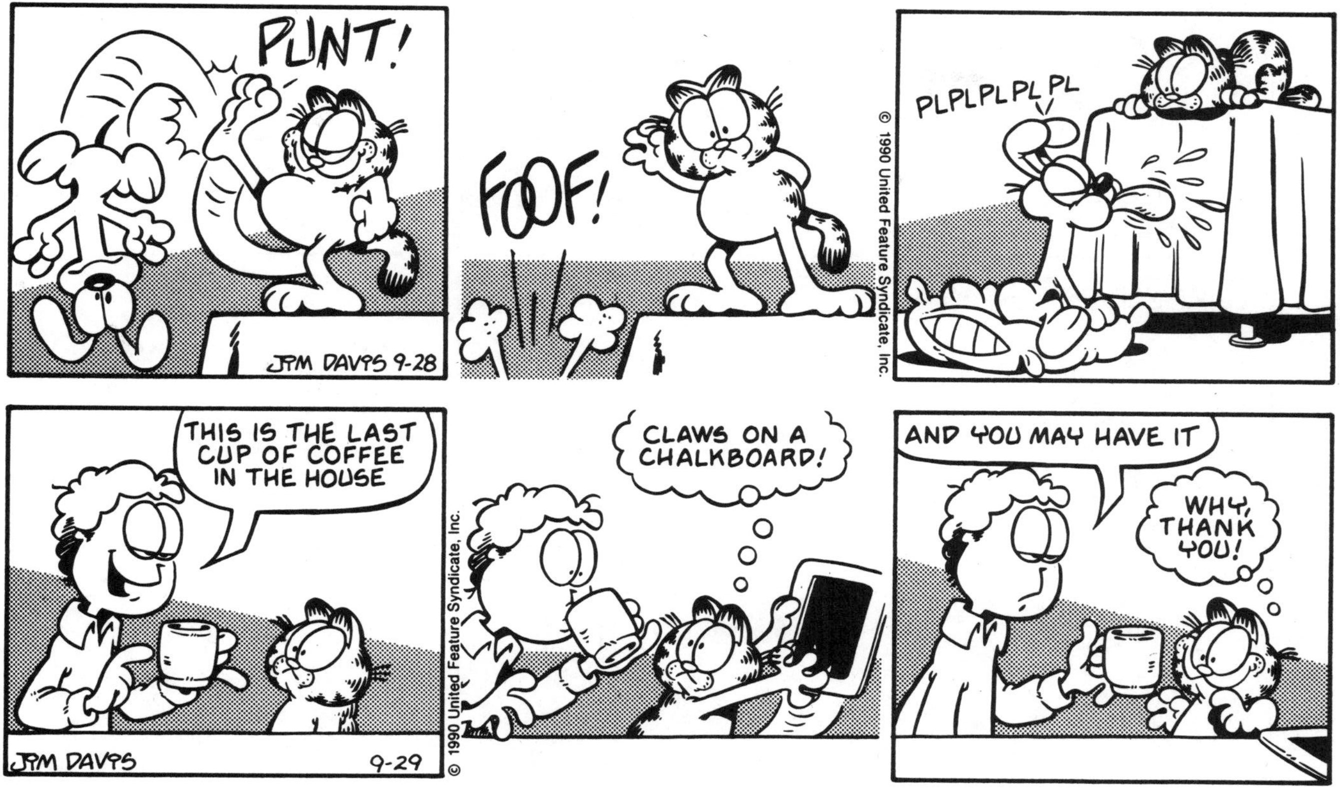
PLINT!
JIM DAVIS 9-28
FOOF!
© 1990 United Feature Syndicate, Inc.
PLPLPLPLPL
THIS IS THE LAST CUP OF COFFEE IN THE HOUSE
JIM DAVIS 9-29
© 1990 United Feature Syndicate, Inc.
CLAWS ON A CHALKBOARD!
AND YOU MAY HAVE IT
WHY, THANK YOU!

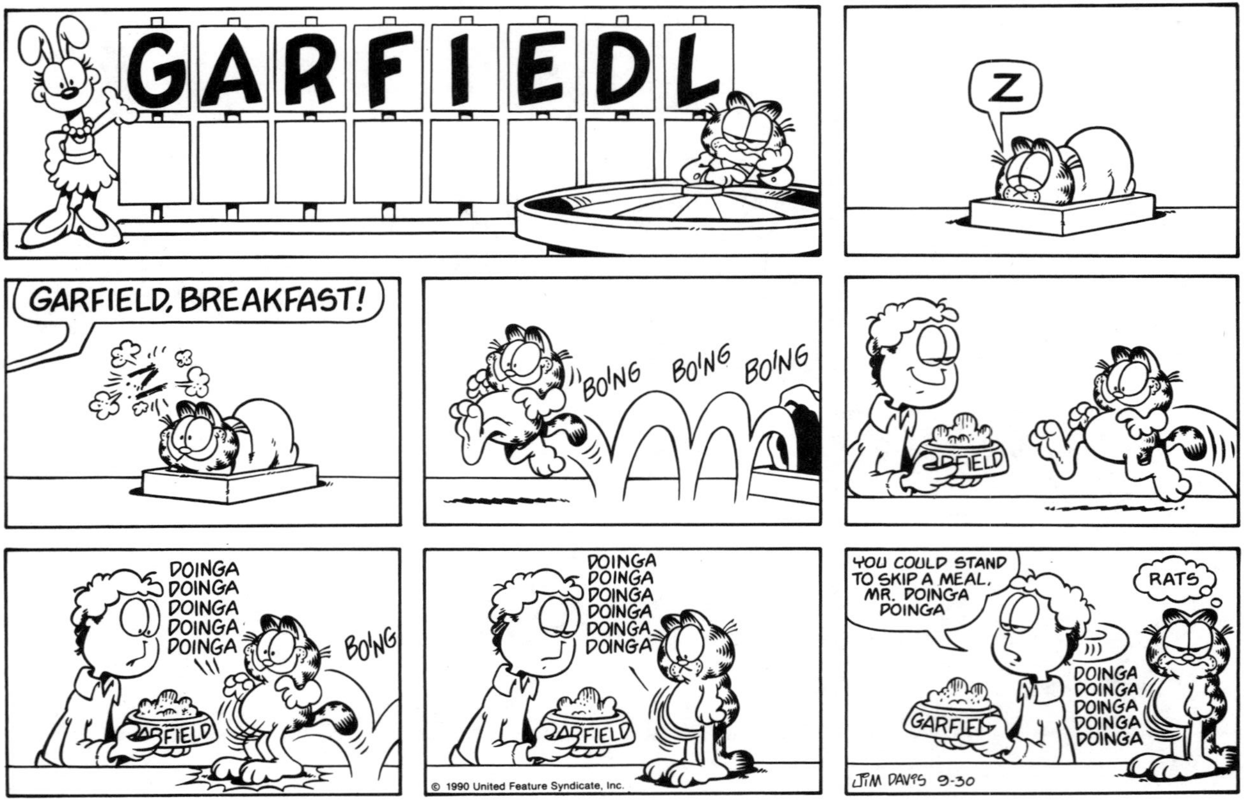
GARFIEDL
Z
GARFIELD, BREAKFAST!
Z
BOING BOING BOING
GARFIELD
DOINGA DOINGA DOINGA DOINGA DOINGA
GARFIELD
BOING
DOINGA DOINGA DOINGA DOINGA DOINGA DOINGA
GARFIELD
© 1990 United Feature Syndicate, Inc.
YOU COULD STAND TO SKIP A MEAL, MR. DOINGA DOINGA
RATS
DOINGA DOINGA DOINGA DOINGA DOINGA
GARFIELD
JIM DAVIS 9-30

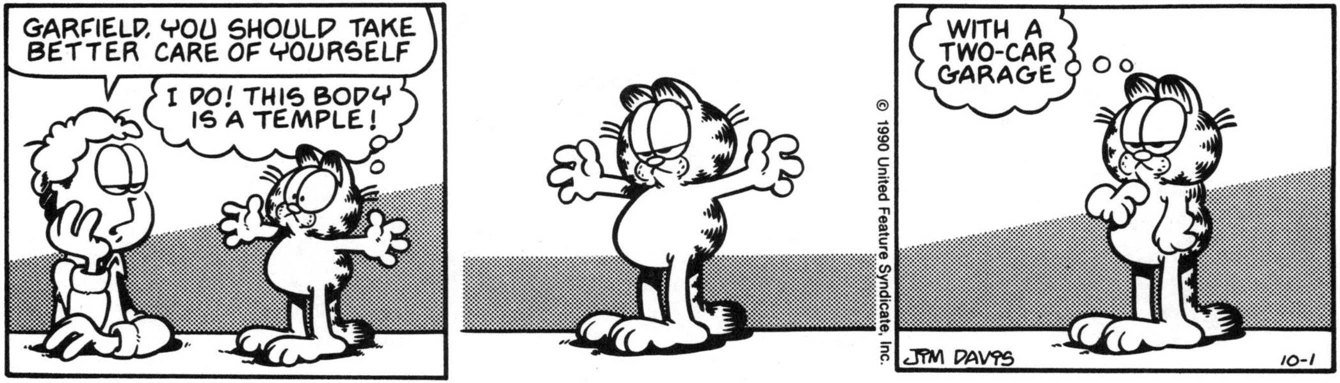
GARFIELD, YOU SHOULD TAKE BETTER CARE OF YOURSELF
I DO! THIS BODY IS A TEMPLE!
WITH A TWO-CAR GARAGE
JIM DAVIS
10-1
© 1990 United Feature Syndicate, Inc.

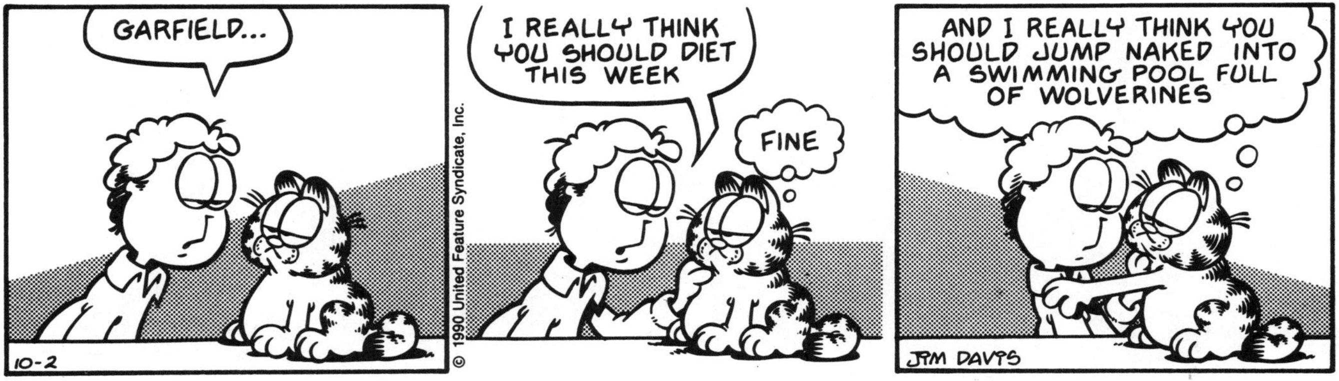
GARFIELD...
I REALLY THINK YOU SHOULD DIET THIS WEEK
FINE
AND I REALLY THINK YOU SHOULD JUMP NAKED INTO A SWIMMING POOL FULL OF WOLVERINES
10-2
JIM DAVIS
© 1990 United Feature Syndicate, Inc.

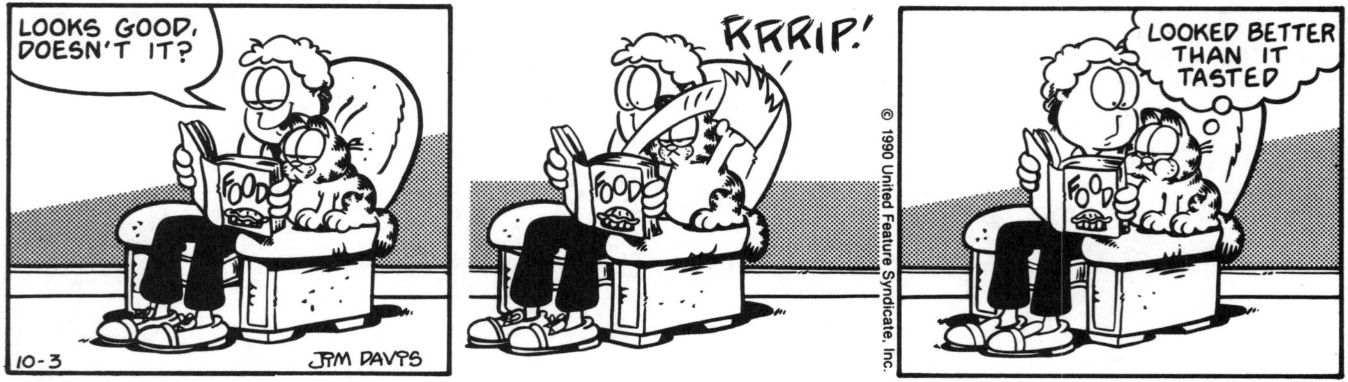
LOOKS GOOD, DOESN'T IT?
10-3
JIM DAVIS
KRRIP!
LOOKED BETTER THAN IT TASTED

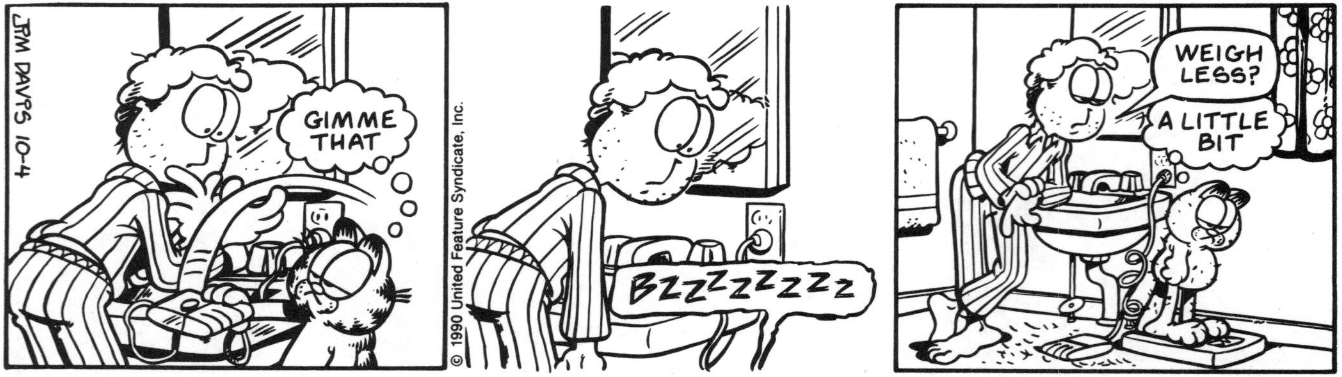
JIM DAVIS 10-4
GIMME THAT
BZZZZZZZZZ
WEIGH LESS?
A LITTLE BIT

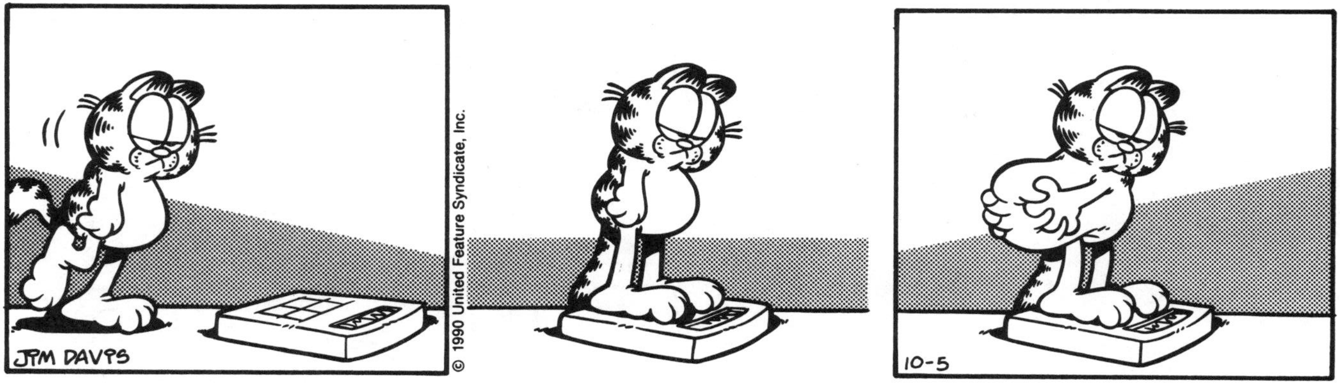
JIM DAVIS
© 1990 United Feature Syndicate, Inc.
10-5

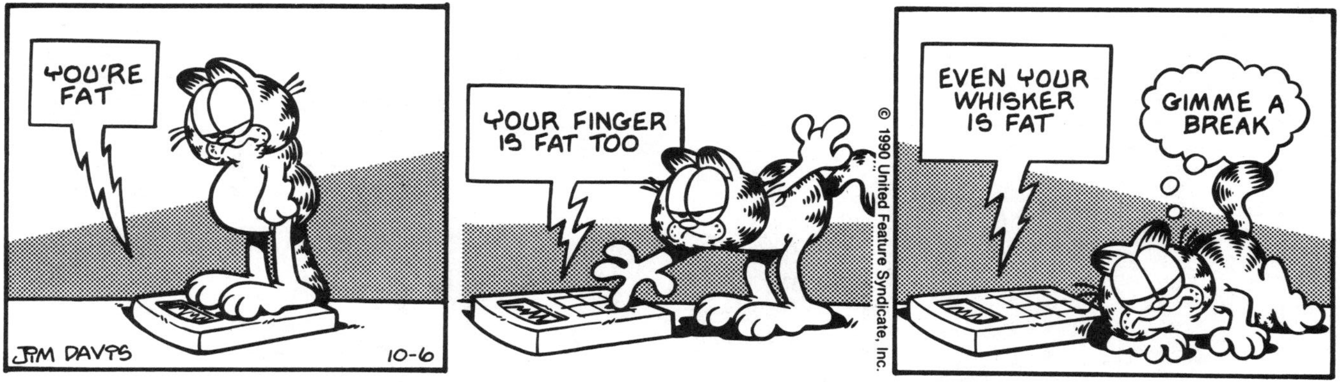
YOU'RE FAT
JIM DAVIS
10-6
YOUR FINGER IS FAT TOO
© 1990 United Feature Syndicate, Inc.
EVEN YOUR WHISKER IS FAT
GIMME A BREAK

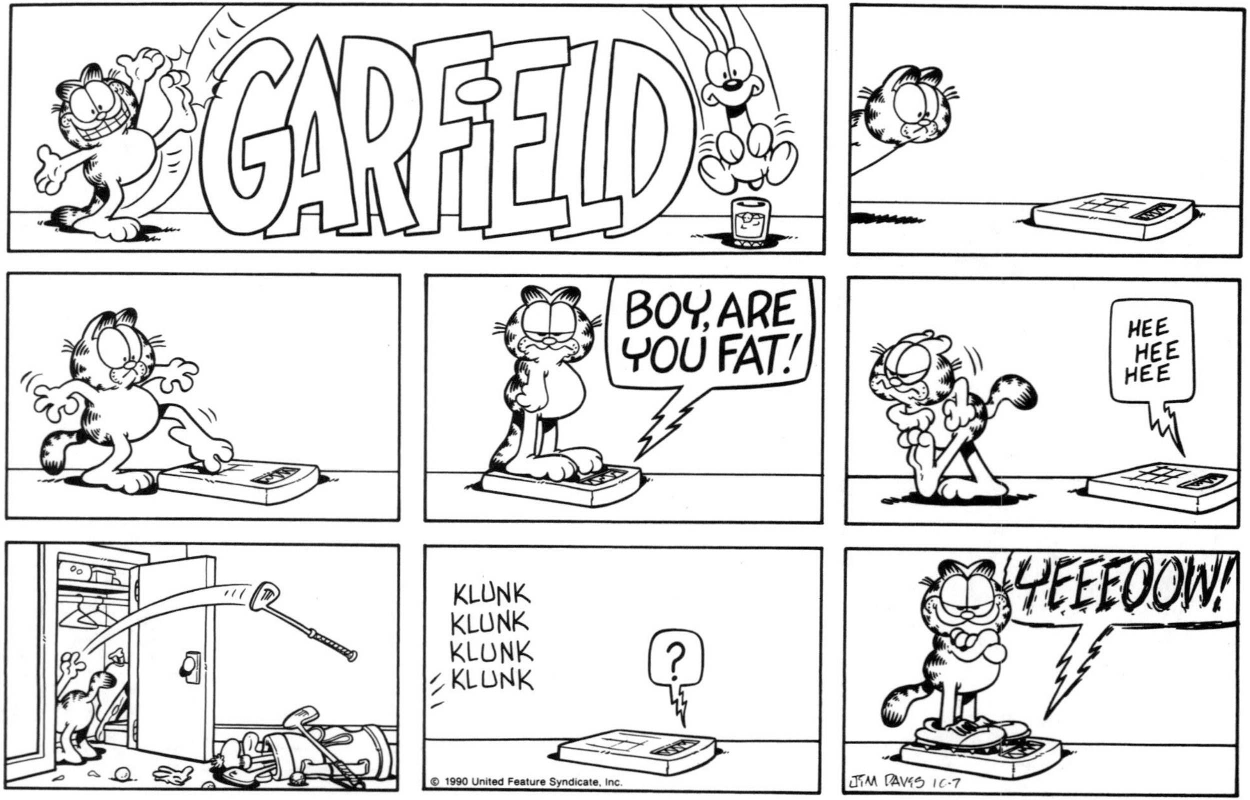
GARFIELD
BOY, ARE YOU FAT!
HEE HEE HEE
KLUNK KLUNK KLUNK KLUNK
?
YEEEOOW!
© 1990 United Feature Syndicate, Inc.
JIM DAVIS 10-7

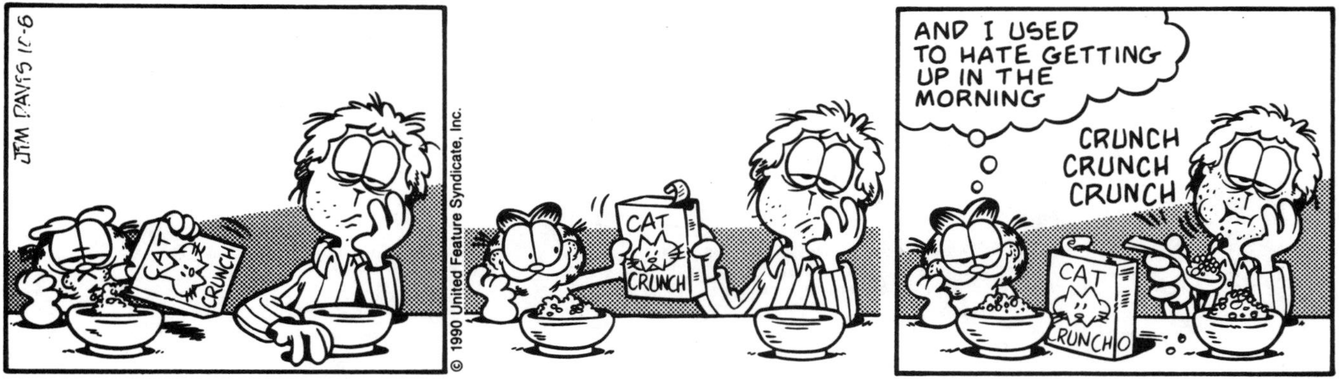
JIM DAVIS 10-6
CAT CRUNCH
CAT CRUNCH
AND I USED TO HATE GETTING UP IN THE MORNING
CRUNCH CRUNCH CRUNCH
CAT CRUNCH

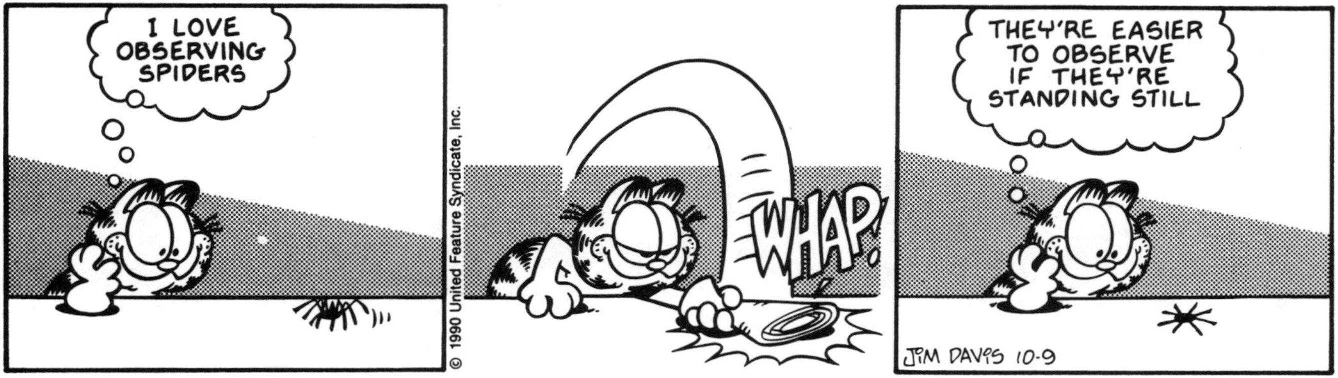
I LOVE OBSERVING SPIDERS
WHAP!
THEY'RE EASIER TO OBSERVE IF THEY'RE STANDING STILL
JIM DAVIS 10-9

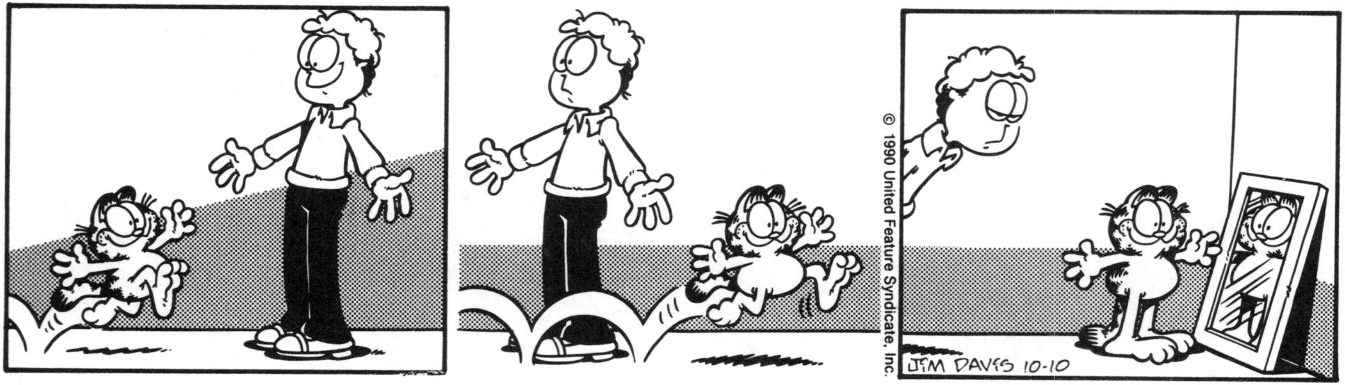
JIM DAVIS 10-10

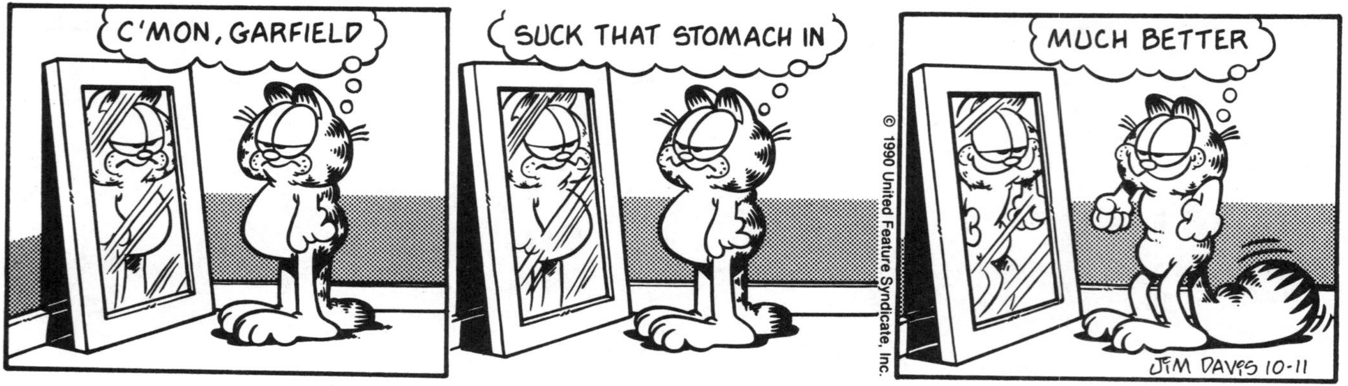
C'MON, GARFIELD
SUCK THAT STOMACH IN
MUCH BETTER
JIM DAVIS 10-11

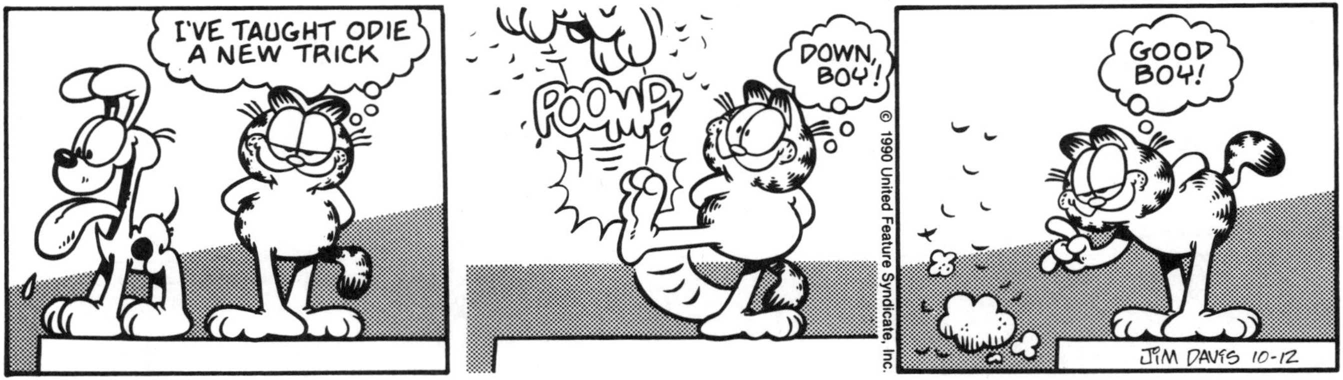
I'VE TAUGHT ODIE A NEW TRICK
POOMP!
DOWN, BOY!
© 1990 United Feature Syndicate, Inc.
GOOD BOY!
JIM DAVIS 10-12

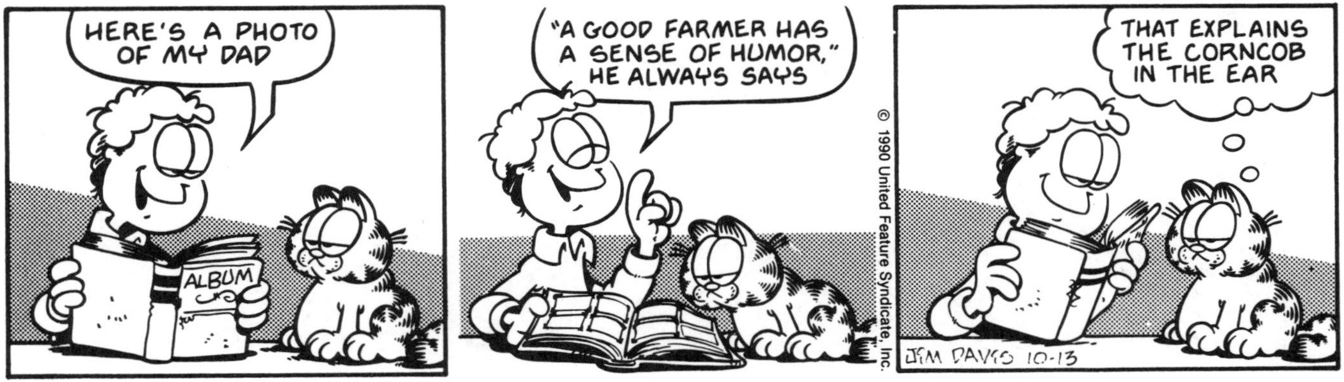
HERE'S A PHOTO OF MY DAD
ALBUM
"A GOOD FARMER HAS A SENSE OF HUMOR," HE ALWAYS SAYS
© 1990 United Feature Syndicate, Inc.
THAT EXPLAINS THE CORNCOB IN THE EAR
JIM DAVIS 10-13

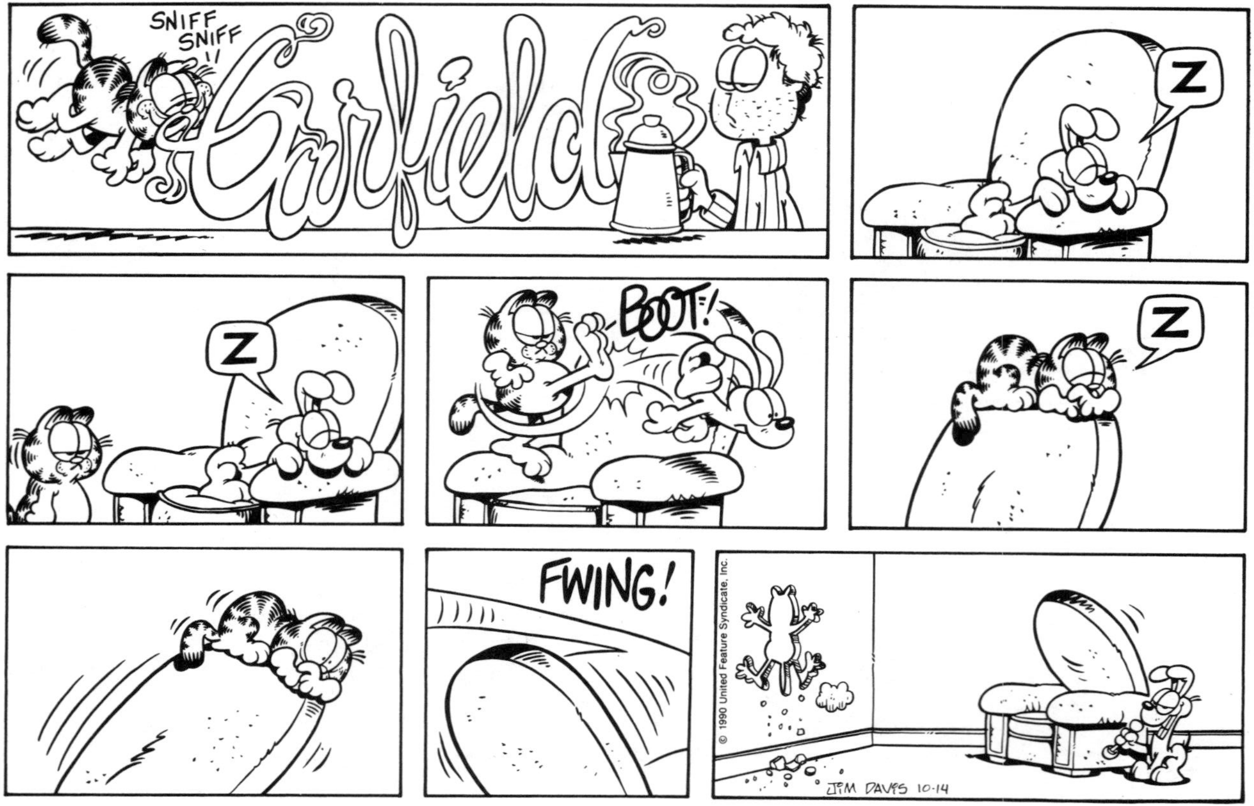
SNIFF SNIFF
Garfield
Z
Z
BOOT!
Z
FWING!
© 1990 United Feature Syndicate, Inc.
JIM DAVIS 10-14

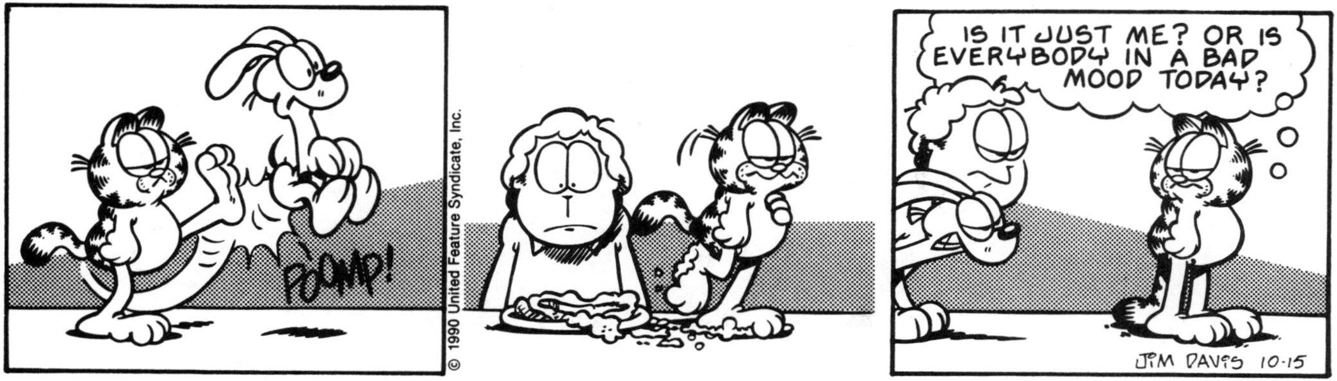
POOMP!
IS IT JUST ME? OR IS EVERYBODY IN A BAD MOOD TODAY?
JIM DAVIS 10-15

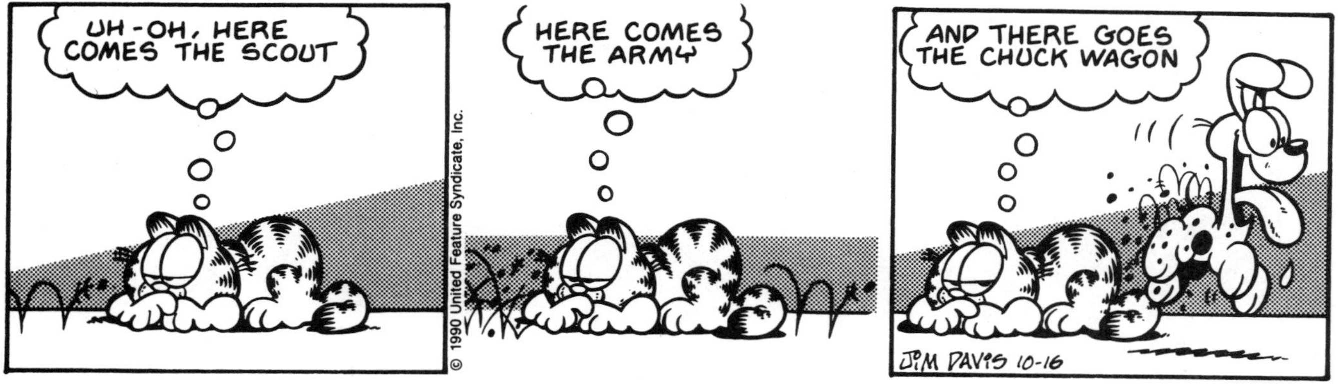
UH-OH, HERE COMES THE SCOUT
HERE COMES THE ARMY
AND THERE GOES THE CHUCK WAGON
JIM DAVIS 10-16

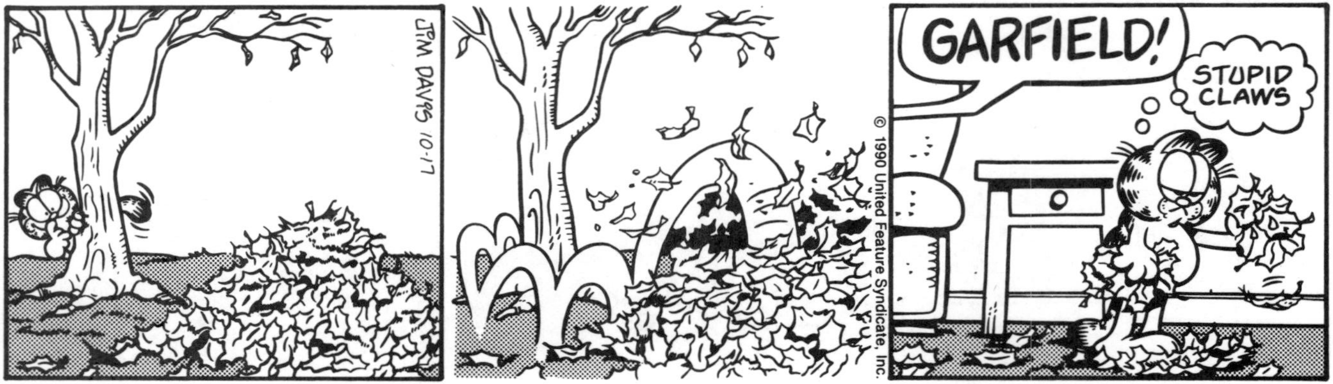
JIM DAVIS 10-17
© 1990 United Feature Syndicate, Inc.
GARFIELD!
STUPID CLAWS

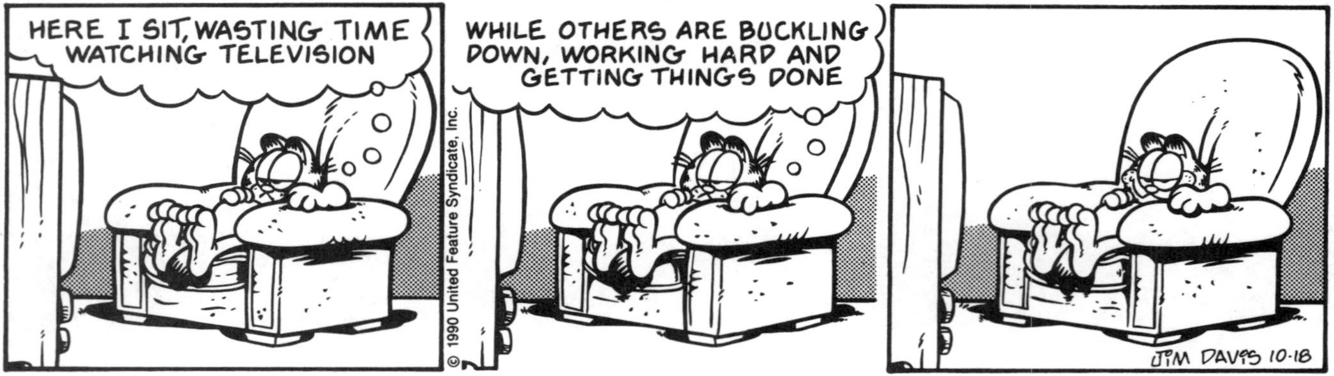
HERE I SIT, WASTING TIME WATCHING TELEVISION
© 1990 United Feature Syndicate, Inc.
WHILE OTHERS ARE BUCKLING DOWN, WORKING HARD AND GETTING THINGS DONE
JIM DAVIS 10-18

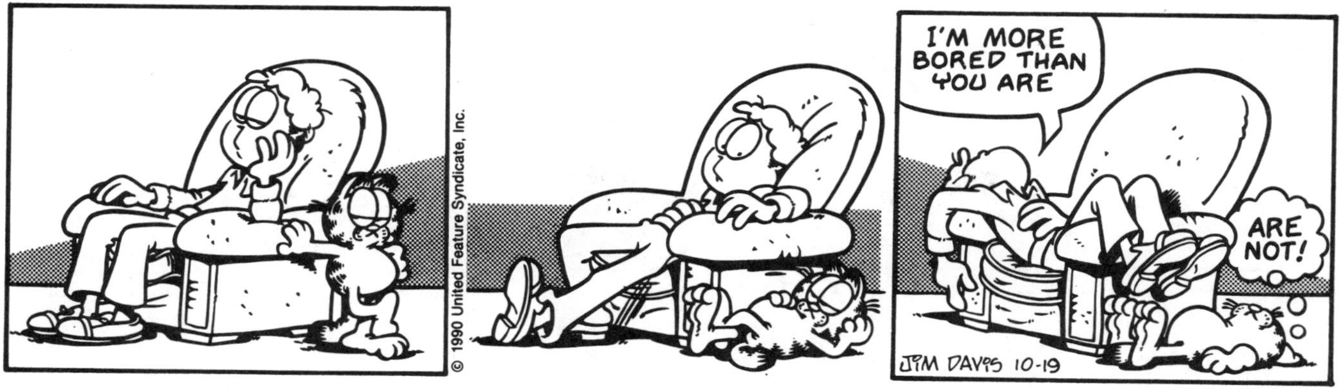
I'M MORE BORED THAN YOU ARE
ARE NOT!
JIM DAVIS 10-19

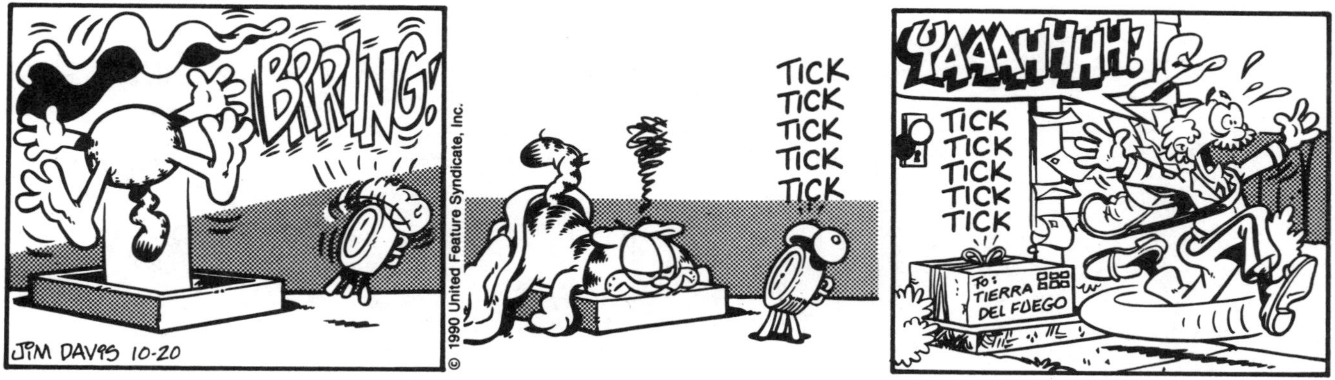
BRRING!
JIM DAVIS 10-20
TICK
TICK
TICK
TICK
TICK
YAAAHHHH!
TICK
TICK
TICK
TICK
TICK
TO: TIERRA DEL FUEGO

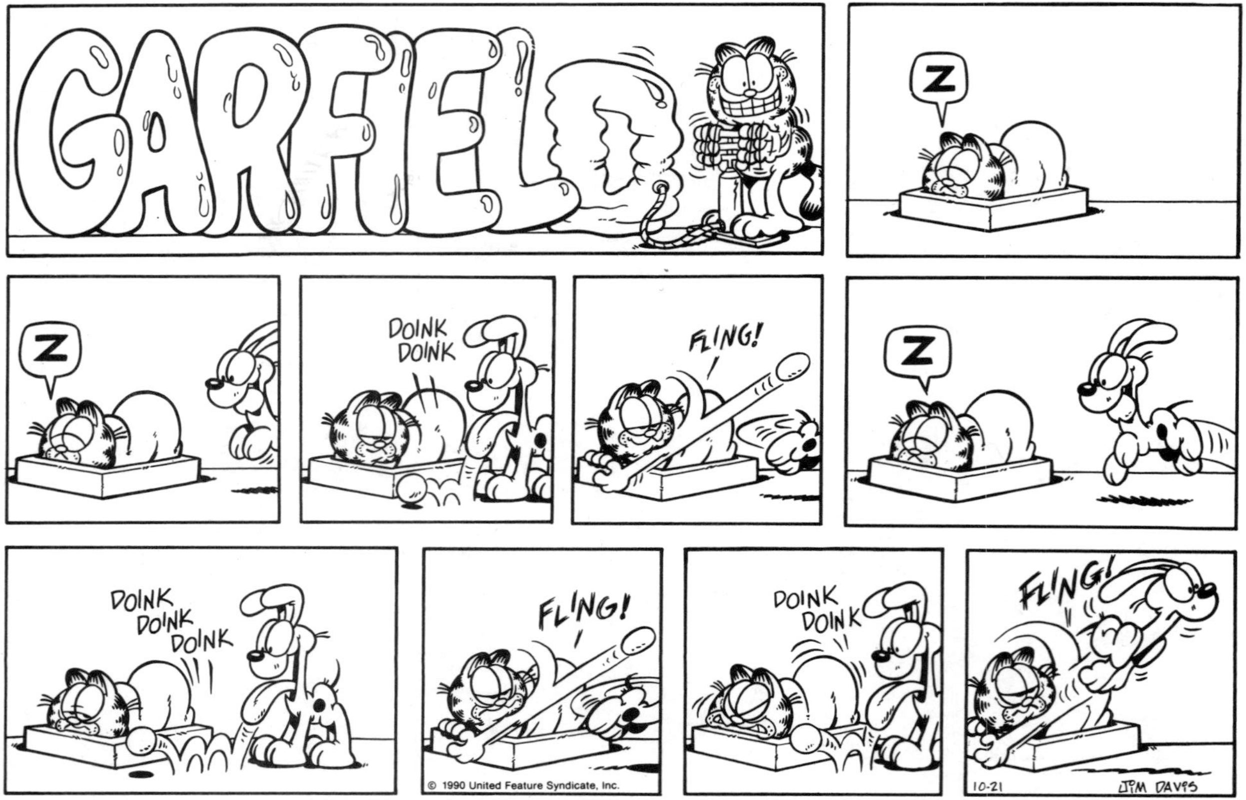
GARFIELD
Z
Z
DOINK DOINK
FLING!
Z
DOINK DOINK DOINK
FLING!
© 1990 United Feature Syndicate, Inc.
DOINK DOINK
FLING!
10-21
JIM DAVIS

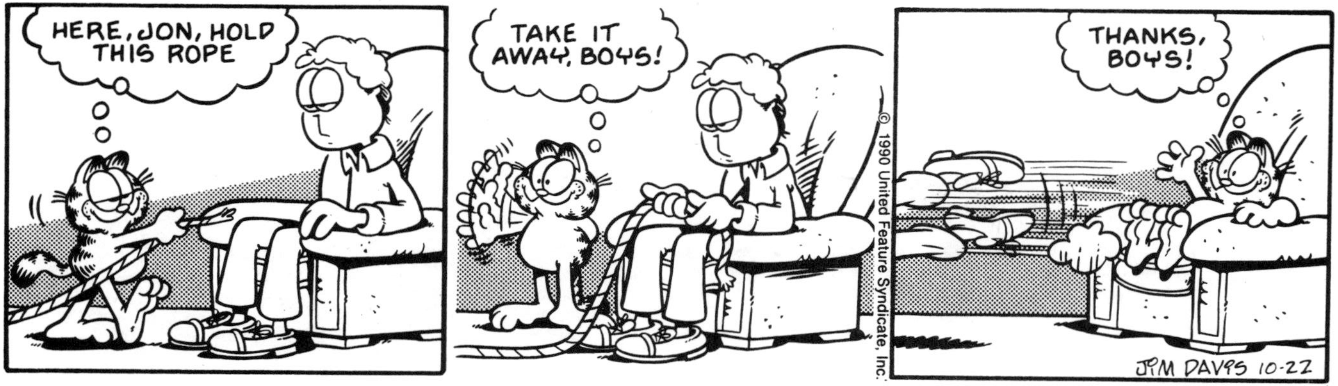
HERE, JON, HOLD THIS ROPE
TAKE IT AWAY, BOYS!
© 1990 United Feature Syndicate, Inc.
THANKS, BOYS!
JIM DAVIS 10-22

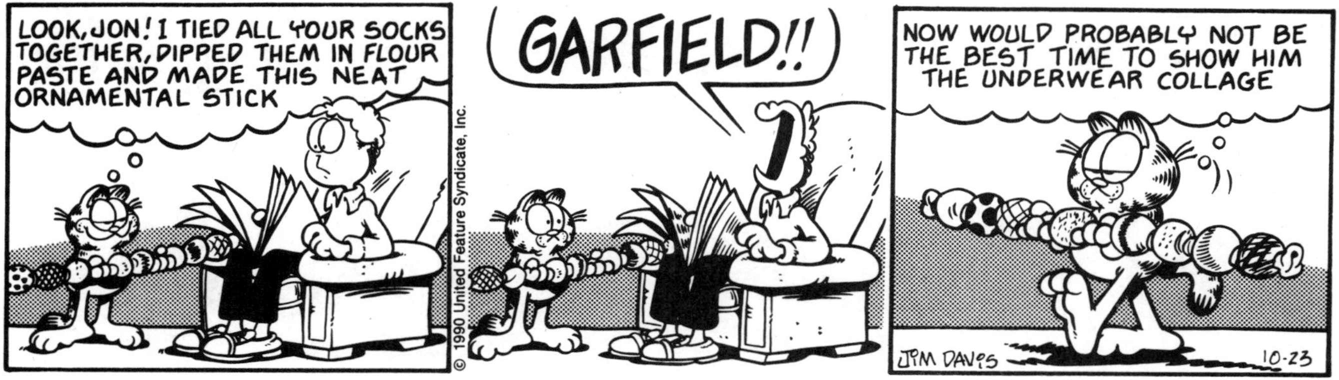
LOOK, JON! I TIED ALL YOUR SOCKS TOGETHER, DIPPED THEM IN FLOUR PASTE AND MADE THIS NEAT ORNAMENTAL STICK
© 1990 United Feature Syndicate, Inc.
GARFIELD!!
NOW WOULD PROBABLY NOT BE THE BEST TIME TO SHOW HIM THE UNDERWEAR COLLAGE
JIM DAVIS 10-23

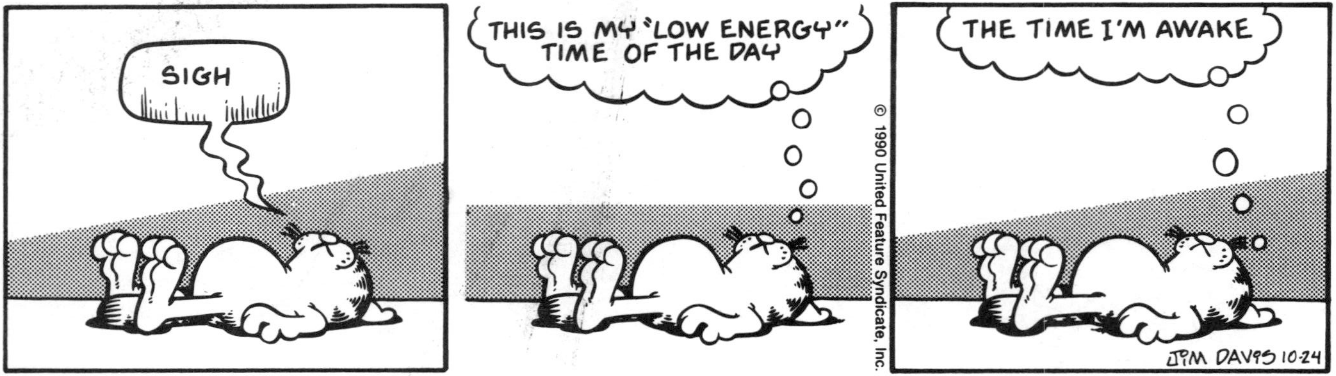
SIGH
THIS IS MY "LOW ENERGY" TIME OF THE DAY
THE TIME I'M AWAKE
JIM DAVIS 10-24

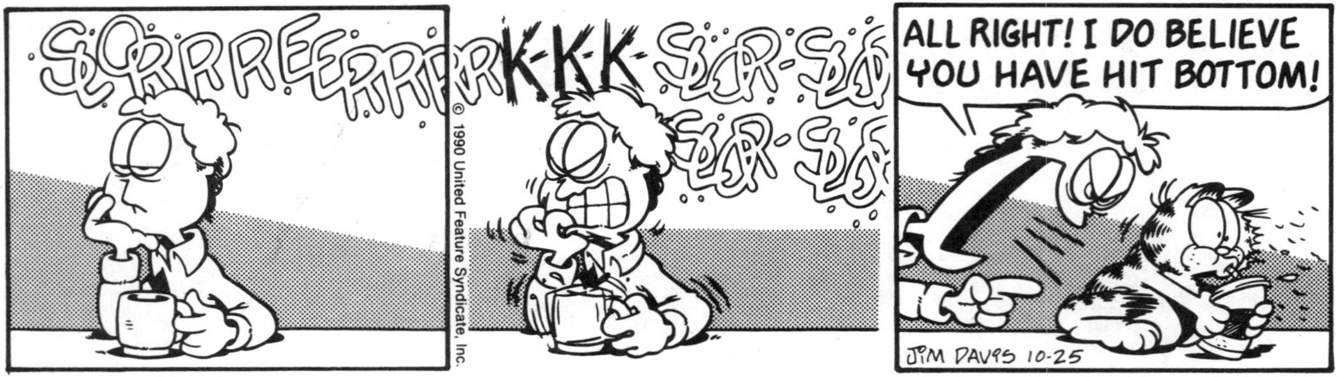
ALL RIGHT! I DO BELIEVE YOU HAVE HIT BOTTOM!
JIM DAVIS 10-25

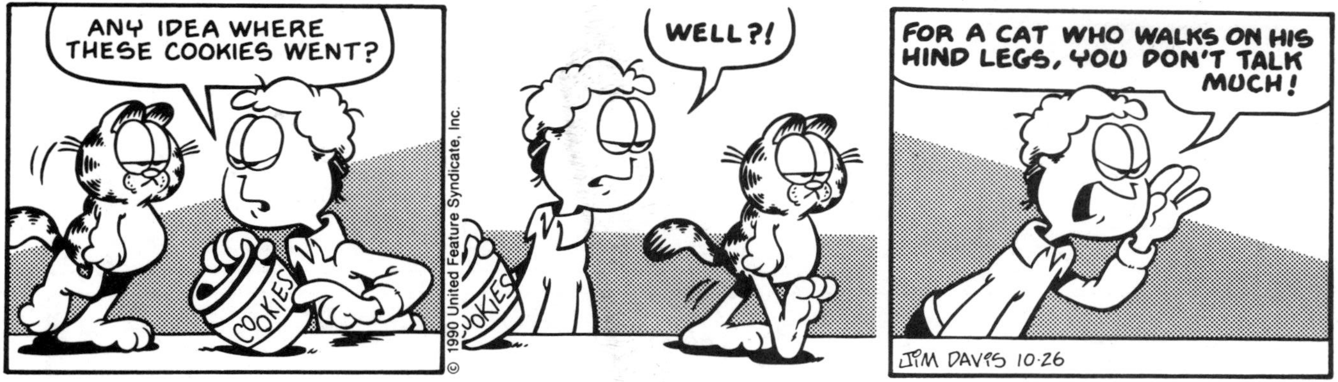
ANY IDEA WHERE THESE COOKIES WENT?
COOKIES
COOKIES
WELL?!
FOR A CAT WHO WALKS ON HIS HIND LEGS, YOU DON'T TALK MUCH!
JIM DAVIS 10-26
© 1990 United Feature Syndicate, Inc.

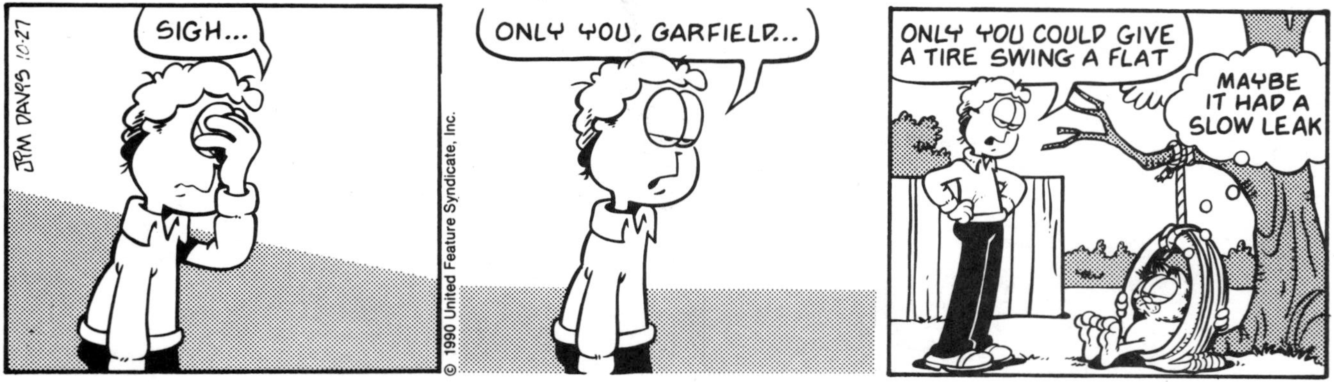
JIM DAVIS 10-27
SIGH...
ONLY YOU, GARFIELD...
ONLY YOU COULD GIVE A TIRE SWING A FLAT
MAYBE IT HAD A SLOW LEAK
© 1990 United Feature Syndicate, Inc.

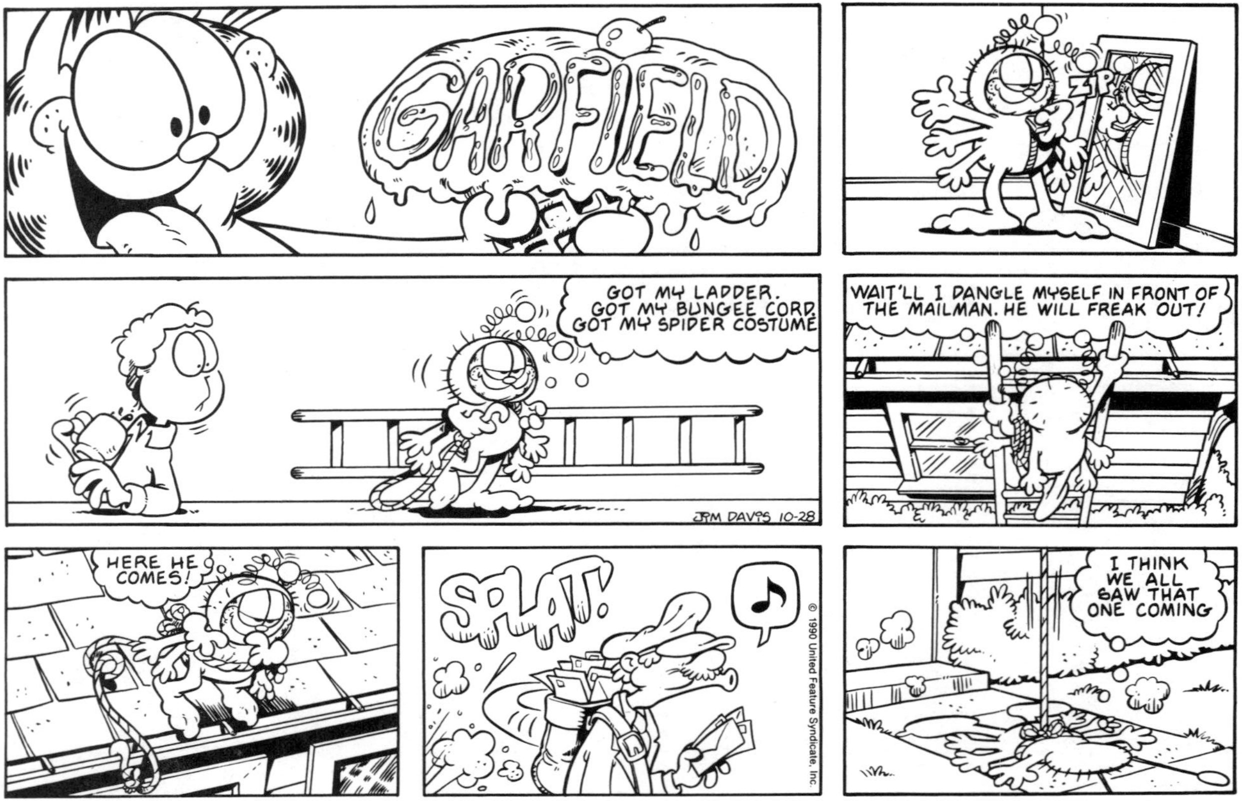
GARFIELD
ZIP
GOT MY LADDER. GOT MY BUNGEE CORD. GOT MY SPIDER COSTUME
JIM DAVIS 10-28
WAIT'LL I DANGLE MYSELF IN FRONT OF THE MAILMAN. HE WILL FREAK OUT!
HERE HE COMES!
SPLAT!
I THINK WE ALL SAW THAT ONE COMING

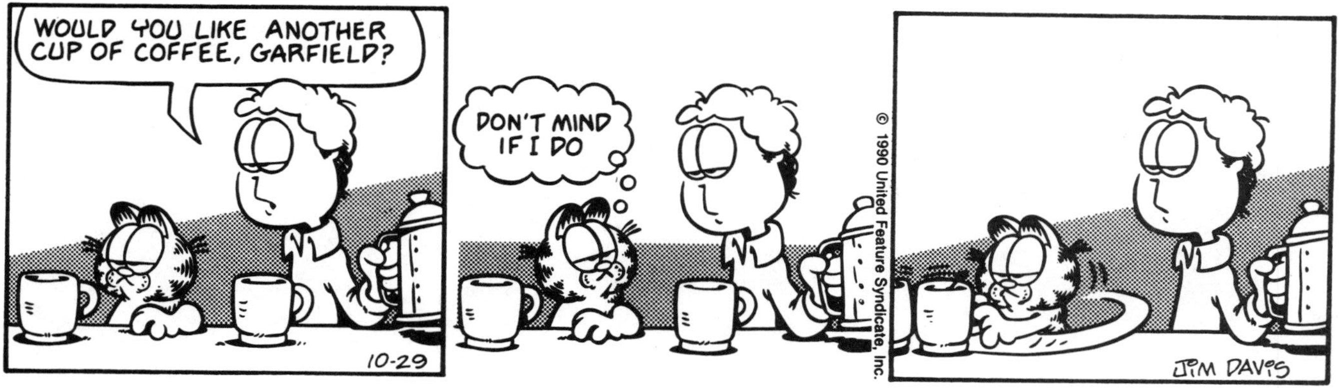
WOULD YOU LIKE ANOTHER CUP OF COFFEE, GARFIELD?
10-29
DON'T MIND IF I DO
© 1990 United Feature Syndicate, Inc.
JIM DAVIS

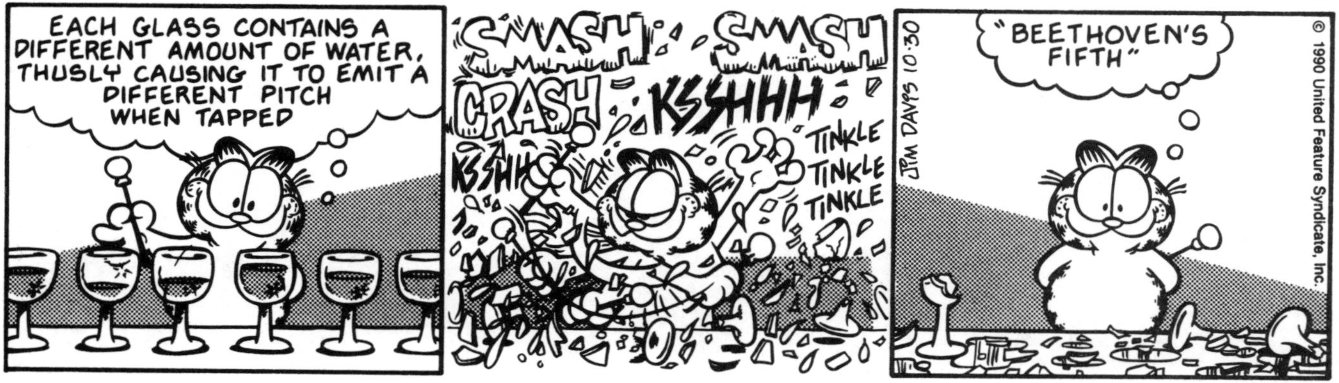
EACH GLASS CONTAINS A DIFFERENT AMOUNT OF WATER, THUSLY CAUSING IT TO EMIT A DIFFERENT PITCH WHEN TAPPED
SMASH SMASH
CRASH KSSHHH
KSSHH
TINKLE TINKLE TINKLE
JIM DAVIS 10·30
"BEETHOVEN'S FIFTH"
© 1990 United Feature Syndicate, Inc.

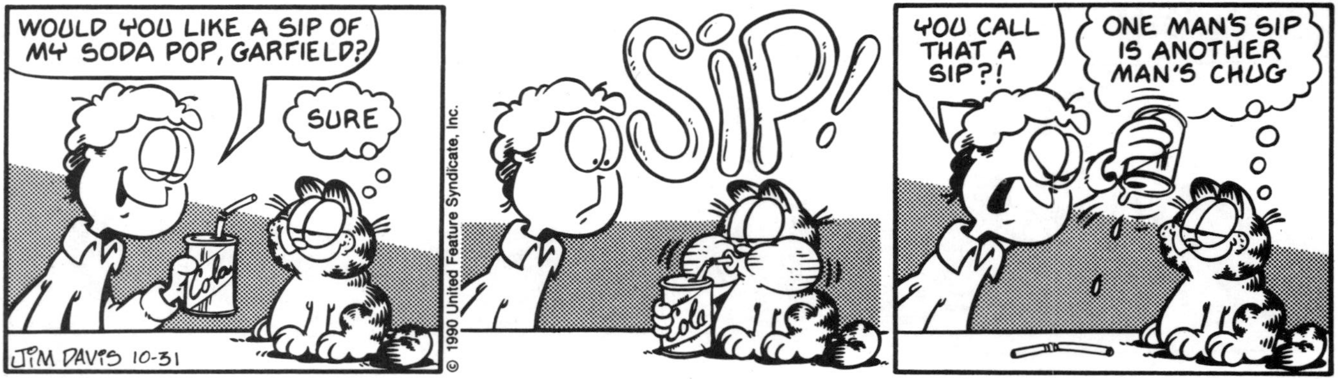
WOULD YOU LIKE A SIP OF MY SODA POP, GARFIELD?
SURE
JIM DAVIS 10-31
Cola
SIP!
Cola
YOU CALL THAT A SIP?!
ONE MAN'S SIP IS ANOTHER MAN'S CHUG

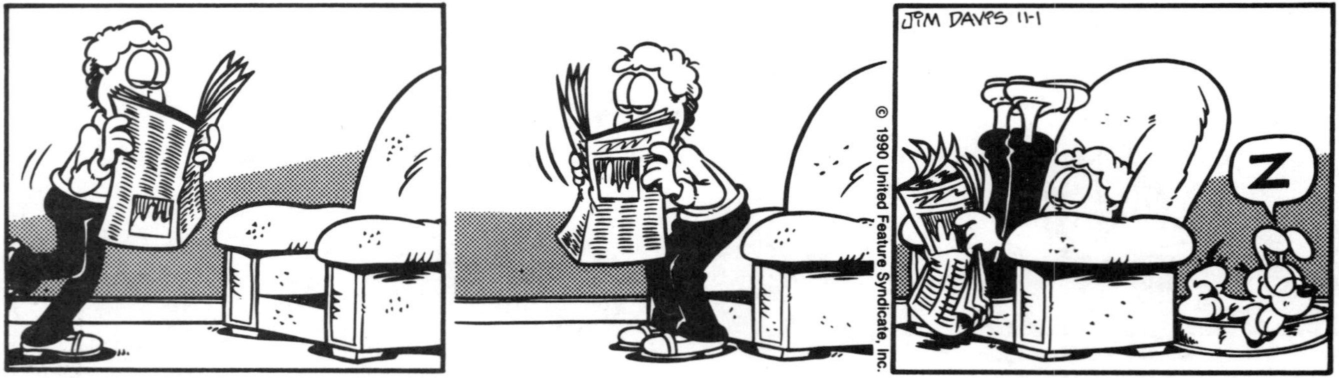
JIM DAVIS 11-1
Z

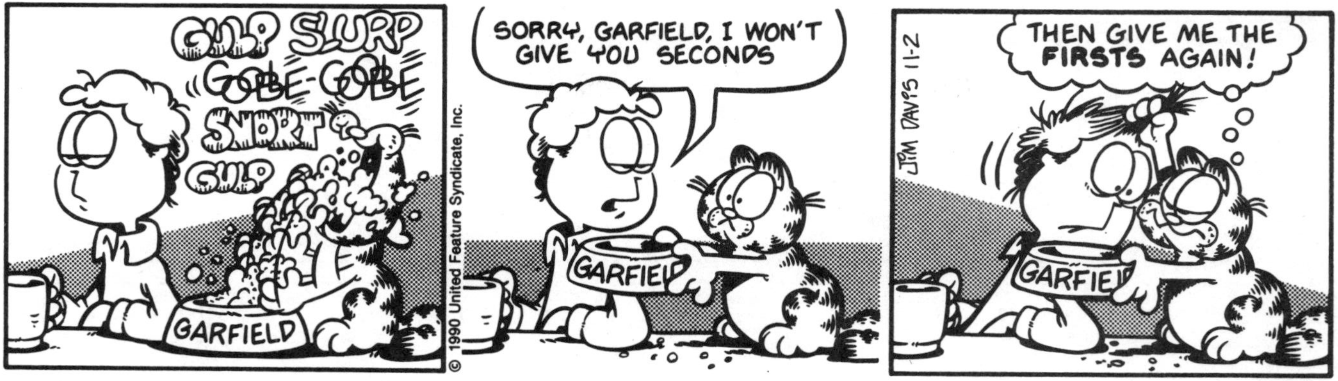
GULP SLURP
GOBBLE-GOBBLE
SNORT
GULP
GARFIELD
© 1990 United Feature Syndicate, Inc.
SORRY, GARFIELD, I WON'T GIVE YOU SECONDS
GARFIELD
JIM DAVIS 11-2
THEN GIVE ME THE FIRSTS AGAIN!

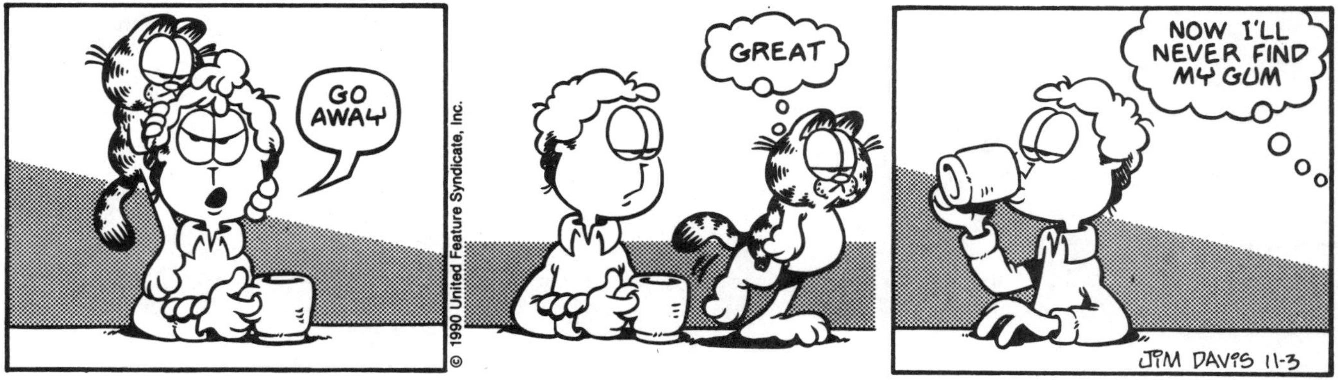
GO AWAY
© 1990 United Feature Syndicate, Inc.
GREAT
NOW I'LL NEVER FIND MY GUM
JIM DAVIS 11-3

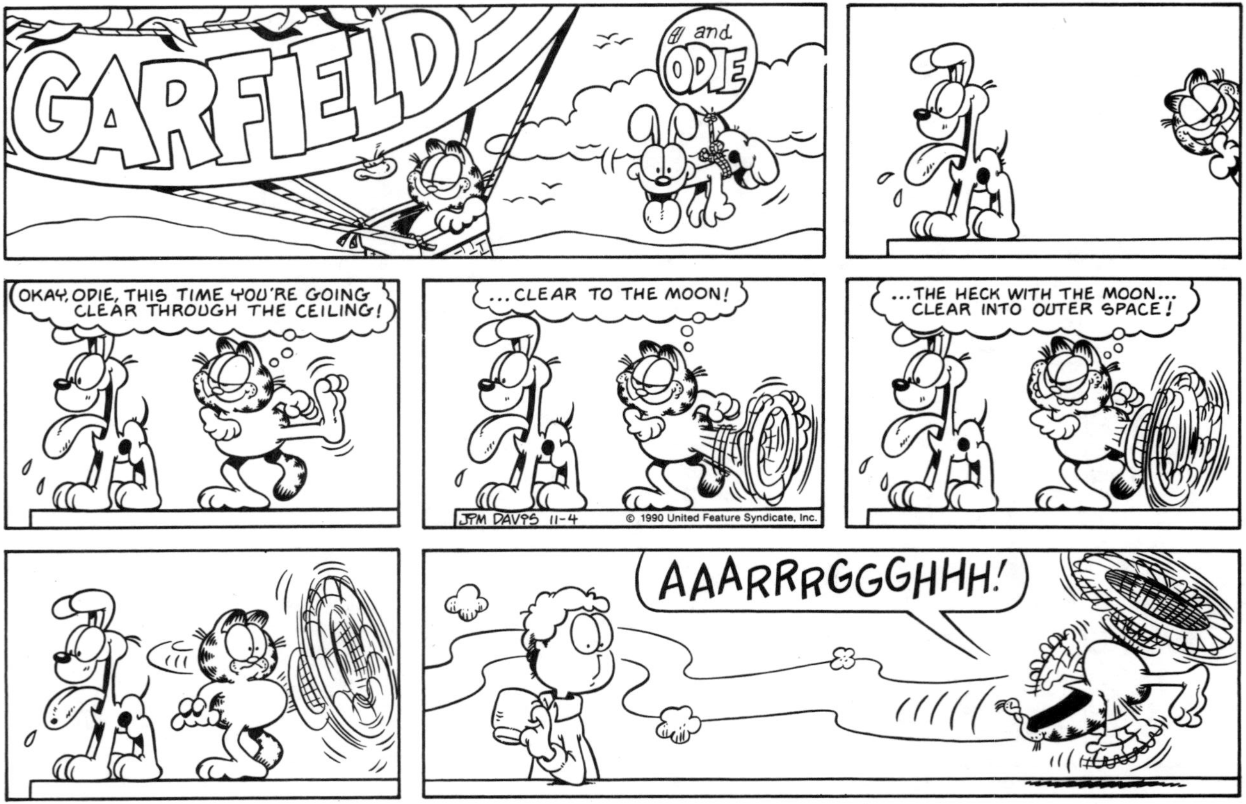
GARFIELD
and ODIE
OKAY, ODIE, THIS TIME YOU'RE GOING CLEAR THROUGH THE CEILING!
...CLEAR TO THE MOON!
JIM DAVIS 11-4
© 1990 United Feature Syndicate, Inc.
...THE HECK WITH THE MOON... CLEAR INTO OUTER SPACE!
AAARRRRGGGHHH!

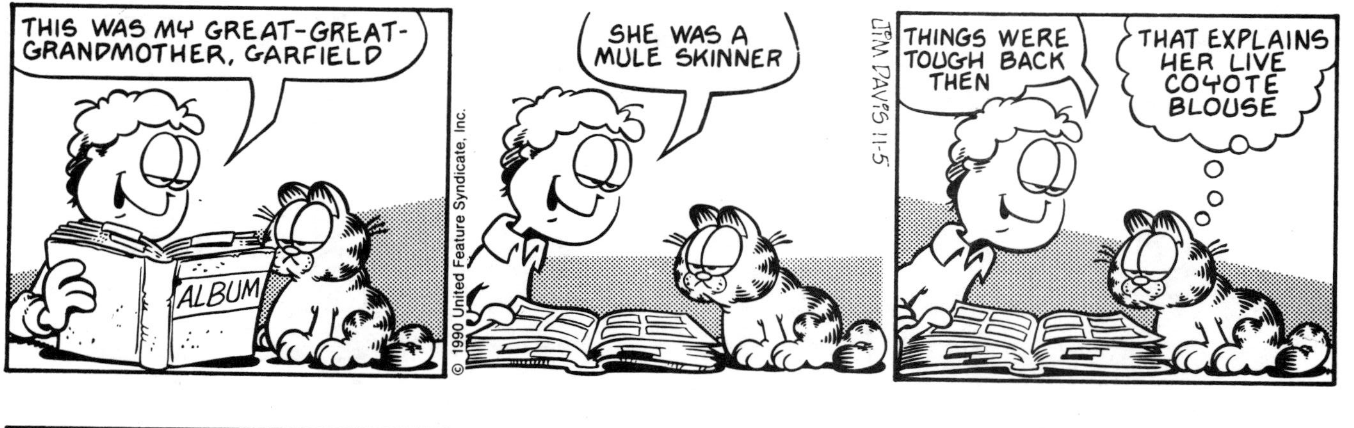
THIS WAS MY GREAT-GREAT-GRANDMOTHER, GARFIELD
ALBUM
SHE WAS A MULE SKINNER
THINGS WERE TOUGH BACK THEN
THAT EXPLAINS HER LIVE COYOTE BLOUSE
JIM DAVIS 11-5
© 1990 United Feature Syndicate, Inc.

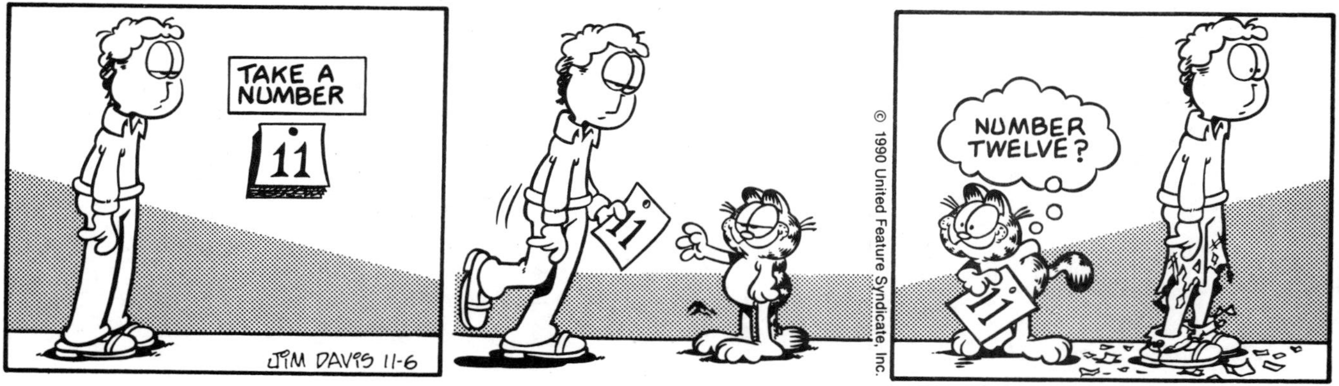
TAKE A NUMBER
11
JIM DAVIS 11-6
11
NUMBER TWELVE?
11
© 1990 United Feature Syndicate, Inc.

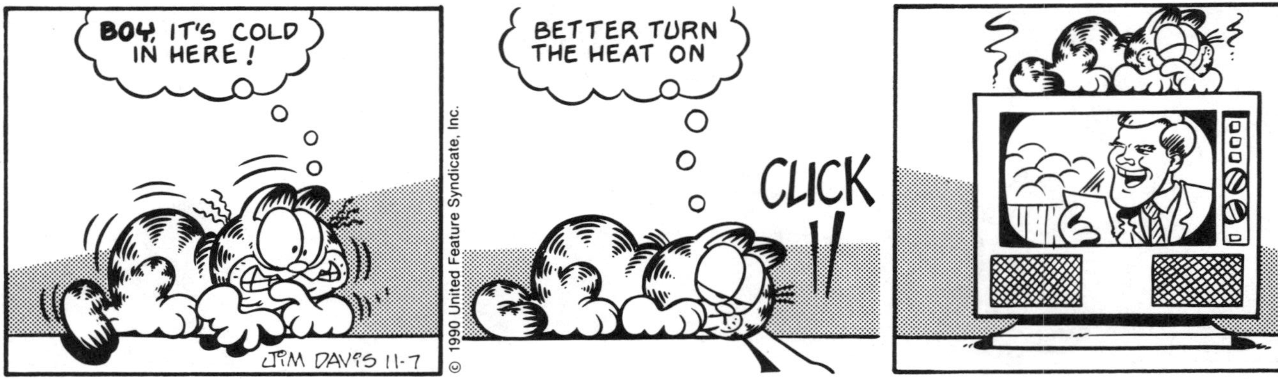
BOY, IT'S COLD IN HERE!
JIM DAVIS 11-7
BETTER TURN THE HEAT ON
CLICK
© 1990 United Feature Syndicate, Inc.

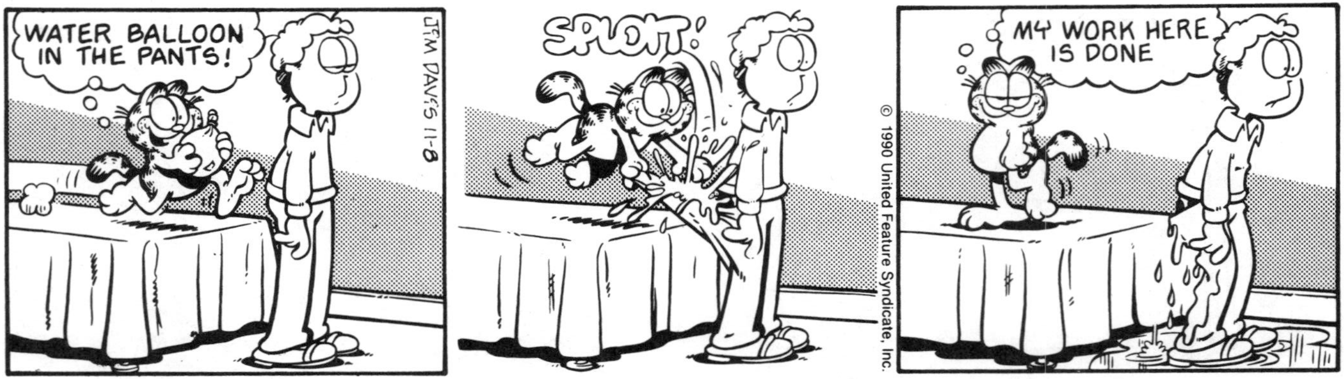
WATER BALLOON IN THE PANTS!
JIM DAVIS 11-8
SPLOIT!
MY WORK HERE IS DONE
© 1990 United Feature Syndicate, Inc.

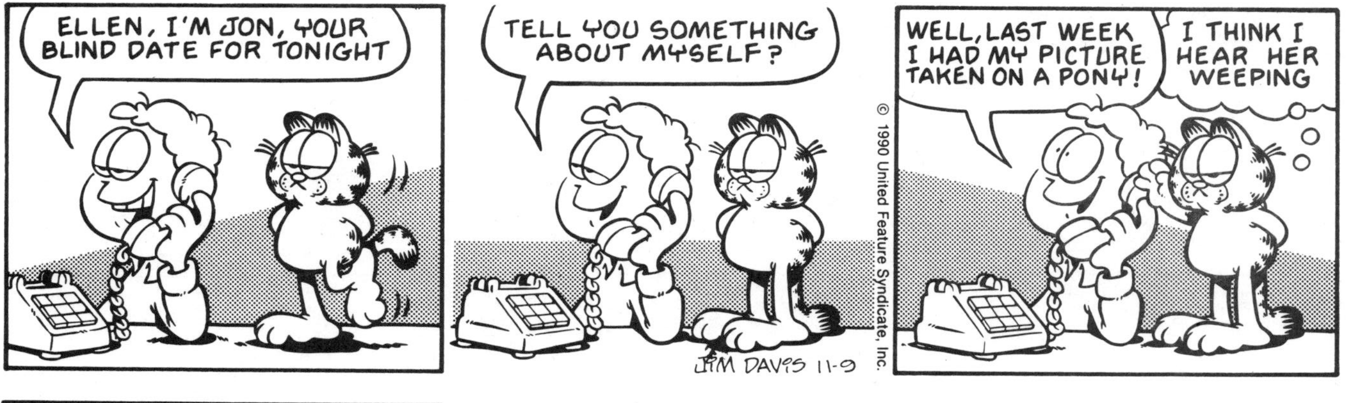
ELLEN, I'M JON, YOUR BLIND DATE FOR TONIGHT
TELL YOU SOMETHING ABOUT MYSELF?
WELL, LAST WEEK I HAD MY PICTURE TAKEN ON A PONY!
I THINK I HEAR HER WEEPING
JIM DAVIS 11-9

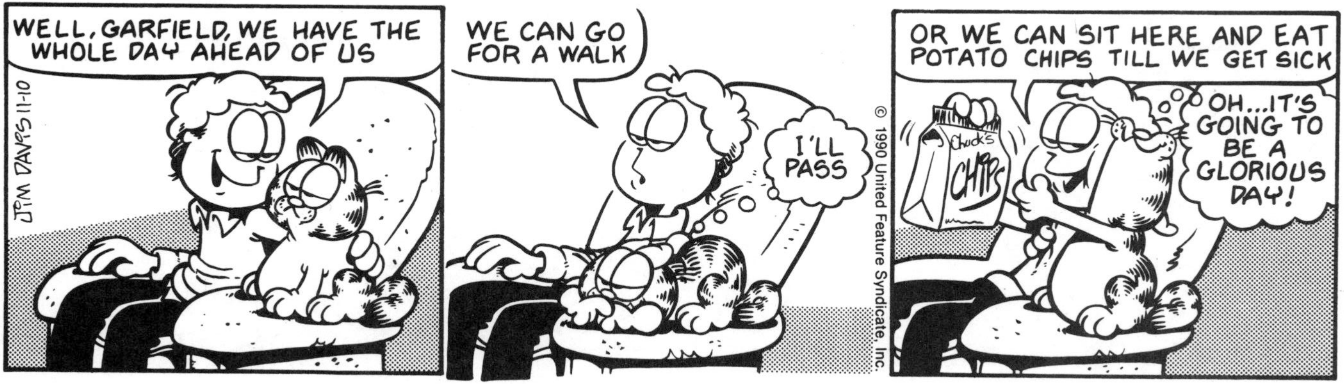
WELL, GARFIELD, WE HAVE THE WHOLE DAY AHEAD OF US
JIM DAVIS 11-10
WE CAN GO FOR A WALK
I'LL PASS
OR WE CAN SIT HERE AND EAT POTATO CHIPS TILL WE GET SICK
Chuck's CHIPS
OH...IT'S GOING TO BE A GLORIOUS DAY!

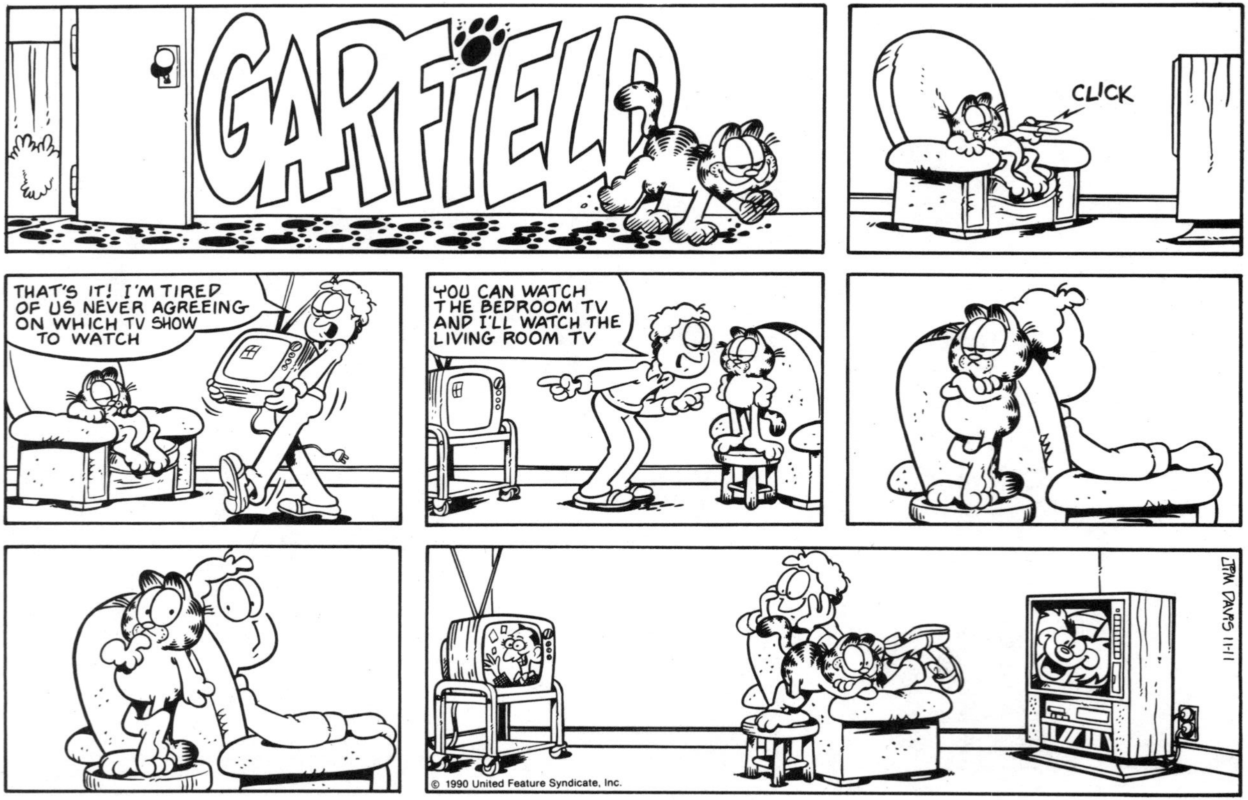
GARFIELD
CLICK
THAT'S IT! I'M TIRED OF US NEVER AGREEING ON WHICH TV SHOW TO WATCH
YOU CAN WATCH THE BEDROOM TV AND I'LL WATCH THE LIVING ROOM TV
JIM DAVIS 11-11
© 1990 United Feature Syndicate, Inc.

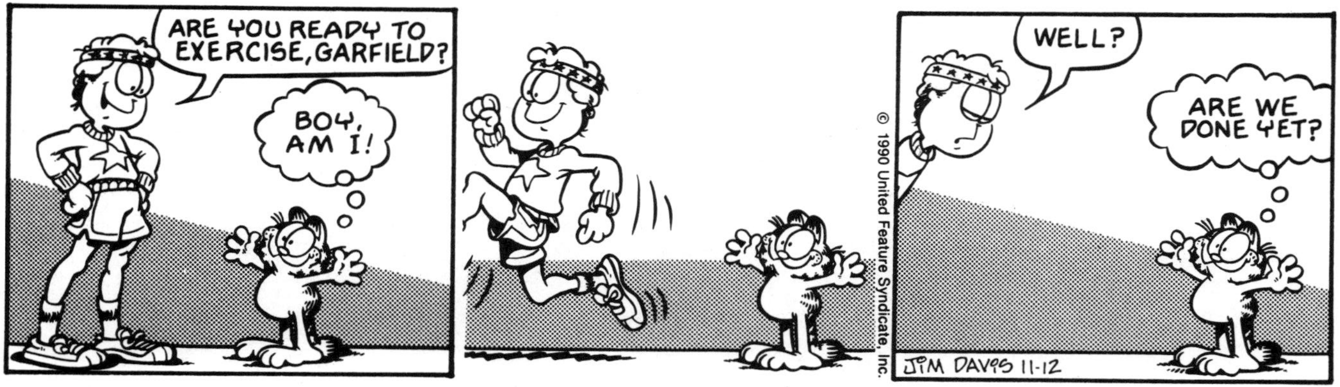
ARE YOU READY TO EXERCISE, GARFIELD?
BOY, AM I!
WELL?
ARE WE DONE YET?
JIM DAVIS 11-12

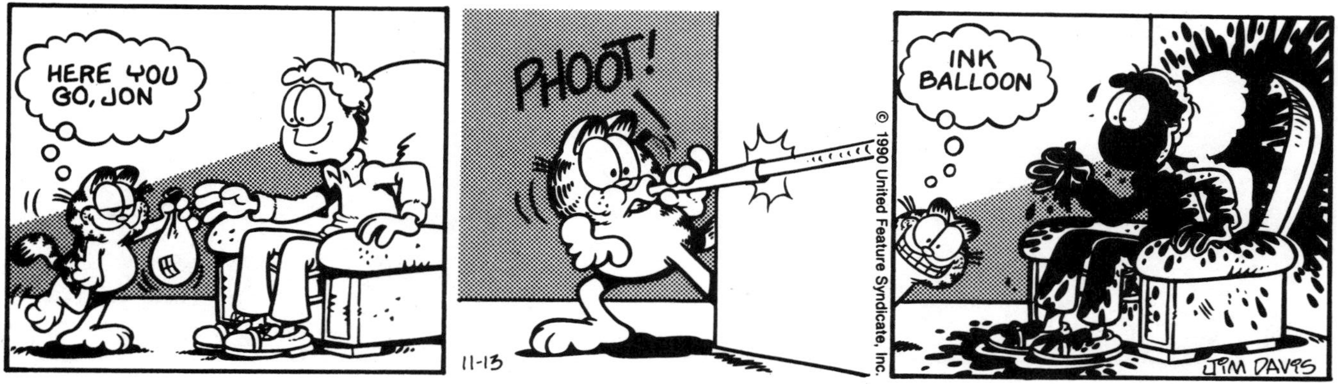
HERE YOU GO, JON
11-13
PHOOT!
INK BALLOON
JIM DAVIS

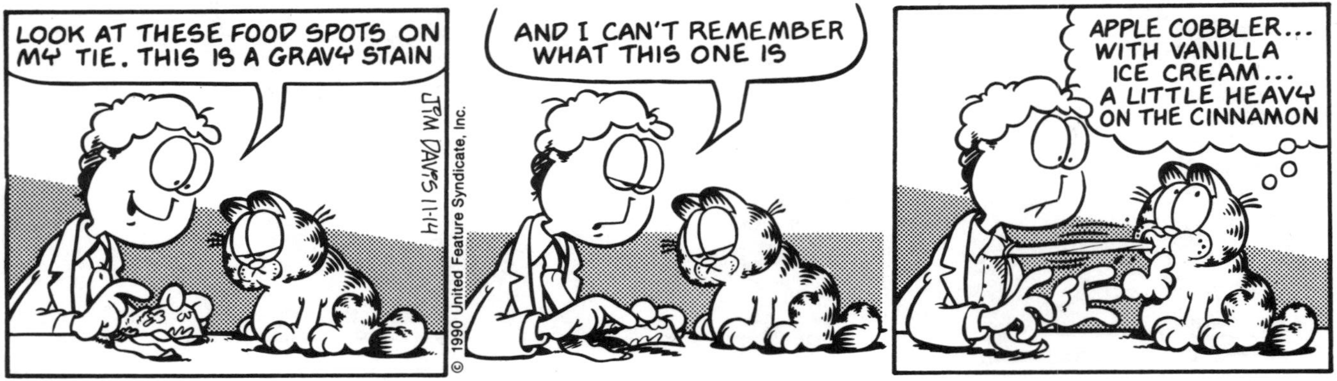
LOOK AT THESE FOOD SPOTS ON MY TIE. THIS IS A GRAVY STAIN
JIM DAVIS 11-14
© 1990 United Feature Syndicate, Inc.
AND I CAN'T REMEMBER WHAT THIS ONE IS
APPLE COBBLER... WITH VANILLA ICE CREAM... A LITTLE HEAVY ON THE CINNAMON

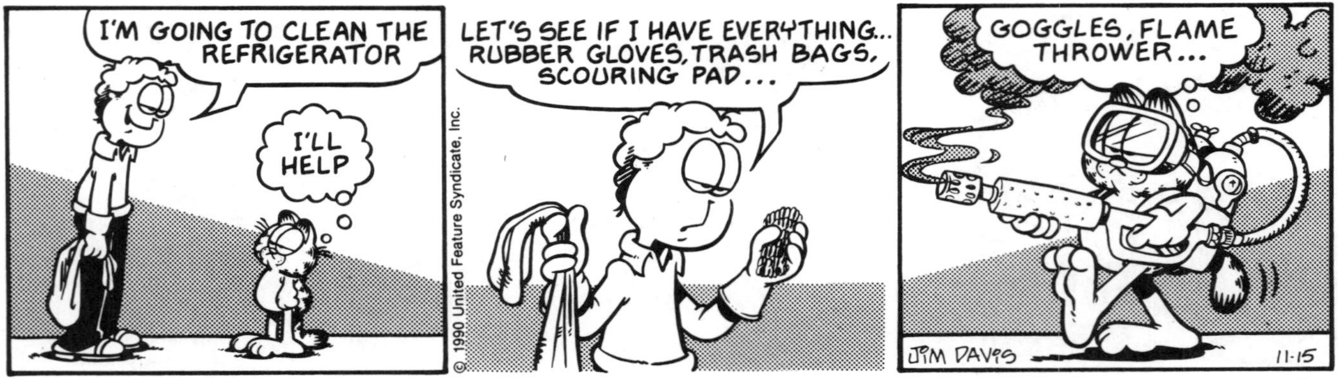
I'M GOING TO CLEAN THE REFRIGERATOR
I'LL HELP
© 1990 United Feature Syndicate, Inc.
LET'S SEE IF I HAVE EVERYTHING... RUBBER GLOVES, TRASH BAGS, SCOURING PAD...
GOGGLES, FLAME THROWER...
JIM DAVIS
11-15

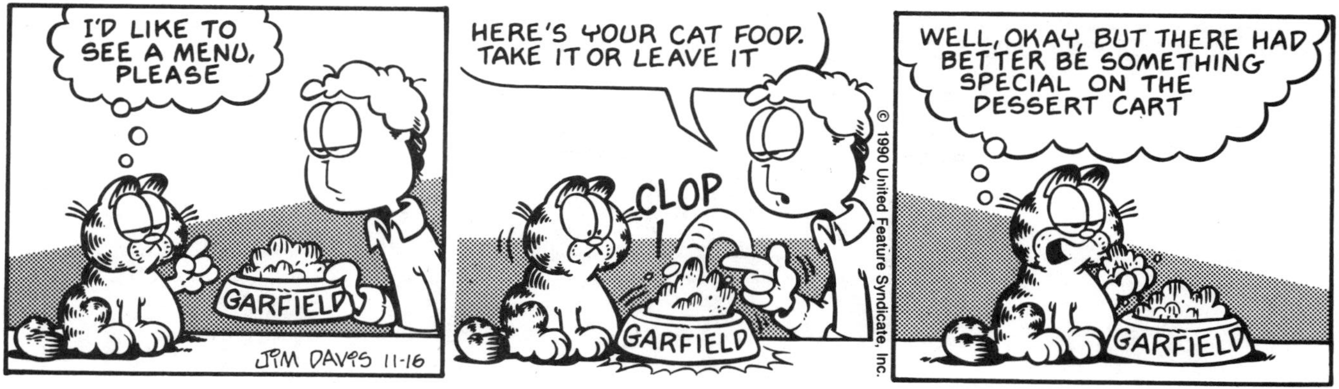
I'D LIKE TO SEE A MENU, PLEASE
GARFIELD
JIM DAVIS 11-16
HERE'S YOUR CAT FOOD. TAKE IT OR LEAVE IT
CLOP
GARFIELD
© 1990 United Feature Syndicate, Inc.
WELL, OKAY, BUT THERE HAD BETTER BE SOMETHING SPECIAL ON THE DESSERT CART
GARFIELD

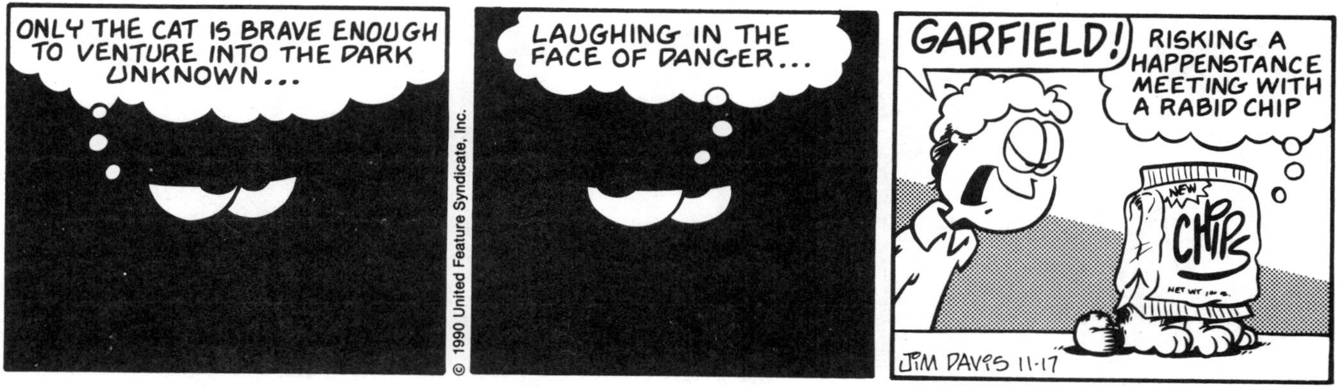
ONLY THE CAT IS BRAVE ENOUGH TO VENTURE INTO THE DARK UNKNOWN...
© 1990 United Feature Syndicate, Inc.
LAUGHING IN THE FACE OF DANGER...
GARFIELD!
RISKING A HAPPENSTANCE MEETING WITH A RABID CHIP
NEW
CHIPS
JIM DAVIS 11-17

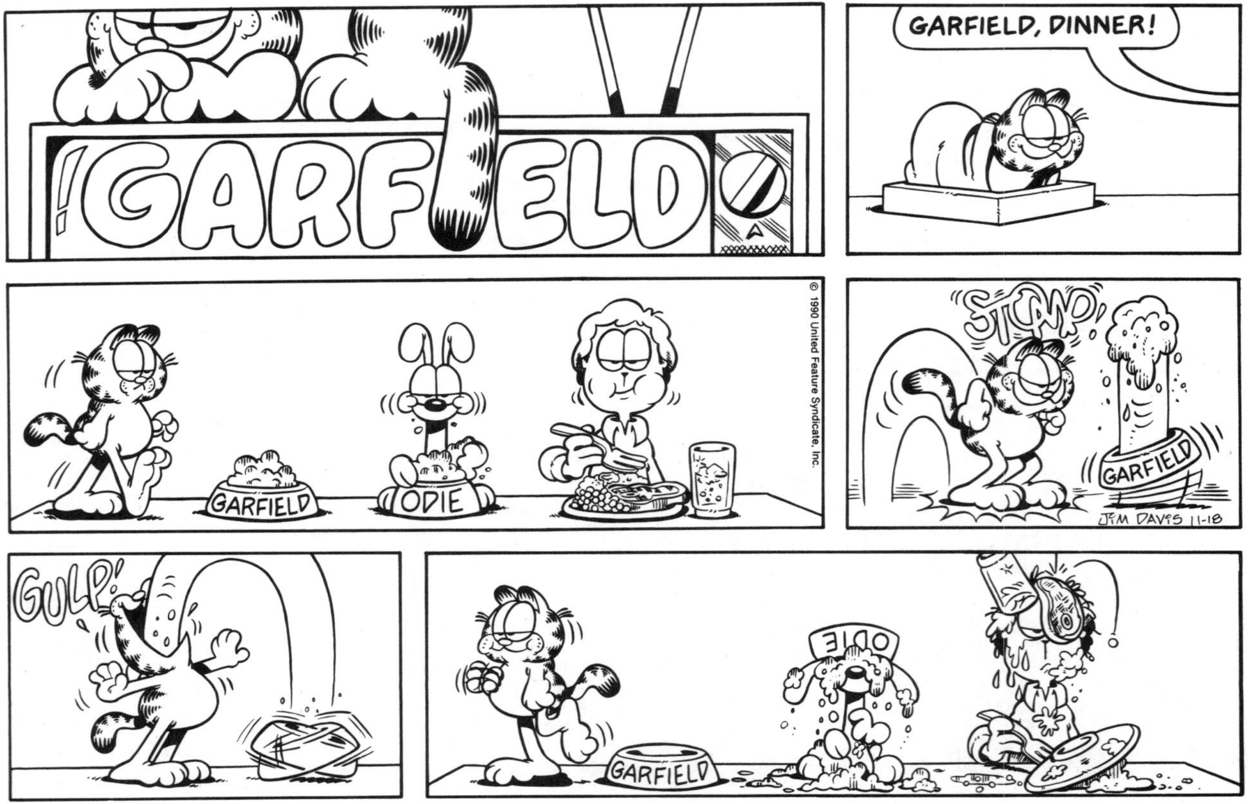
GARFIELD
GARFIELD, DINNER!
GARFIELD
ODIE
STOMP!
GARFIELD
JIM DAVIS 11-18
GULP!
GARFIELD
ODIE

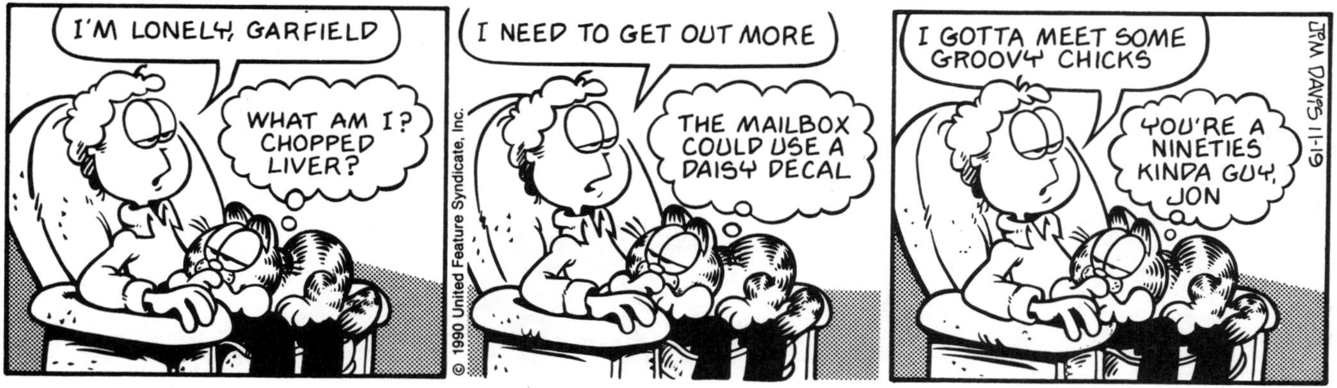
I'M LONELY, GARFIELD
WHAT AM I? CHOPPED LIVER?
© 1990 United Feature Syndicate, Inc.
I NEED TO GET OUT MORE
THE MAILBOX COULD USE A DAISY DECAL
I GOTTA MEET SOME GROOVY CHICKS
YOU'RE A NINETIES KINDA GUY, JON
JIM DAVIS 11-19

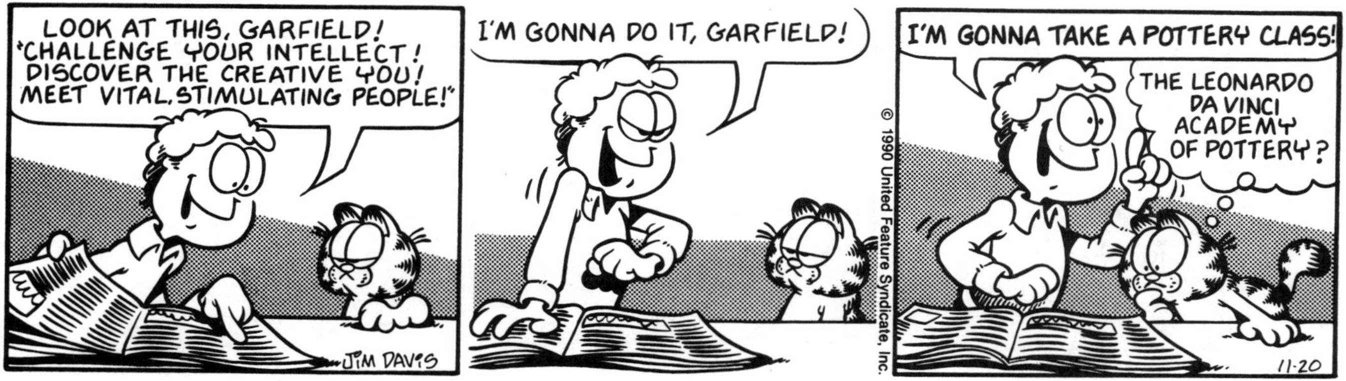
LOOK AT THIS, GARFIELD! "CHALLENGE YOUR INTELLECT! DISCOVER THE CREATIVE YOU! MEET VITAL, STIMULATING PEOPLE!"
JIM DAVIS
I'M GONNA DO IT, GARFIELD!
© 1990 United Feature Syndicate, Inc.
I'M GONNA TAKE A POTTERY CLASS!
THE LEONARDO DA VINCI ACADEMY OF POTTERY?
11-20

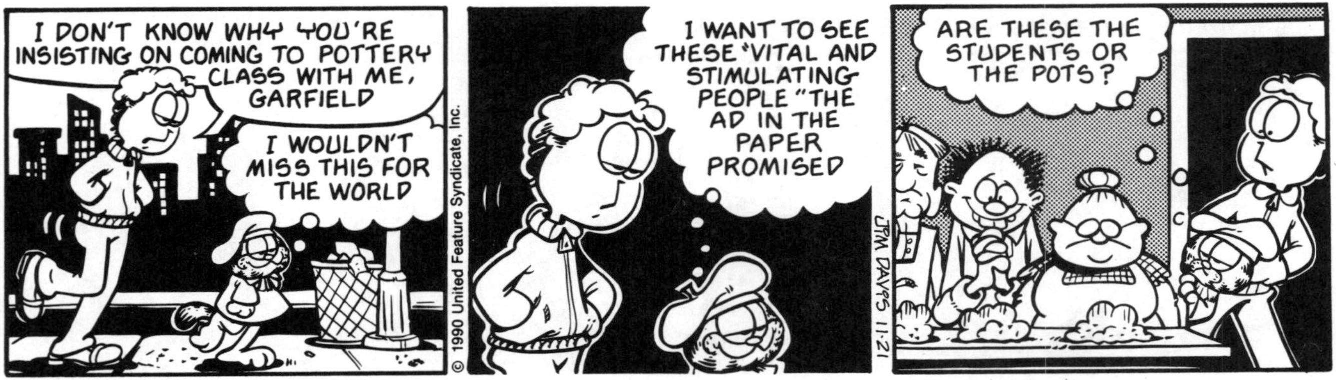
I DON'T KNOW WHY YOU'RE INSISTING ON COMING TO POTTERY CLASS WITH ME, GARFIELD
I WOULDN'T MISS THIS FOR THE WORLD
I WANT TO SEE THESE "VITAL AND STIMULATING PEOPLE" THE AD IN THE PAPER PROMISED
ARE THESE THE STUDENTS OR THE POTS?
© 1990 United Feature Syndicate, Inc.
JIM DAVIS 11·21

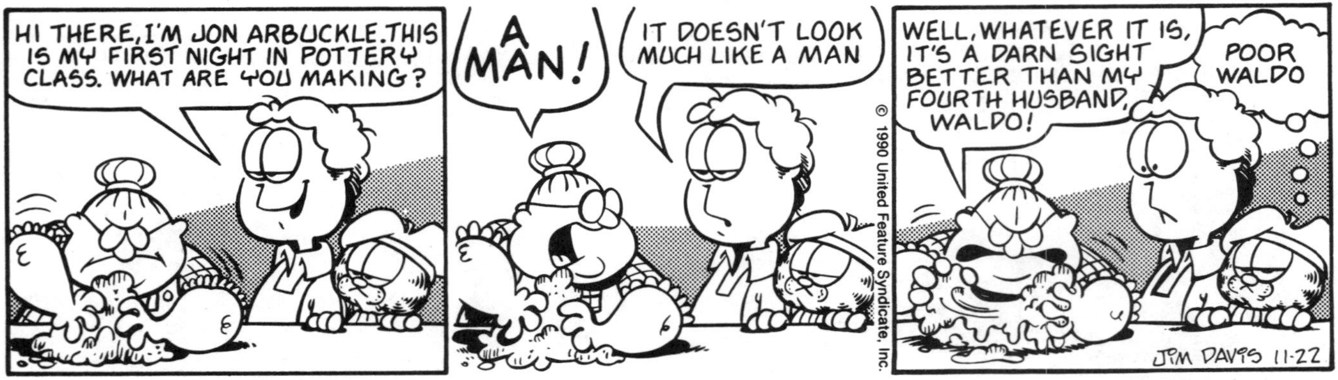
HI THERE, I'M JON ARBUCKLE. THIS IS MY FIRST NIGHT IN POTTERY CLASS. WHAT ARE YOU MAKING?
A MAN!
IT DOESN'T LOOK MUCH LIKE A MAN
WELL, WHATEVER IT IS, IT'S A DARN SIGHT BETTER THAN MY FOURTH HUSBAND, WALDO!
POOR WALDO
© 1990 United Feature Syndicate, Inc.
JIM DAVIS 11·22

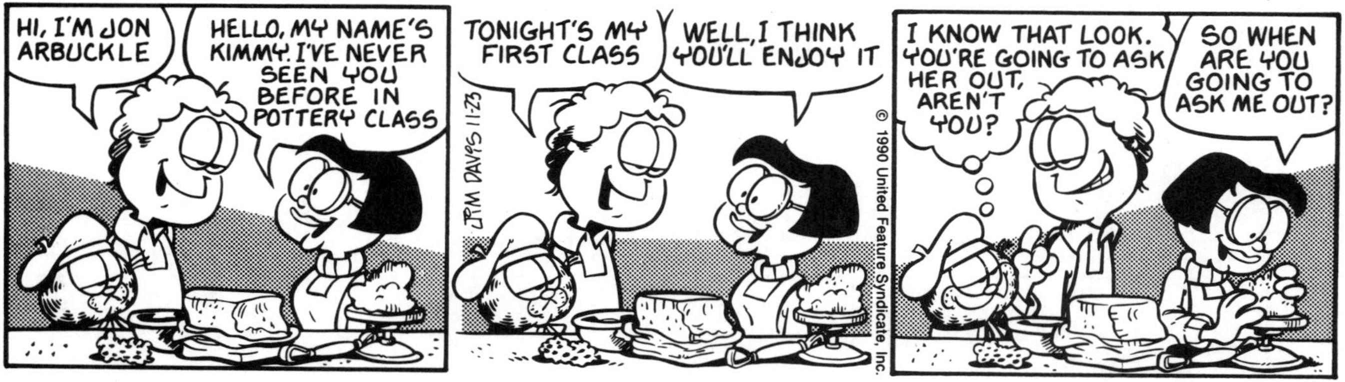
HI, I'M JON ARBUCKLE
HELLO, MY NAME'S KIMMY. I'VE NEVER SEEN YOU BEFORE IN POTTERY CLASS
JIM DAVIS 11-23
TONIGHT'S MY FIRST CLASS
WELL, I THINK YOU'LL ENJOY IT
© 1990 United Feature Syndicate, Inc.
I KNOW THAT LOOK. YOU'RE GOING TO ASK HER OUT, AREN'T YOU?
SO WHEN ARE YOU GOING TO ASK ME OUT?

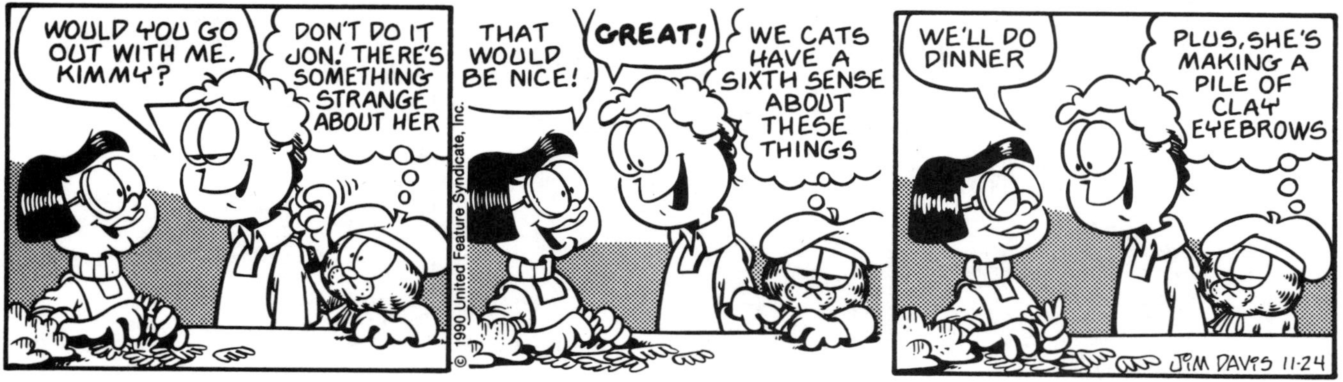
WOULD YOU GO OUT WITH ME, KIMMY?
DON'T DO IT JON! THERE'S SOMETHING STRANGE ABOUT HER
© 1990 United Feature Syndicate, Inc.
THAT WOULD BE NICE!
GREAT!
WE CATS HAVE A SIXTH SENSE ABOUT THESE THINGS
WE'LL DO DINNER
PLUS, SHE'S MAKING A PILE OF CLAY EYEBROWS
JIM DAVIS 11-24

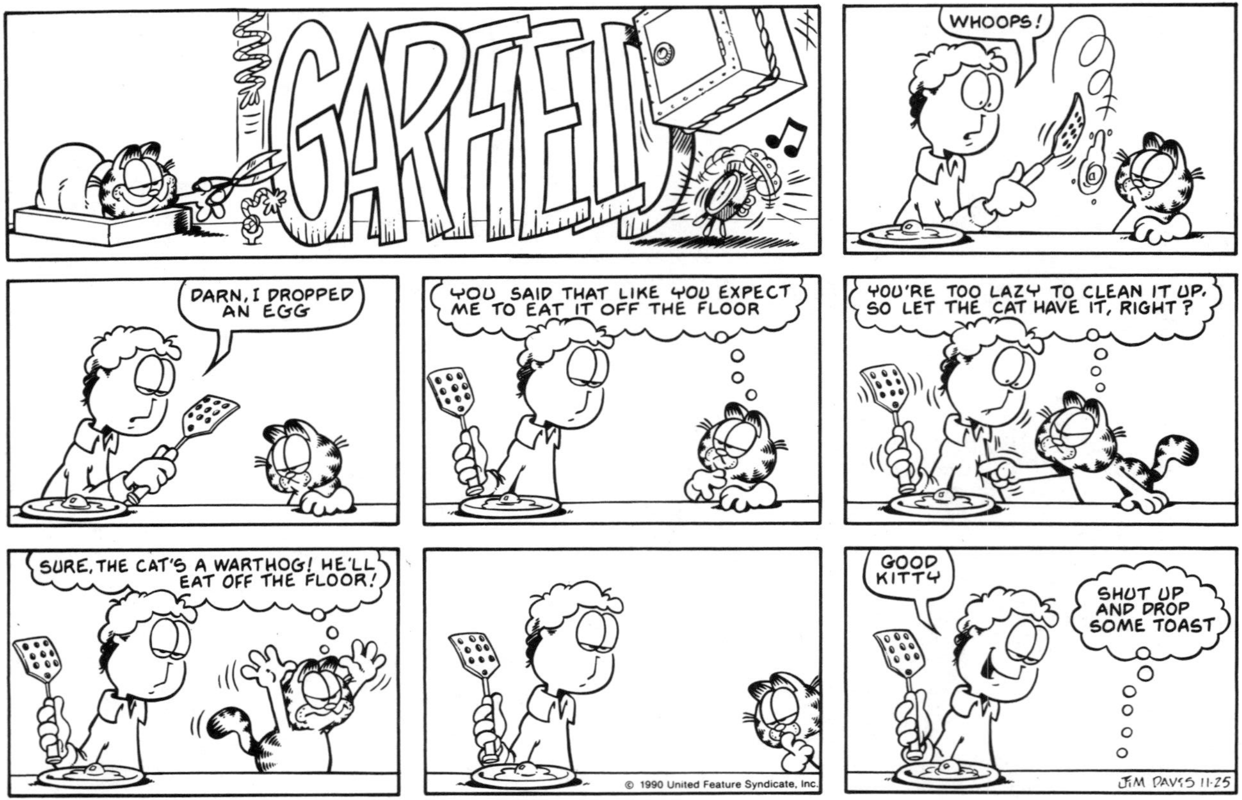
GARFIELD
WHOOPS!
DARN, I DROPPED AN EGG
YOU SAID THAT LIKE YOU EXPECT ME TO EAT IT OFF THE FLOOR
YOU'RE TOO LAZY TO CLEAN IT UP, SO LET THE CAT HAVE IT, RIGHT?
SURE, THE CAT'S A WARTHOG! HE'LL EAT OFF THE FLOOR!
© 1990 United Feature Syndicate, Inc.
GOOD KITTY
SHUT UP AND DROP SOME TOAST
JIM DAVIS 11-25

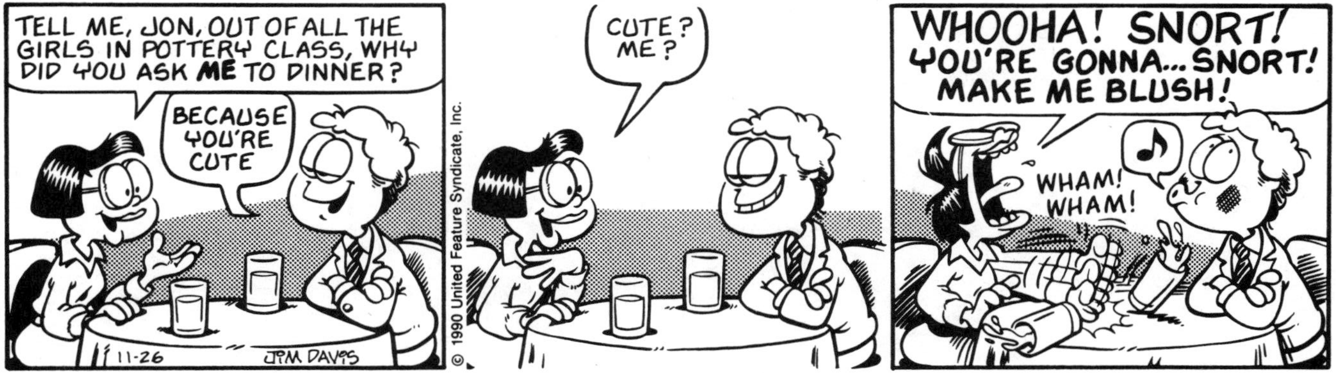
TELL ME, JON, OUT OF ALL THE GIRLS IN POTTERY CLASS, WHY DID YOU ASK **ME** TO DINNER?
BECAUSE YOU'RE CUTE
11-26
JIM DAVIS
CUTE? ME?
WHOOHA! SNORT! YOU'RE GONNA... SNORT! MAKE ME BLUSH!
WHAM! WHAM!

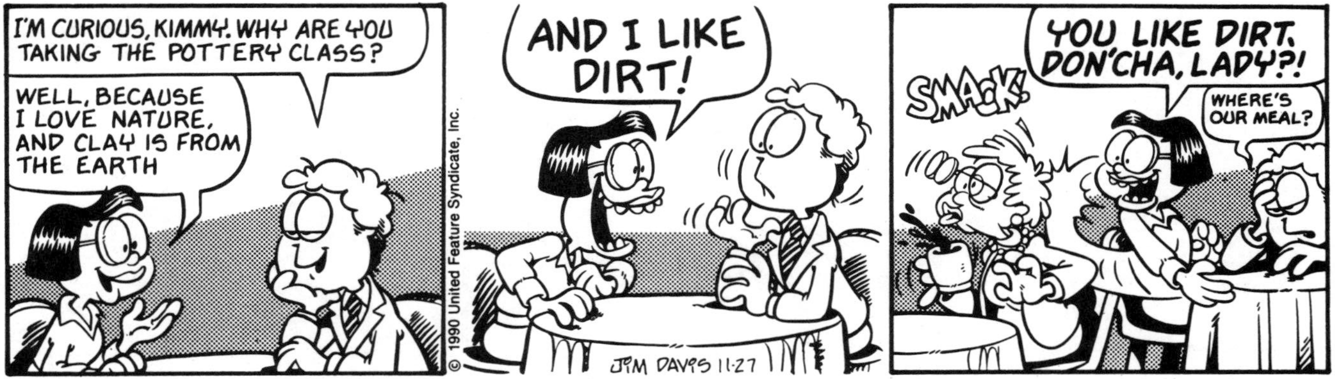
I'M CURIOUS, KIMMY. WHY ARE YOU TAKING THE POTTERY CLASS?
WELL, BECAUSE I LOVE NATURE, AND CLAY IS FROM THE EARTH
AND I LIKE DIRT!
JIM DAVIS 11-27
SMACK!
YOU LIKE DIRT, DON'CHA, LADY?!
WHERE'S OUR MEAL?

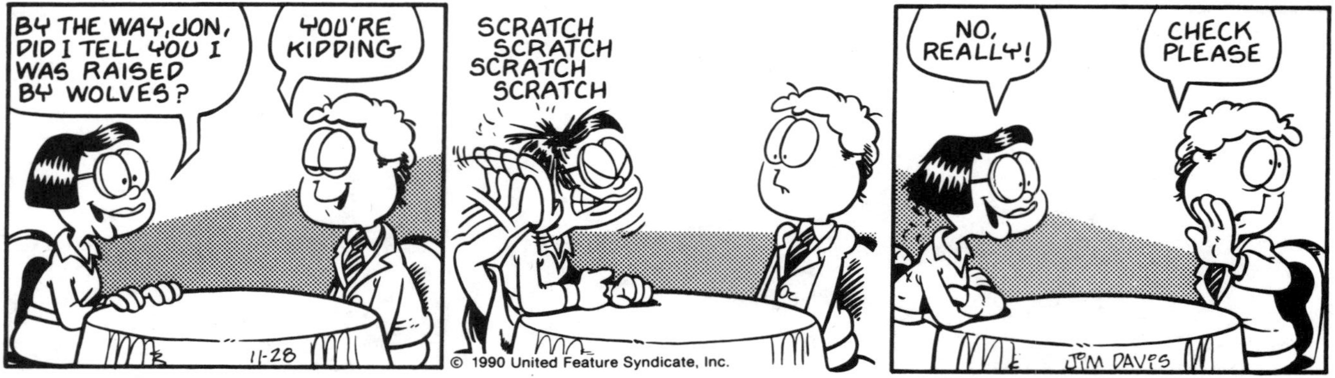
BY THE WAY, JON, DID I TELL YOU I WAS RAISED BY WOLVES?
YOU'RE KIDDING
11-28
SCRATCH SCRATCH SCRATCH SCRATCH
© 1990 United Feature Syndicate, Inc.
NO, REALLY!
CHECK PLEASE
JIM DAVIS

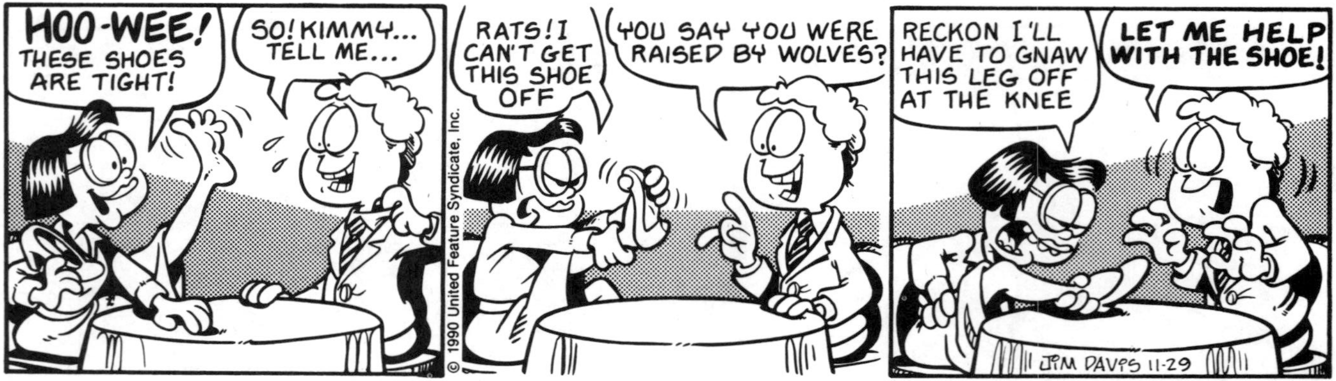
HOO-WEE! THESE SHOES ARE TIGHT!
SO! KIMMY... TELL ME...
© 1990 United Feature Syndicate, Inc.
RATS! I CAN'T GET THIS SHOE OFF
YOU SAY YOU WERE RAISED BY WOLVES?
RECKON I'LL HAVE TO GNAW THIS LEG OFF AT THE KNEE
LET ME HELP WITH THE SHOE!
JIM DAVIS 11-29

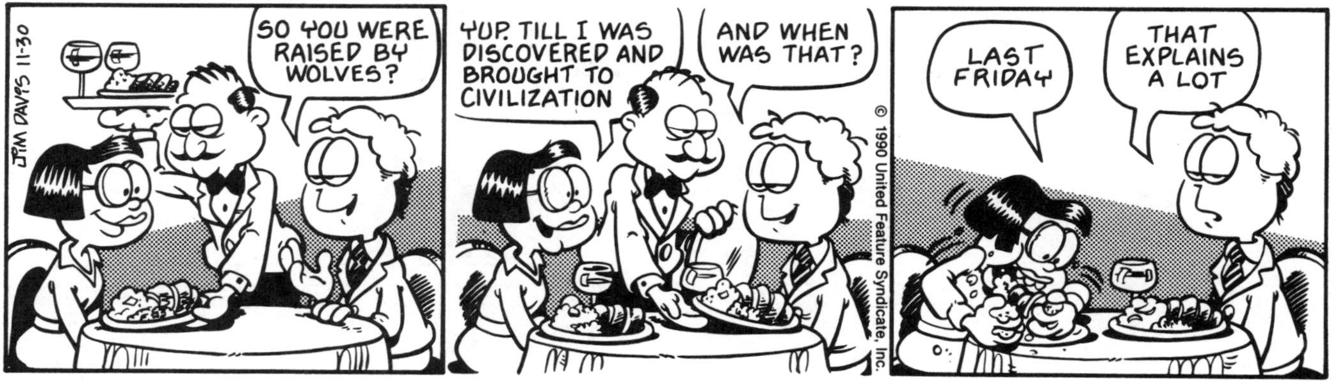
JIM DAVIS 11-30
SO YOU WERE RAISED BY WOLVES?
YUP. TILL I WAS DISCOVERED AND BROUGHT TO CIVILIZATION
AND WHEN WAS THAT?
© 1990 United Feature Syndicate, Inc.
LAST FRIDAY
THAT EXPLAINS A LOT

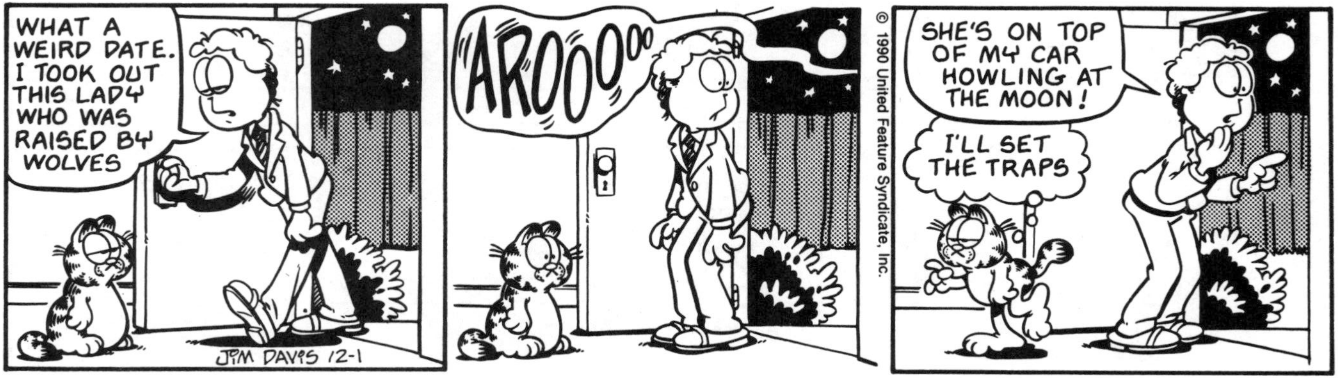
WHAT A WEIRD DATE. I TOOK OUT THIS LADY WHO WAS RAISED BY WOLVES
JIM DAVIS 12-1
AROOOOOO
© 1990 United Feature Syndicate, Inc.
SHE'S ON TOP OF MY CAR HOWLING AT THE MOON!
I'LL SET THE TRAPS

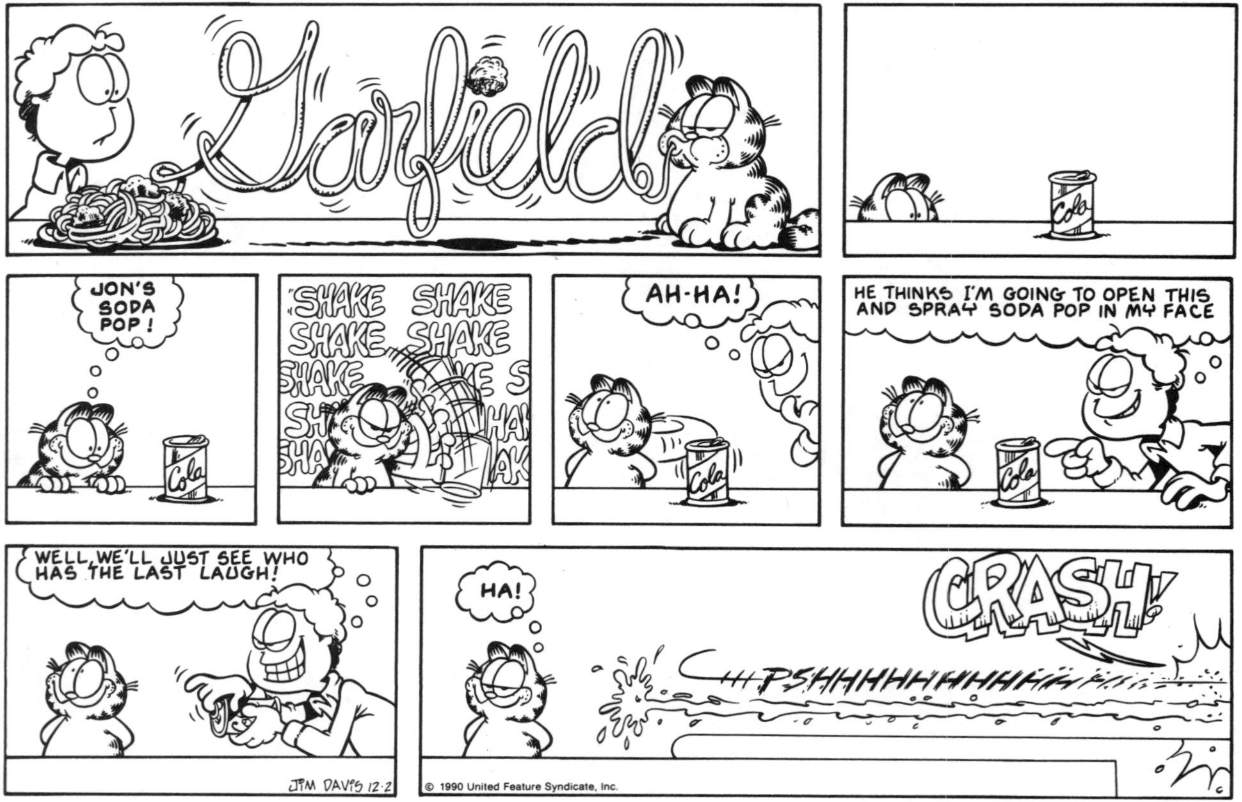
Garfield
Cola
JON'S SODA POP!
SHAKE SHAKE SHAKE SHAKE
AH-HA!
HE THINKS I'M GOING TO OPEN THIS AND SPRAY SODA POP IN MY FACE
WELL, WE'LL JUST SEE WHO HAS THE LAST LAUGH!
JIM DAVIS 12-2
HA!
CRASH!
PSHHHHHHHHHHHH
© 1990 United Feature Syndicate, Inc.

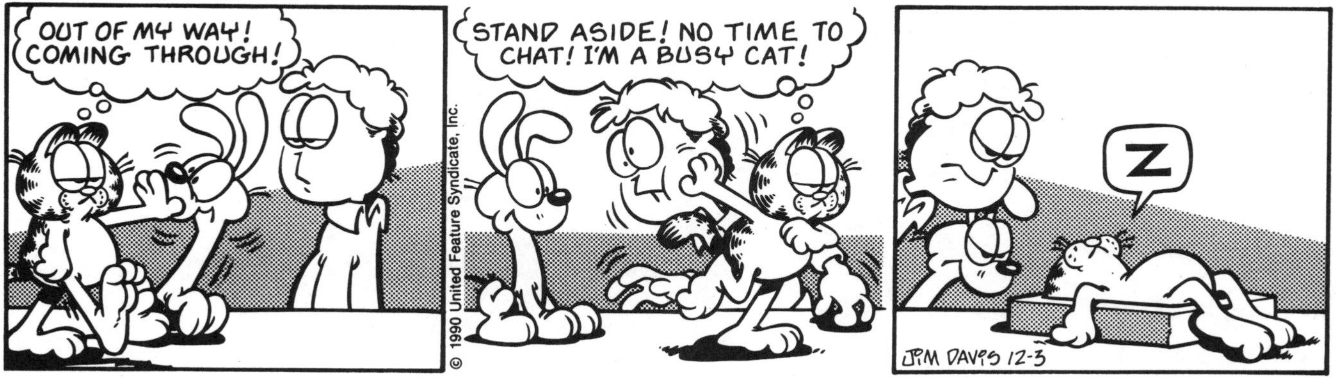
OUT OF MY WAY! COMING THROUGH!
STAND ASIDE! NO TIME TO CHAT! I'M A BUSY CAT!
Z
© 1990 United Feature Syndicate, Inc.
JIM DAVIS 12-3

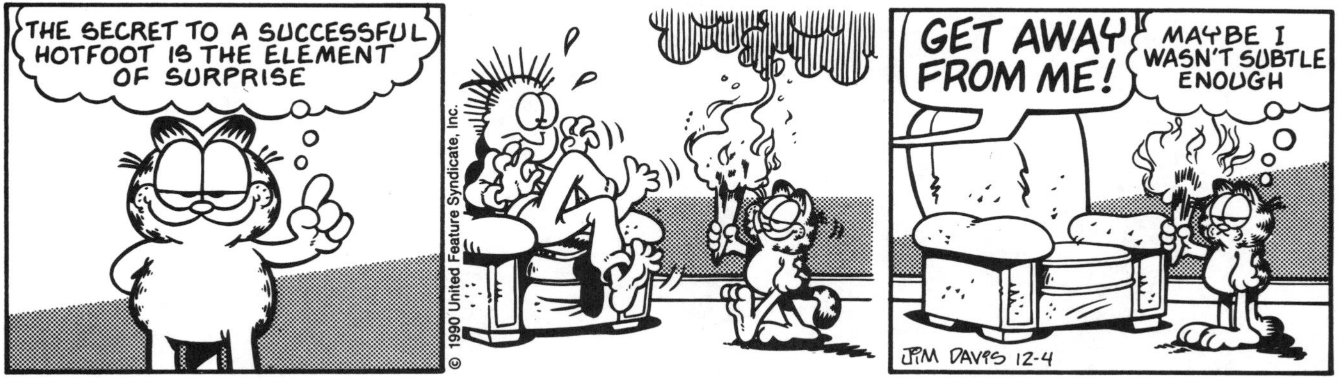
THE SECRET TO A SUCCESSFUL HOTFOOT IS THE ELEMENT OF SURPRISE
GET AWAY FROM ME!
MAYBE I WASN'T SUBTLE ENOUGH
© 1990 United Feature Syndicate, Inc.
JIM DAVIS 12-4

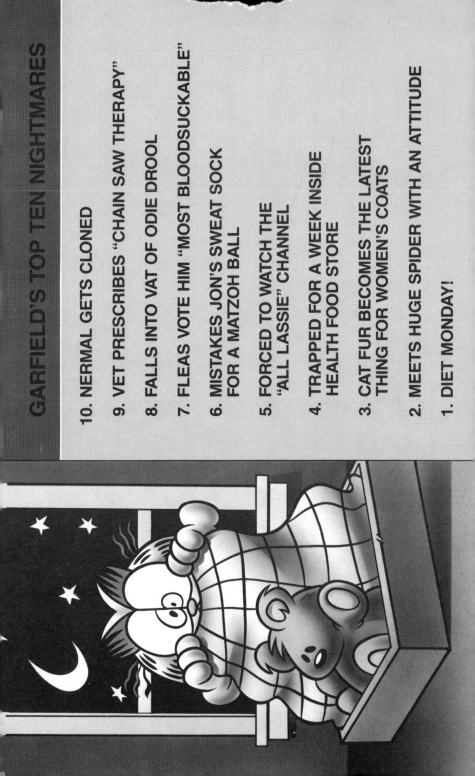

GARFIELD'S TOP TEN NIGHTMARES

10. NERMAL GETS CLONED

9. VET PRESCRIBES "CHAIN SAW THERAPY"

8. FALLS INTO VAT OF ODIE DROOL

7. FLEAS VOTE HIM "MOST BLOODSUCKABLE"

6. MISTAKES JON'S SWEAT SOCK
   FOR A MATZOH BALL

5. FORCED TO WATCH THE
   "ALL LASSIE" CHANNEL

4. TRAPPED FOR A WEEK INSIDE
   HEALTH FOOD STORE

3. CAT FUR BECOMES THE LATEST
   THING FOR WOMEN'S COATS

2. MEETS HUGE SPIDER WITH AN ATTITUDE

1. DIET MONDAY!